ENVIRONMENT AND SOCIETY
IN EASTERN EUROPE

ENVIRONMENT AND SOCIETY IN EASTERN EUROPE

Edited by

ANDREW TICKLE
and
IAN WELSH

 LONGMAN

Addison Wesley Longman Limited
Edinburgh Gate
Harlow
Essex CM20 2JE
United Kingdom
and Associated Companies throughout the world

*Published in the United States of America
by Addison Wesley Longman, New York*

Visit Addison Wesley Longman on the world-wide web at
http://www.awl-he.com

© Addison Wesley Longman Limited 1998

Photo of Josef Vavroušek © Andrew Tickle 1989

First published 1998

ISBN 0 582 22763 1

British Library Cataloguing-in-Publication Data
A catalogue record for this book is available from the British Library

Library of Congress Cataloging-in-Publication Data
A catalog record for this book is available from the Library of Congress

Set by 35 in 10/12 pt Times
Printed in Malaysia,PP

To Josef Vavroušek
(1944–95)

CONTENTS

CONTRIBUTORS

Dr Sonja Boehmer-Christiansen is a Reader in the Research Institute for Environmental Science and Management at the University of Hull. A political scientist and native of Dresden in the former East Germany, her previous publications include *Acid Politics: environmental and energy policies in Britain and Germany* (1991, with Jim Skea).

Professor György Enyedi is an Academician at the Centre for Regional Studies, the Hungarian Academy of Sciences. His publications include *State of the Hungarian Environment* (1990, with Don Hinrichsen) and *Cities and Social Transformation in Central Europe* (forthcoming).

Dr Natalia Mirovitskaya is at the Nicholas School of the Environment, Duke University. Her previous research has focused on native peoples and gender issues in the former Soviet Union.

Dr Viktória Szirmai is a senior research fellow at the Institute of Sociology, the Hungarian Academy of Sciences. She has published widely on interest relations within Hungarian environmental politics and policy and is currently working on environmental conflict management issues.

Dr Andrew Tickle lectures in geography at Birkbeck College, London, and was a visiting fellow of the School of Slavonic and East European Studies (SSEES), University of London. He has worked closely with environmental groups in central and eastern Europe since 1988 and co-founded Greenpeace in Czechoslovakia.

The late **Ing Josef Vavroušek**, CSc, was Czechoslovakia's first federal minister of the environment. After leaving formal politics he became a visiting fellow of the Cambridge-based Global Security Programme and vice-dean of social sciences at Charles University, and founded a new Czech environmental NGO, the Society for Sustainable Living (STUŽ).

Dr Ian Welsh lectures in sociology at Cardiff University. He has a longstanding interest in environmental sociology spanning nuclear, climate change and road-building issues. He is the author of *Mobilising Modernity: The Nuclear Moment* (forthcoming), which addresses the significance of the nuclear case for contemporary debates about ecological and reflexive modernization.

Professor Jacek Wódz is professor of sociology at the Silesian University, Katowice, and professor of political sciences at the Institute d'Études Politiques de Bordeaux. Recently published work (with Kazimiera Wódz) has addressed identity and politics at local and regional scales in central Europe.

Professor Kazimiera Wódz is professor of sociology and vice-dean of social sciences at the Silesian University, Katowice. Her works include *Regional Identity, Regional Consciousness* (1995) and more recently she has researched regional industrial decline, restructuring and sustainable development in Katowice province.

FOREWORD
dedicated to Josef Vavroušek

We find ourselves on the threshold of a new millennium. Our civilization is entering it considerably divided, egotistical, and short-sighted. The loss of respect for the 'order of being', which we did not create, but of which we are merely a part; for the secret inner meaning which this order possesses; and for its memory, which connects man to the eternal, has led us into a deep crisis. In the pursuit of increased production and consumption, we have lost interest in the fact that it has taken nature millions of years to produce that which we consume over the course of a single year; that the environment, upon which our existence depends, is being ruthlessly and often senselessly destroyed; that most of the burden of debt that we have incurred on our environment will be painfully redeemed by future generations, for whom our current production will only be a giant heap of waste.

I believe that we must look for the solution in the domain of the human spirit. It is necessary for the egotism of reason to be balanced by humility and sensitivity. The resurgence of the human spirit, and of human responsibility for the world is an opportunity for us to free ourselves from our addiction to growth and consumption.

Josef Vavroušek was one of those who succeeded in analysing, defining and, above all, suggesting alternatives to this state of affairs. His profound knowledge of many scientific disciplines allowed him to understand the web of mutual relationships between economics, sociology and ecology and thus to participate in solving the global crisis of responsibility by his contribution to the conception of 'sustainable living'. However, it was primarily the awareness of oneness with nature, respect for life in all its forms and for nature as a whole, as well as humility in the face of the 'order of being' and respect for the free will of man, which gave hope and life to his conception of 'sustainable living'. Josef believed that the only truly inexhaustible resource was human invention, which would lead us to the unveiling of the secret of the continuous self-renewal of life in nature. He believed that the human spirit could surpass nature only when it proves to be capable of taking responsibility for other beings, for nature, and for the future.

In his vision of 'sustainable living', Josef suggested new models of behaviour, new systems of values and life aspirations which were founded on quality of life and not on the quantity of material goods consumed. Likewise, this concept implored that the right of future generations to an equivalent quality of life and environment be respected. Josef was convinced that the common interests of humankind in conserving an environment of high quality could overcome growing conflicts due to economic, national, religious or other interests. For this reason he called a high-level meeting in Dobříš in 1991 under the title 'Environment for Europe'. In spite of (or rather because of) it all, he was often publicly damned and doubted. Even though he was able to understand others and see things through their eyes, and – in his global understanding of connections and mutually connected individual fates – able to defend the interests of even his opponents, he remained misunderstood by many. It seemed that he was always a step ahead of others in his visions and in his ideas.

Josef's tragic parting is a challenge to all of us – it is up to each one of us to determine how we will assume our part of our collective global responsibility; how we will tame the egotism of our thoughts and accept humility in the face of being and its order, and how we will justify our actions before our grandchildren.

Václav Havel
Prague, 25 February 1998

PŘEDMLUVA
věnovaná Josefovi Vavrouškovi

Ocitáme se na prahu třetího tisíciletí. Naše civilizace do něho vstupuje značně rozpolcená, pyšná a krátkozraká. Ztráta respektu k řádu bytí, který jsme nevytvořili, ale jehož jsme pouhé součásti, k tajemnému vnitřnímu smyslu, jejž tento řád má, k jeho paměti, jež člověka propojuje s věčností, nás přivedla do hluboké krize. V honbě za vyšším růstem výroby a spotřeby nás přestalo zajímat, že to, co spotřebujeme během jediného roku, příroda vytvářela milióny let, že životní prostředí, na kterém jsme existenčně závislí, bezohledně a často i nesmyslně ničíme, že tento dluh na zdevastovaném prostředí budou bolestně splácet především budoucí generace, pro které naše současná výroba bude už jen obrovská kupa odpadků.

Věřím, že řešení musíme hledat ve sféře lidského ducha. Pýchu rozumu je třeba vyvážit pokorou a citem. Vzpamatování lidského ducha a lidské odpovědnosti za svět je pro nás šancí, jak se vymanit z naší drogové závislosti na růstu výroby a spotřeby.

Josef Vavroušek byl jedním z těch, kteří dokázali tento stav věcí analyzovat, pojmenovat a především navrhnout alternativy. Jeho hluboké znalosti mnoha vědních disciplín mu umožnily pochopit vzájemná přediva vztahů mezi ekonomikou, sociologií a ekologií a přispět tak k řešení globální krize odpovědnosti svým podílem na koncepci "trvale udržitelného života". Ale bylo to především vědomí sounáležitosti s přírodou, úcta k životu ve všech jeho formách a i k přírodě jako celku, pokora vůči řádu bytí a respekt vůči svobodné vůli člověka, které daly jeho pojetí této koncepce naději a život. Josef věřil, že jediným skutečně nevyčerpatelným zdrojem je lidská invence, která nás povede k odhalování tajemství neustále se obnovujícího života v přírodě. Věřil, že lidský duch dokáže předčit přírodu jen tehdy, bude-li schopen přejmout odpovědnost také za druhá stvoření, za přírodu, za budoucnost.

Josef ve své vizi trvale udržitelného života navrhl nové modely chování, nové stupnice hodnot a životních cílů, které byly založeny na kvalitě života, nikoli na kvantitě spotřebovávaných statků. Tato koncepce rovněž požadovala, aby bylo respektováno právo budoucích generací na stejně kvalitní život a prostředí. Josef byl přesvědčen, že společný zájem lidstva na zachování kvalitního životního prostředí může překonat narůstající konflikty ekonomických, národnostních, náboženských nebo jiných zájmů. Proto také v roce 1991 svolal v Dobříši setkání na vysoké úrovni s názvem "Životní prostředí pro Evropu". Přesto, anebo spíše právě pro to všechno, byl často veřejně zatracován a zpochybňován. Zatímco on dokázal chápat druhé, dívat se na věci i jejich očima a ve svém globálním chápání souvislostí a vzájemného propojení dílčích osudů hájit i zájmy svých oponentů, zůstával mnohými nepochopen. Jakoby byl ve svých vizich a představách vždy o krok dopředu před ostatními.

Josefův tragický odchod je pro nás všechny velkou výzvou – je na nás na každém, jak se zhostíme svého dílu naší globální odpovědnosti, jak zkrotíme pýchu svého myšlení a přijmeme pokoru vůči bytí a jeho řádu, jak obhájíme naše činy před našimi vnuky.

Václav Havel

V Praze dne 25. února 1998

PREFACE

This book was originally conceived in 1991, when the revolutions of 1989 were recent events and the literature on the environment in eastern and central Europe was limited. Since then the academic literature on the environment within the social sciences and the revolutions in central and eastern Europe has grown enormously. For us these two concerns have never been easily separable and indeed one of the main objectives of this book has been to deal with the social and environmental transformation of this region as intimately related processes. Our approach to the environment is thus social and cultural as well as one which engages with the organic environment which is commonly associated with nature.

If the intervening years have seen major upheavals in central and eastern Europe then this has also been true of our lives. The original sole editorship of the volume was abandoned in 1992 after a sustained period of illness which has periodically continued to interrupt progress on this and other tasks. The closer involvement of a second editor (Andrew Tickle) with the project has enabled the work to assume wider ambitions and resulted in a close and productive working relationship between social and natural scientists. We have learned much from each other and will continue to do so into the foreseeable future. Entry into parenthood and moves within the academic labour market have further added to the delay in completing the book. Serendipitously these delays have allowed us to produce a much more considered volume than would otherwise have been possible.

In the face of the numerous delays we can only thank everyone associated with this project for their patience and forbearance. In particular we thank our contributors and Chris Harrison at Addison Wesley Longman for their support and tolerance over what has been a rather difficult period; our partners and children also know something of the social costs associated with the book. In addition, we acknowledge the financial help of the School of Geography and Environmental Management, Middlesex University; the Centre for Extra-Mural Studies, Birkbeck College, and the School of Social and Administrative Studies, Cardiff University. The Council and Director of the School of Slavonic and East European Studies (SSEES), University of London, are also thanked for the award of an Honorary Visiting Fellowship to Andrew Tickle in 1996–97.

We thank Taylor & Francis for their permission to reproduce part of Jacek Wódz's paper from *Society and Natural Resources* within the chapter on Poland. We are indebted to Jana Lihocká, Pavla Alchin, David Short and Frank and Krystyna Carter for help with translations, Carina Sandberg for her bibliographic research early in the project and Jaqueline Swift for her painstaking efforts preparing the manuscript. Matthew Smith, Shuet-Kei Cheung and Ann Barham are also to be thanked for ensuring the production period went smoothly.

Finally, we are of course particularly grateful to Václav Havel and the staff of the Office of the President for his foreword to this volume, which is dedicated to our mutual friend and colleague Josef Vavroušek,[1] who was tragically killed during the book's completion.

Andrew Tickle
Ian Welsh

London and Cardiff, February 1998

NOTE

1. For a further appreciation of Josef Vavroušek's life and work see Prins, G., Segall, I. and Gott, R. 'Green velvet revolutionary' *The Guardian*, 10 April 1995, London.

CHAPTER 1

THE 1989 REVOLUTIONS AND ENVIRONMENTAL POLITICS IN CENTRAL AND EASTERN EUROPE

Ian Welsh and Andrew Tickle

INTRODUCTION

This chapter provides an introduction to the role of the environment in the central and eastern European revolutions of 1989. Existing accounts of the revolutions have tended to emphasize the pursuit of freedom and democracy through political and economic reforms, either neglecting the environment completely or treating it as a marginal issue. Whilst there is a wealth of material which details the nature of environmental problems in central and eastern Europe, including the former Soviet Union (FSU) (see for example DeBardeleben, 1985; Ziegler, 1987; Stewart, 1992; Carter and Turnock, 1993; Pryde, 1995), accounts of how the environment acted as a focus for political mobilizations are much rarer (although see Jancar-Webster, 1993). In particular there have been few systematic attempts to explain why the environment was so important in the mobilization phase leading up to the 1989 revolutions; why the environment initially became a central component of the political parties which emerged; why the responses of western states took the form they did; how environmental issues subsequently became sidelined, and finally what the consequences of this are for the future of environmental politics in the FSU and central and eastern Europe.

There is even less attention given to the place of environmental politics in this region within the context of western approaches to the environment in the closing years of the twentieth century. The 1989 revolutions coincided with a marked 'global turn' in environmental politics as international summitry leading to global environmental conventions took centre stage, most notably in relation to the 1992 United Nations Conference on Environment and Development (UNCED) in Rio de Janeiro (the 'Earth Summit'). Given this global trend, the sudden collapse of communism offered an opportunity to restructure whole economies around clean production techniques. However, this perhaps unique political and economic opportunity was not seized.

Instead the dominant western view, which achieved ascendancy in the aftermath of the revolutions, was a triumphalist assertion of liberal political and economic forms (Fukuyama, 1989; Sachs, 1990). The World Bank and the IMF applied their well-honed structural development formulae to the FSU and central and eastern

Europe with disastrous results. By imposing privatization, marketization, tradable currencies and reduced social expenditure, the economic infrastructure of the former Council for Mutual Economic Assistance (CMEA) states was completely destroyed. The impacts of this destruction have been critiqued comprehensively by Gowan (1995). Using a range of UN, World Bank, IMF and World Health Organisation sources, he produces a dispassionate argument which can be summarized in the following manner.

The central impacts of the West's economic approach to the former eastern bloc resulted in intense downward pressure on wage levels. Between January 1990 and the end of 1992 these fell by 33.9 per cent in Poland, 21.5 per cent in Czechoslovakia and 14 per cent in Hungary (Gowan, 1995: 20). At the start of the 1990s exports to EC countries boomed but then slumped under the impact of protectionist measures and successful western take-overs. By 1993 the FSU had a trade deficit with the EC of US$7.2 billion (pp. 21, 27). The IMF has calculated that it will take until 2010 for even the most 'successful' of the restructured economies, such as Poland, to return to 1989 living standards (Gowan, 1995: 55). Economic restructuring imposed significant material hardship upon the vast majority of the population of the region.

UNICEF estimated that there have been 800,000 excess deaths between 1989 and 1993 in Russia, Ukraine, Bulgaria, Hungary and Poland as a direct consequence of these actions (Gowan, 1995: 22). As the important insight that poverty and environmental degradation go hand in hand (World Commission on Environment and Development, 1987) was beginning to guide development aid to the 'third world', economic hardship and environmental degradation were being actively created in eastern and central Europe.

A further part of the accompanying western triumphalism centred on the idea that solutions to environmental problems would be found through market mechanisms far more effectively than through communist central planning. We do not share this faith in the ability of the market alone to produce environmental gains, and indeed argue that the widely discredited system of central planning provides important examples demonstrating the continued importance of the state in a regulatory mode.

In relation to these events we advance a series of arguments. We argue that the importance of environmentalism within the revolutions arises from the fact that it represented one of the few politically significant spheres of independent (i.e. extra-party) organization within civil societies, which had been harshly suppressed though never completely crushed under communism. We hold this argument in common with some other commentators (see Jancar-Webster, 1993). The argument is extended here, however, by emphasizing the historical importance of the environment as an area enjoying legitimacy within the structures of the communist party. This element of our argument emphasizes the scientific, political and rank-and-file purchase of the environment within the party apparatus. The increasing acceptance of an environmental agenda within Marxism–Leninism is thus seen as providing one important prefigurative channel through which social and political forces, such as extensive nature conservationist networks, came into being (DeBardeleben, 1985; see also Chapters 2 and 4 of this volume). Rather than an immediate mobilization around demands for democratic reforms, the environment thus plays an important prefigurative role in the resultant transformations.

The explanatory power of this historical argument is of course limited and we draw attention to a number of more recent factors. These include changes in the occupational structure of the former eastern bloc modelled on Soviet methods of forced industrialization, the importance of cultural products in precipitating change with particular importance being attached to the media, forms of intellectual leadership, and – in certain countries – the resilience of parts of civil society in the face of decades of repression.

Whilst wishing to advance these general arguments we also recognize the importance of differences arising from each country's experiences of Soviet domination and the legacy of their particular cultural and social forms. From a sociological perspective, the diverse nationalities subsumed by the Soviet model inevitably produced an equally diverse set of responses, particularly as each of the ex-communist societies struggled to come to terms with the legacy of Soviet domination. The difficult and painful task of economic reconstruction has been accompanied by the equally urgent task of finding a new identity in a post-communist world where all the old certainties had suddenly been dissolved. This process is inevitably complex, with each society drawing upon different historical and cultural traditions. This complexity is further compounded by sudden exposure to models of contemporary civil society drawn from 'advanced' capitalist states. To Gowan, the deliberate exportation of a neo-liberal conception of civil society promoting a minimalist state and the expression of personal freedom and identity through market-based consumption is a crucial part of the West's economic restructuring strategy (Gowan, 1995: 49).

Within this amalgam of change the environment's role as catalyst will inevitably vary. For example, in Poland and East Germany workers' movements and religious institutions played crucial, though very different, roles in nurturing political mobilizations for democracy and the environment during the 1980s.

These organizing themes have prioritized certain countries which have historically fulfilled particularly important roles in relation to both the Soviet Union and the West. East Germany, Czechoslovakia, Poland and Hungary represented both a geopolitical buffer between Russia and the NATO allies in the post-war period whilst simultaneously providing a source of 'modern' industrial capacity within the former CMEA. The transitions in these countries assume particular importance due to these historic associations. We concentrate on these countries and their relation to the FSU as we believe that the most significant insights are to be found here.

In particular we want to question several of the core assumptions which became established during and after the 1989 revolutions. Perhaps prime amongst those is the argument, originally advanced by Fukuyama (1989), that the fall of communism represented 'the end of history' as all that remained was liberalism. According to this view the collapse of the eastern bloc demonstrated the flawed nature of communist central planning and, by default, vindicated market mechanisms as the most effective means of allocating resources within a society. The western media's identification of intense pockets of environmental degradation within the region was taken as proof that communism held the environment in complete disregard, with the corollary that the market would find better solutions.

We are not convinced by these arguments and take the view that market mechanisms alone cannot achieve either sustainable development or an equitable and just society (see Eckersley, 1992; Mulberg, 1992). The need for planning which retains some autonomy from narrowly conceived economic goals represents for us a crucial area where democratically representative institutions and groups must guide development practices through the political codification of ethical and moral principles. In this sense we are not convinced by the argument that a liberal political model alone can fulfil this ambition either. Our main reservation here relates to the liberal reliance upon an abstract and universally present individual shaped by common commitments, for example 'rational' discourse, free association as defined by the rule of law, the right to free speech and so on. The capacity of liberal civil society to accommodate difference and diversity has been severely tested in the West by issues of 'race', class, gender, sexuality and environmental concerns (see for example Weeks, 1994). These concerns have brought into question the legitimacy of a civil society which in practice has privileged white male heterosexual interests above all others.

In the former eastern bloc, where liberal economic reforms have proceeded apace, the ensuing quest for renewed civil societies has unleashed unexpected social forces which stretch liberal political and social forms even further. Amongst these has been the emergence of various forms of nationalism, a process bloodily demonstrated in the former Yugoslavia and numerous former Soviet republics – a trend which it would be premature to regard as declining (Zizek, 1990). In central and eastern Europe as a whole the construction and questioning of regime legitimacy within the new democracies occurred simultaneously without the luxury of accumulated historical experience which accompanies such reflection in the West. The intensity of the search for new civil society in central and eastern Europe has to be understood, in part, as an attempt to rebuild a sense of both national and civic culture in the midst of these tensions.

Soviet communism systematically repressed and distorted expressions of civil society throughout its tutelage over its eastern European empire. In many of the countries considered here the models of civil society available in the 1990s are reconstructions of those existing before Soviet domination. It is our contention that the combination of these archaic civil societies with the rapid economic and political transformations make Fukuyama's (1989) prediction of liberal world dominance premature. In Vavroušek's words the post-war liberal system is 'melting down' because it was 'unable to prevent or solve many of the interlinked problems which create environmental insecurity' (1993: 89). The call of the past is mediated by the pull of the brave new world of privatization and both are mediated through the lens of material hardship and the more recent memory of the limited but adequate certainties of central planning.

The position taken here is a much less comfortable one than the standard triumphalist assertion of liberal ascendancy. The nature of the pyrrhic victory over communism is revealed in the crises of identity experienced by prominent western nations following the collapse of the much vaunted 'new world order' which briefly surfaced at the time of the Gulf War in 1990. The collapse of the Cold War removed the structural alignment of national identities based on the neat juxtaposition of ideological opposites and has precipitated a quest for new roles, meanings and identities. An environmental post-modern world was seen in embryonic form as the Berlin Wall was torn down (Lash, 1990). Though the conceptual work necessary to define a green post-modernism remains to be done, some of the issues raised here remain crucial to the formulation of such a path.

DEMOCRACY AND THE 'VELVET REVOLUTIONS'

It is difficult to communicate the impact of the abrupt abolition of an entire way of thinking and living. A Russian sociologist confided that after seventy years of Marxism–Leninism being the only acceptable basis for analysis it was suddenly totally discredited. The response to this was not the emergence of many competing sociological paradigms, rather people waited to be told what the 'new line was to be'.[1] This anecdote reflects the important insight that Soviet Marxism–Leninism has never been a simple reflection of the works of Marx and Lenin, rather it has been a contingent doctrine subject to continual reinterpretation by a changing *nomenklatura* (DeBardeleben, 1985: 7). The intense distrust of this cadre following the revolutions resulted in few clearly articulated alternatives to communist domination, at least amongst the general populace. This kind of cultural shock is not confined to the heartland of Russia; following unification Germans used the term *'die Mauer im Kopf'* – the wall in the head – to describe the enormous task of coming to terms with radically changed circumstances in terms of embedded social, cultural and political practices (Hamilton, 1992: 7).

The years of communist domination produced an idealized view of western democracy, the pursuit of which became one of the implicit objectives of the 'velvet revolutions'. One reason why these revolutions won the enthusiastic support of western political leaders such as Margaret Thatcher lay precisely in the fact that they could be claimed to demonstrate popular demand for one of the cornerstones of capitalism. The emphasis placed on bourgeois freedoms – freedom of speech, freedom of assembly, freedom to travel, free elections and so on – lacked an appreciation of the limitations of these freedoms once established, and perhaps more importantly lacked any recognition of the problems of achieving initial legitimacy for such a democracy.

Liberal democracy was seized upon as the only apparently certain means of eliminating the old *nomenklatura*, thus banishing communism once and for all. The use of round-table discussions to facilitate the transition to democracy was uneven and the hopelessly tight timetables gave such forums little time to establish either their own legitimacy or meaningful political agendas (Welsh, 1994: 385). The result was not a transition to an ordered capitalist system but the dominance of chaos and crisis (Touraine, 1992: 134) as new centres of identity, purpose and direction began to compete.

In this competition it is easy to underestimate the potency of the pre-existing environmental networks throughout the countries discussed here. Positive freedoms, particularly those of association and expression, became key political demands mobilized by groups such as Ekoglasnost in Bulgaria (e.g. Fisher, 1993a: 95). Environmentalists throughout the region began to argue for *glasnost* from below, demonstrating the new-found vitality of the grass-roots movements. Freedom from communist central planning and access to environmental information were themes which found ready support within pre-existing conservation and environmental networks. Particularly in urban areas the environment and social welfare issues were indivisible due to the chronic health impacts of industrial pollution (Friendly and Feshbach, 1992; Carter and Turnock, 1993; Feshbach, 1995). As these concerns reached wider and wider constituencies environmental dissidents, who had demonstrated their integrity and courage by speaking out before the arrival of *glasnost*, became increasingly trusted and influential political leaders.

In some countries the submerged networks of environmental activists quickly became the framework for the revolutions of 1989. Often environmentalists built on and developed earlier anti-nuclear networks established during the European Nuclear Disarmament campaigns of the 1980s. These networks provided links with west Europeans, particularly in East Germany, where the well-established German Green Party provided a ready source of collaboration (Tismaneanu, 1989: 104). These networks extended east into the Ukraine and other countries, including the Baltic states (Kux, 1991).

During the initial stages of democratic state formation following the revolutions, social, political, economic and environmental realignment became so closely interwoven as to be indivisible. Activists, accustomed to dealing only with environmental issues, suddenly found themselves acting as political representatives, often as members of provisional or recently elected governments, dealing with the entire spectrum of issues confronted within the transition. The move from opposition to government is an extraordinarily difficult one to make, even after years of being the official opposition, as the British Labour Party discovered when it assumed office for the first time in 1924. Compared with this, assuming political leadership in any of the countries discussed here was like stepping into a maelstrom. This had some immediate political consequences. One was the democratization of the old communist parties, which has subsequently led to the election of reform communist governments in countries such as Hungary, Romania, Poland[2] and Bulgaria. A second consequence has been the dependency of the new governments upon former communist bureaucrats and managers for the necessary knowledge and skills to run the state. A third has been the entry of opportunists, sometimes under the guise of environmentalism, with an eye to ready profits flowing from privatization and marketization. These political factions all have different views on important issues. Most centrally, the debate over the scope, rate and depth of marketization has dominated domestic political debate, displacing the environment from its brief position of prominence. This amalgam of pressures leaves the place of the state in achieving both environmental and social gains ill defined and much disputed. We return to this in the final chapter.

INTELLECTUAL LEADERSHIP

One of the most important features which made the revolutions of 1989 possible was the intellectual leadership of Gorbachev in breaking with the established political wisdom of the *nomenklatura*. Gorbachev acted decisively in pursuit of a transformed communism through the twin initiatives of *glasnost* and *perestroika*. These initiatives were introduced into a range of Soviet policy spheres, where they had both intended and unintended consequences. The initiative caught western governments, commentators and analysts unawares. The social and political sciences also failed to offer any substantial warning that change of a fundamental nature was about to occur. It is a sanguine reflection that these disciplines continue to be most effective as codifiers of what is.

If the 1980s demonstrated one thing clearly, it was the importance of charismatic leaders in promoting significant change through the presentation of a seemingly coherent vision claiming to break decisively with what had gone before. Thatcher, Reagan and Gorbachev all demonstrated Weber's insight that charismatic leadership must periodically reinvigorate established polities, producing a temporary amelioration in, if not escape from, the iron cage of bureaucracy. The importance of key figures in periods of intense change serves to underline the manner in which social and personal factors combine to produce transformations which social theory alone is ill equipped to predict (Polyani, 1944; Glasman, 1994).

The charismatic nature of Gorbachev's leadership was further enhanced by the inflexible and increasingly hardline stances taken by other eastern European leaders. Long after it had become clear that Gorbachev would not permit any Soviet intervention in the internal affairs of the countries dealt with here, their communist leaders continued to attempt to cling onto power (Kusin, 1986; Adomeit, 1990; Stokes, 1991). Gorbachev's agenda was thoroughgoing and extended to all areas of policy in recognition of the need to transform the malaise which had come to dominate the USSR since the 1970s. It was perhaps this shared commitment to total transformation which led Margaret Thatcher to describe Gorbachev as 'someone I can do business with'. Gorbachev's attempt to reconstitute Soviet communism beyond the degrees of manoeuvre permitted by traditional readings of Marxism–Leninism complicates the simplistic interpretation of collapse due to internal inefficiency which has dominated much western literature.

Whilst the revolutions of 1989 have been widely interpreted as the finale of an outdated political and economic system collapsing under the weight of its own illegitimacy and inefficiency, it is important not to lose sight of Gorbachev's attempt to shape the transition to produce a coherent, if massively reformed, socialist system (Adomeit, 1990; Stokes, 1991). From the beginning Gorbachev strove to reorient the CMEA around a fifteen-year economic modernization plan concentrating on electronics, automated production, atomic energy, materials science and biotechnology (Kusin, 1986: 43). The CMEA also drew up detailed environmental action programmes during this final phase of communism. The CMEA countries were thus developing a modernization package similar to the European Community's FAST programme immediately prior to their transformation. Gorbachev's foreign policy was designed to provide the necessary funds for this modernization in two ways. By advancing rapidly towards significant nuclear and conventional arms reduction he sought an escape from the military burden imposed on the USSR by the West, particularly the United States.[3] In this he echoed earlier attempts by Brezhnev, within the Helsinki process,[4] to reduce the economic burdens of the 'arms race'. Resources released from the military burden would be available for modernization, whilst the reduced military threat posed by the Soviet Union would make the country a more acceptable business partner and site for inward investment.[5] *Glasnost* and *perestroika* were thus crucial to the success of Gorbachev's wider aim of a reinvigorated communist party equipped with a modernized agenda which broke decisively with Russian insularity at home and confrontation abroad.

In terms of foreign policy, one of the few areas where the Soviets had maintained a dialogue with the West throughout the Cold War was in fact the environment.[6] Collaboration on the environment gave eminent Russian academicians in atmospheric modelling a key role in establishing the credibility of nuclear winter as a consequence of any large-scale nuclear war. This, combined with the possibility of accidental nuclear war, produced some of the most telling arguments against deterrence (Smoker, 1988) and drew early attention to the importance of 'globalism' as a political and analytical domain undermining the autonomy of national actors (Welsh, 1988: 43).

The acceptance of the environment as an area within which Marxism–Leninism could 'do business' with the West lent it a certain legitimacy within the party apparatus, something which perhaps reflected the considerable legacy of ecological science within the USSR (Gare, 1993). In terms of attempts to bridge the gap between the arts and sciences made famous by C.P. Snow's notion of two cultures, the Soviets had mounted some innovative educational initiatives in this area, including attempts to bring together aesthetic and scientific approaches towards the environment (Senkevich, 1991).

Such initiatives have to be read as part of a strategic theoretical and legislative programme addressing the environment within Marxism–Leninism (Volgyes, 1974; DeBardeleben, 1985; Jancar, 1987). These scientific, cultural and political expressions of environmental awareness were accompanied by the active state promotion of conservation groups from the 1920s onwards (Yanitsky, 1993; Mirovitskaya, this volume). In common with the growth of western environmentalism, these conservation groups became the seedbed of more politically oriented environmental movements. In the lead-up to the revolutions of 1989 membership of recognized conservation movements within the region grew rapidly, as did their more clandestine counterparts. According to Yanitsky (1993) the 'crossover membership' meant that the environment began to have an active constituency throughout the apparatus of the communist party from factory committees upwards. Public acquiescence in the official line was marked by the private acknowledgement that Marxism–Leninism did not have solutions to the problems it confronted. Anecdotally, Yanitsky describes the party as being over by some time in the late 1970s, a date that has also been suggested for Czechoslovakia (Kabele, 1993: 767). From this point the environment became increasingly discussed in the private residences of party *apparatchiks* and intellectuals, something reflected in the growth in environmental legislation throughout the later years of communist rule. The important point here is that this constellation of forces within Soviet communism gave the environment legitimacy based on the support of a diverse range of groupings within the party and beyond the party-state. It took the revolutions of 1989 to introduce the only element missing from this constellation when compared with the West – formal environmental non-governmental organizations (ENGOs).

Growth in the legitimacy of the environment within Soviet communism is differentially reflected in the countries considered in other chapters of this volume. Influences specific to each country produced specific nuances. As Tickle and Vavroušek point out for Czechoslovakia, environmentalism also drew on the romantic and aesthetic movements in the Austro-Hungarian period. Elsewhere, for example, religious institutions played an important role in the development of autonomous environmental movements (Fisher, 1993a: 94–96; Joppke, 1995; Hicks, 1996).

ENVIRONMENT, SOCIETY AND NATURE

The environment has become the focus of a burgeoning literature in both the natural and social sciences in recent years. This massive growth in publication belies the fact that the environment remains an intensely contested term with a range of meanings. The major contours of these debates revolve around the extent to which the environment should be conceived as a domain where objective scientific knowledge derived from the 'natural' sciences should hold sway. According to this view the environment can be understood through the discerning of 'laws of nature' which assume a reality independent of humans. This 'realist' view (Bhaskar, 1975; Benton, 1989), ascendant until the 1970s, has since come under increasing criticism by those who argue that nature and the environment are 'socially constructed' (Haraway, 1992; Ross, 1994; Yearly, 1994; Hannigan, 1996). As no consensus over these debates is in sight it is crucial that the reader understands the approach taken to these issues here.

We are centrally concerned with the environment as a site which plays a crucial role in focusing insights from a wide range of academic disciplines. These include the biological and physical sciences, economics, politics, philosophy and sociology. In laying competing claims to explanatory power in relation to this site, disciplines enter into a dialectical redefinition of both the environment and disciplinary boundaries. Such perturbations can increase interdisciplinary rivalry, appear to reduce analytical purchase and lead to extremely charged debates. This background noise can obscure the need for interdisciplinary work in this area (see Becher, 1989; Arizpe, 1991). By focusing on the role of the environment in the revolutions of 1989 we believe that the implications of these debates can be given substance in ways which advance the understanding of the revolutions and wider choices relating to environmental policy and politics which confront all nations.

The term *ecology* is taken here to denote a science, with a long tradition in both West and East, which deals with the inter-relationships between different species and their habitats. As Enzensberger famously commented, this science only becomes contentious when it includes the human species as this makes the consideration of a range of ideological, moral and ethical issues inescapable (1974). To this view the contentious nature of an ecology which embraces humans arises from the incorporation of social and political issues which undermine claims to scientific credibility. Social and ethical concerns are inseparable from, indeed are vital to, any adequate understanding of the environmental. The term *environmentalism* thus expresses human concerns for, and intervention in, the environment. Many forms of environmentalism are possible, including extreme right-wing variants, making the alignment between environmental and social policy positions a crucially important political arena.

Under the dominance of the biological and natural sciences the term *environment* has tended to become synonymous with 'nature' and the 'natural'. For present purposes any such definition is far too restrictive. The environment can refer to any site which sustains biological life irrespective of its relation to 'nature'. Most obviously the built environment has little direct relation to the organic *processes* which form the basis of classical habitat ecology.[7] A more extreme example would be the interior of the Russian Mír space station, which constitutes a totally engineered environment. In a social scientific sense this distinction obviously depends upon whether humans are part of nature or regarded as separate or above nature.

The Enlightenment view that humankind enjoyed a separation from the rest of nature found practical expression with the advent of modern industrial societies, playing a crucial formative role in both East and West. For our present purposes one of the most important similarities between these two apparently opposed political systems has been the belief that 'nature' could be made subordinate to human will through science and technology (Merchant, 1983).

In this view 'nature' became the subject of a long and complex process of social construction which meant that what is commonly understood as 'natural' has changed over time within particular societies and been an area of competing definition between societies. Another consequence of these processes has been that 'human nature' has been both constructed and contested as a site through which the natural sciences could extend their overall control over nature to include humans. Science and technology have thus contributed to the domination of both nature and people. A common feature of these processes involves dominant social categories, such as male superiority, being projected onto 'nature', where they are observed and then read back onto human societies as 'objective' evidence of, for example, gender differences (Haraway, 1992; Ross, 1994). What is understood as natural is thus always historically contingent and profoundly dependent upon competing sets of ideas about the social. For Haraway, this means that discourse is always a form of material practice, that is, part of the struggle over the definition of human–human and human–nature relationships. For Ross, the crucial challenge is to maintain a distinction between wisdom about nature and the supposed wisdom *of* nature which predetermines social roles. We are thus operating with a distinctly constructivist view of 'nature' and the environment which recognizes the inevitably contingent status of 'hard' scientific knowledge and rejects the view that 'nature' can provide any model for how societies should be. The works of Haraway and Ross also provide a possible bridge between the assertion of human separation from nature and the opposite view, associated with 'deep ecologists' (see Devall and Sessions, 1985; Fox, 1990), which would regard humans as 'just' another species. As O'Neill (1993) argues, the human capacity to decide consciously to prioritize other species over immediate material or aesthetic interests distinguishes humankind from other species. Humans are of nature but also constitute nature.

Bridges of this sort are rare in a period when the relationship between the environment (understood as sets of ecological processes) and society is undergoing intense redefinition. We believe that the revolutions of 1989 can illuminate this process of redefinition and in protean form reveal some of the wider stakes which ride upon its outcome. This belief is based on the indivisible unity between environment and society, the social and the natural. Without society there can be no environment and without an environment capable of supporting certain forms of life there can be nothing which resembles society, or for that matter humans. The future of society and the future of what it will mean to be human have increasingly become seen as tied to the fate of the planet. The prospect of environmental degradation so intense as to require permanent mechanical aids to make human life possible raises the prospect of a future as cyborgs. Others suggest we have already passed that point.[8]

There is then a crisis of 'nature' in both senses of the word – as a system of ecological processes capable of supporting oxygen-dependent life forms and the identity of what we regard as the most evolved such life form – humans. These crises call into question the fundamental tenets of the post-war international order and the systems of national governance upon which this was based. Lest these claims seem too far-fetched, let us relate them back via the words of a late contributor to this book. In 1993, Josef Vavroušek wrote:

> It is in the basic interests of all human beings to have clean air and water, unspoiled soils, healthy forests and conserved natural resources, biological diversity, the beauty of harmonious land-scape and many other gifts of nature. And this is also our responsibility, not only for future generations of humanity, but for all living beings as well as non-living elements of nature. (p. 91)

Vavroušek, a Czech scientist precipitated into formal politics by the 'velvet revolution' as the Czechoslovak Federal Minister of the Environment (see Chapter 4), placed responsibility upon society for the biological and aesthetic integrity of all nature in full recognition of the complexity and difficulty involved in reconciling, for example, competing perceptions of a harmonious landscape. The environment thus becomes a site through which the economic, political and scientific agendas of societies have to be directed towards longer-term objectives, abandoning the short-termism of most economic and political activity.

This approach to politics, developed in part during the revolutions, linking the health of human societies to the robustness of the environment, had the potential to redraw the political landscape of the closing years of the twentieth century. Such a politics could have begun to redress centuries of human economic activity which have treated the environment as an externality, a free good representing an endless source of raw materials and a sink for pollution of all kinds. It is this indissoluble link between human rights, human welfare and the environment which we believe links the initial revolutions of 1989, making them more than just the overthrow of a particular political and economic regime.

Whilst the relationship between the environment and the revolutions is a complex one, the environment constituted one of the few areas where immanent expressions of civil society remained possible under successive Soviet and allied regimes. The environment constituted a long-standing thread of social and political activity within the closed societies of the FSU and central and eastern Europe. When that political and economic system was finally manoeuvred into a position of collapse by a range of external and internal pressures, environmentalism represented one of the few free spaces within which any form of organization outside the state existed. Submerged environmental movements became highly visible political movements in incredibly short time spans, precipitating trusted environmental activists into positions of political leadership. If there has been one event singled out by commentators as significant in this respect it has been the accident at the Chernobyl nuclear power station.

The implications of Chernobyl

The accident at the nuclear power plant at Chernobyl[9] in 1986 has been widely interpreted by commentators on the environment in central and eastern Europe (Gould, 1990; Feshbach, 1995; Dawson, 1996). Some have argued that Chernobyl 'changed nothing' (Yanitsky, 1993) but the majority regard the accident as one of the formative moments in social movement activism in the FSU (Massey Stewart, 1992; DeBardeleben and Hannigan, 1995). Yanitsky's arguments are true only in the narrow sense that political and economic expediency within the Ukraine resulted in the remaining reactors being pressed back into electricity production following the accident. IMF and World Bank insistence on world prices being paid for gas has intensified Ukrainian enthusiasm for more nuclear power. Beyond this we find that the Chernobyl accident acted as an important focus for a range of existing social and political pressures already present in relation to environmental issues (Young and Launer, 1991).

Coming at the height of Gorbachev's *glasnost* initiative, the Chernobyl accident revealed that freedom of information did not extend to major reactor accidents. This reinforced the demands of both scientists and environmentalists for free access to information and an end to state suppression of such data. It took a further reactor accident at Tomsk in 1993 to prompt Yeltsin to order a comprehensive audit of all nuclear facilities and their potential hazards (Feshbach, 1995: 4). The Chernobyl accident seriously undermined the supposed superiority of Soviet science and technology, providing a powerful example of the drawbacks of the giganticism associated with Soviet ambitions. That the modernist drive of the Soviet super-state could result in such a catastrophe represented a further major blow to the legitimacy of scientific socialism. The accident also heightened tensions with the Soviet allies in eastern Europe, amongst whom access to nuclear power had been a symbol of trust and status. Popular protests in these countries, in Poland, Czechoslovakia and Hungary, formed a significant point of access for western ENGOs, adding weight to the already burgeoning domestic environmental critiques. The accident clearly contributed to political destabilization within the Soviet Union itself. Some Ukrainians regarded it as an act of nuclear genocide (Goldman, 1992: 9), whilst in the Baltic states of Latvia and Estonia the presence of other large RBMK reactors gave environmentalism a prominent place in arguments for independence (Pryde, 1992: 13).

The accident simultaneously jeopardized *perestroika*, as the West learned of it not from the Russians but from abnormally high levels of radiation detected by Swedish monitoring stations. An important Russian response was the ready acceptance of international delegations offering scientific and technical assistance. Whilst assistance in the initial stabilization of the Chernobyl reactor was refused, the subsequent safety evaluation of similar reactors, the assessment of future nuclear programmes and the evaluation of the radiological impact of the accident have all been areas of international collaboration. Recently this has been politically mediated by Russia's increasing participation within the G-7 group. In that respect, it should be noted that scientific collaboration has not remained completely decoupled from the political pursuit of aid, something which has prevented the compilation of coherent data in a number of areas, including the radiological evaluation of the accident.

Chernobyl impacted on environmentalism in a number of ways. It further legitimized environmentalists' demands for freedom of information; provided a powerful example of the existence of a pan-European environment, with the cloud of fallout travelling north-east and then south over Italy before returning north and west over France and the UK, where it 'rained out' over North Wales and Cumbria; illustrated the dangers associated with high-risk technologies; provided the most important source of radiological data since the atomic bombs dropped on Hiroshima and Nagasaki by the western allies in 1945; and provided a strong impetus to various environmental movements' campaigns in the central and east European states which possessed Russian-built reactors. Furthermore, the European Union became more interested in nuclear safety behind the former 'Iron Curtain' than ever before and nuclear technology became an area where development aid was readily forthcoming.[10] The accident was constructed as an opportunity for the western nuclear industry to develop new markets at a time when new domestic orders were drying up and existing contracts were beginning to be cancelled.[11]

The prospect of a western take-over in nuclear science and technology inside the FSU needs care. The tremendous pride and prestige associated with Soviet nuclear science and technology cannot be simply replaced by off-the-shelf western products. The Soviets' enormous scientific and technological commitment in this area produced an immense scientific and technical cadre. The morale and integrity of this cadre remain crucial to the management and containment of nuclear materials. The decline in status and wage levels of Russian nuclear scientists since the 1989 revolutions has been linked with evidence of a significant increase in an illicit trade in highly enriched fissile material (Kramer, 1986; Feshbach, 1995: 27–30). The proliferation implications of this trade are especially serious given the existence of a number of client states wealthy enough to acquire nuclear weapons by this means. The Russian nuclear enterprise is also keen to re-equip its eastern European neighbours and develop an integrated trade in the whole nuclear fuel cycle, though this may be thrown into doubt by the thorny issue of where to site nuclear waste repositories. Such technical and economic exchanges will play an important role in the ultimate geopolitical alignment of central and eastern Europe. Currently, however, most of the former Soviet bloc satellites are determined to follow East Germany (GDR) into the EU and NATO. This raises profoundly important issues beyond the scope of this book, including the future of supranational military organizations such as NATO. Whether such Cold War organizations can be reformed and find a new identity and purpose in a post-Cold-War age remains one of the most important geopolitical issues to emerge from the revolutions of 1989.

Chernobyl clearly structured the subsequent trajectories of environmentally sensitive issues in both internal and external senses. Tragically, the chaos which dominated the initial clean-up operations extended into the subsequent radiological evaluation of the accident, jeopardizing the prospects of reliable dose response data from release pathways with more relevance to civil radiological protection than the standards currently derived from bomb survivors. Whilst agreeing with Fisher (1993a: 89) that Chernobyl contributed to rather than created environmentalism, it is important to recognize that the roots of environmentalism in central and eastern Europe extend even further back into history than is commonly acknowledged.

The sources of environmentalism are thus far more diverse than many commentators acknowledge. There are both differences and similarities with the evolution of environmentalism in a range of western countries here. Whilst commentators like Yanitsky (1993) emphasize the differences, we do not want to lose sight of the similarities, which we believe will become increasingly important to the future development of environmental politics in this region, something we discuss more fully in the final chapter of this volume.

GENDER, ENVIRONMENT AND THE REVOLUTIONS

In the West the relationship between gender and environmental activism is widely acknowledged, even if there is no ready consensus about the significance of eco-feminism (Merchant, 1992; Mies and Shiva, 1993; Jackson, 1995). Irrespective of this, eco-feminism has mounted influential critiques of dominant approaches towards the environment which neglect the social reproduction of humans and the centrality of women within this. From this view, for example, environmental management, stewardship and the use of economic instruments to achieve environmental objectives reflect male approaches emphasizing control and dominance over both nature and women.

At the heart of these concerns lies the gendered distribution of both formal and informal power. This prioritizes the importance of gender in both the public and private spheres, with the relationship between these spheres being particularly important for the nature of the resultant civil society. The recognition that established liberal notions of civil society are in fact gendered has been a relatively recent object of academic analysis (Walby, 1994). That women have a crucial stake in the civil societies which are emerging in central and eastern Europe is beyond question and clearly illustrated by opposition to a ban on abortions in countries such as Poland, where the influence of the Catholic Church is particularly strong.

The stakes for women throughout central and eastern Europe have been particularly high. Under communism women had access to a wide range of occupational categories frequently denied them in the West. Despite this women were still under great pressure to become mothers, with medals being given to those with large families. Tensions between womens' reproductive and productive capacities represented a constant dynamic within which access to social welfare provision, particularly housing, health, education and childcare, remained endemic within the eastern bloc (Mieczkowski, 1985).

Given the centrality of the World Bank and IMF in the economic, political and social restructuring of eastern Europe, Enloe's insight (1989) that all such remodelling assumes traditional roles for women as mothers, wives, and cheap, flexible part-time workers can be expected to have considerable analytical importance. In some countries, women played a significant role in the submerged environmental networks which prefigured the 1989 revolutions. As in the French revolutions, women's experiences formed a central mobilizing theme and women were prominent both on the street and in organizing committees (Dolling, 1991; Einhorn, 1993; Watson, 1993b). This involvement reflected a long-standing commitment within opposition movements organized around human rights issues (Jancar, 1985; Wolchik and Meyer, 1985).

The environmental gains sought in the 1989 revolutions were inseparable from certain rights and provisions to which women are sensitized through their roles as mothers and carers. The relationship between clean air and water and healthy children provides a particularly graphic example of how women's greater involvement in childcare introduces a greater sensibility of the impacts of pollution. The association between poverty and ill health also impacts directly on women within the sphere of domestic consumption, where they 'traditionally' go without to ensure that children and male workers have enough.

Following the revolutions of 1989 every policy sphere contained embedded gender relations and implications. Decisions over the kind of industrial modernization to be undertaken, the structure and objectives of regulatory mechanisms (whether market- or state-driven), the nature of the political democracy to be built, the shape of environmental and welfare policy; all had implicit and explicit consequences for women. Despite this, the recognition of a gendered dimension is often completely absent, even in areas of the literature which deal directly with problems of legitimacy associated with social welfare (see for example Frankland and Cox, 1995).

As in the French revolutions women were steadily excluded, first from roles of prominence and then more generally from the streets throughout the region. Accounts of the transition process emphasizing the importance of political strategy and negotiation in the transition to democracy fail to acknowledge this exclusion (Welsh, 1994). They do, however, reveal the importance of 'round table' discussions widely used as a transitional forum to shape 'founding elections'. These typically comprised around fifty delegates and up to 500 experts meeting intensively over a period of several months. In the crucial period between January 1989 and March 1990 these round tables paved the way for elections in Poland, Hungary, Czechoslovakia, the GDR, Bulgaria and Romania. The constitution of these round tables thus played a central role in establishing the initial political, economic and environmental agendas in central and eastern Europe. Inclusion or exclusion from these groups and the relative weight given to competing voices within them constituted a crucial exercise of power. The problem of establishing initial regime legitimacy within the fledgling democracies was compounded by the plethora of internal voices striving to be heard and the attempts of external bodies, most notably key governmental, financial and commercial institutions. The clamour for 'dialogue' from the West reflected a range of concerns. To the US government, maintaining the stability of deterrence assumed crucial importance, particularly when Ukraine sought to retain a significant proportion of the FSU's nuclear arsenal. Anecdotally, the view was expressed that the further west one went in Russia the more events resembled the American gold rush with prospectors, in this case western corporates, filing claims with whoever appeared to be the most powerful local authority.[12] The view is supported by the comments of Lord Howe, the former UK Foreign Secretary and adviser to the Ukrainian government, who favoured the establishment of 'bandit capitalism', likening this to the 'great robber baron phase of American capitalism' (Gowan, 1995: 48).

In these intermediate forums the twin demands of political and economic reform displaced concerns over gender and the environment[13] during a crucial window of consolidation. The subsequent parliaments of the new democracies contained far fewer women than the socialist assemblies they replaced. This displacement of women from the public sphere coincides with the reassertion of a range of past patriarchal practices subordinating women within the private sphere. In Poland, for example, the Catholic Church quickly reasserted its influence in reclaiming assets nationalized by the state and began a campaign to revoke abortion rights instituted under socialist administrations – an issue that has continued to divide the nation as the new Polish constitution was debated throughout the early part of 1997.

The attempt to confine women to the private sphere coincides with a model of liberal economic development which has been dependent upon women's unpaid labour to service a predominantly male labour force. The standard tariff of IMF and World Bank conditions for loans include reductions in the overall burden of welfare spending as a prerequisite of reduced state expenditure and downward pressure on wages. The formula has a disproportionate impact upon women and other poor groups dependent upon welfare provisions. The economic restructuring which has taken place in eastern Europe has reconstituted the profile of both environmental impacts (see Boehmer-Christiansen, this volume) and the gender order of the affected societies. The role of environmental groups, and women within them, as catalysts of change has been submerged in the subsequent transition to a 'man's world'

(Molyneux, 1990; Watson, 1993a: 472, 1993b). To some commentators, women and the environment were the joint losers in the transition (see Fisher, 1993b and Mirovitskaya, this volume).

The reassertion of traditional forms of female subordination towards the end of the twentieth century is an area we return to in our conclusions as we believe that this represents one sphere of the emergent civil societies where fresh and unanticipated sources of contestation will emerge. In post-war Britain a similar attempt was made to return women to the home to 'breed a new imperial race' (Wilson, 1977). This attempt failed, as similar attempts to confine women in central and eastern Europe are also likely to fail.

THE MEDIA

In considering the importance of the media in the transformation of central and eastern Europe it is worth following some well-established distinctions reflecting the double-edged nature of the media. A central tension here lies between those who emphasize the power of media production to shape perceptions (such as Horkheimer and Adorno) and post-modernists emphasizing the autonomy of the 'reader'[14] and the importance of contextual or constructivist elements through which readers and viewers attribute meaning to media products. These debates become peculiarly salient when applied to the environment in central and eastern Europe in terms of both media representation inside these countries and the depiction of the environment to outside western audiences. In the West, eastern Europe quickly became known as a region suffering some of the worst environmental degradation imaginable as a consequence of the excesses of communism. Images from pollution blackspots cast a graphic picture of environmental and human suffering, with little to counter the impression that this was typical of the entire region. The vast tracts of relatively unpolluted lands remained an invisible backdrop to these striking images.

In eastern Europe the liberalization of the media, particularly television, became a central element of the new public sphere, vital to the growth and functioning of emergent civil societies. Given the long history of absolute state control over the media, it is easy to see why the emergence of media resembling those of the West should be seen in this light. The role of the media in the 1989 revolutions assumed central significance in several respects. Communist regimes in general have proven particularly vulnerable to the spread of 'free' information and this was true in eastern and central Europe in the periods before, during and immediately after the 1989 revolutions. In countries like the GDR, communist party officials frequently complained about the presence of the enemy in every home in the form of a television set capable of receiving West German broadcasts (Tismaneanu, 1989: 92). Arguably, western success in this propaganda war between East and West led to the construction of the Berlin Wall as the only means of halting the exodus of citizens. The destabilization of the regimes in eastern Europe which erupted in 1989 was not, however, the product of deliberate propaganda aimed at the central tenets of Marxism–Leninism by the intelligence communities of the West. As an ideology and organizing principle Marxism–Leninism was already widely discredited throughout the eastern bloc by this time.

Three major media influences can be identified. First was the widespread availability of images portraying ways of life which appeared to encapsulate the forms of freedoms sought within the revolutions. These proved extraordinarily potent, especially amongst the young and professional middle classes. The freedom to enjoy 'decadent' western rock music and participate in domestic 'alternative' cultures serves as a strong case in point (Ramet, 1994). The state's intolerant and authoritarian response to such desires merely fuelled resistance.[15] Attempting to discredit the party line of Marxism–Leninism, as official western propagandists did, was by this time largely pointless as the ideology was unofficially already dead.

Secondly, the availability of information on environmental events inside the region discredited the assurances about *glasnost*, further weakening the legitimacy of state, governments and the party alike. As mentioned above, the accident at Chernobyl was particularly significant in this respect but it would be wrong to see this as the only, or even the crucial example of this process. As the 1980s progressed the environmental consequences of other large-scale Soviet-style projects became subject to similar processes of legitimation stripping.

During and after the revolutions the environment in eastern Europe was extensively portrayed by the western media as a series of disaster areas. Dramatic news items and documentaries depicting scenes of chronic air and water pollution, high-environmental-impact engineering projects and so on made areas such as the 'Black Triangle' (comprising the industrial regions of North Bohemia, southern East Germany and Silesia) household names, leaving the impression of completely despoiled countries. The accumulated stockpiles of nuclear waste and the existence of large tracts of land contaminated by radioactivity, particularly in the FSU, all added to the picture of ecological disaster (Friendly and Feshbach, 1992; Wolfson, 1994; Feshbach, 1995; Pryde, 1995).

Thirdly, and perhaps most importantly for those on the ground, advanced television technology meant that western audiences could witness the revolutions as they happened. These were the first 'real-time TV' revolutions in the history of the world. The idea that the hand of the most powerful state could be stayed by the moral opprobrium of the 'world community' already had credibility amongst antinuclear activists (Welsh, 1987); now the technical means to marshal such opprobrium were readily available. At key junctures the presence of the television media was a factor restraining military commanders unwilling to execute the orders of increasingly desperate hardline political leaders. In Leipzig, for example, Erich Honecker's orders to fire at demonstrators were disregarded by Soviet military commanders and the KGB is said to have supported demonstrations in Prague (Kux, 1991: 5). It also seems likely that media images, particularly on television, speeded the tempo of overall change. In Czechoslovakia and Bulgaria, Russian television (made available in slavish attempts to curry Soviet favour) coverage was politically more open than domestic channels and images of citizens tearing down Hungarian border fences with Austria resulted in many East German citizens fleeing to the West via this hole in the 'Iron Curtain'.

The accumulated cultural capital of resistance built up amongst the street protesters was already the commonplace of environmental activism and activists. Peaceful protests, candlelit vigils, bearing witness, the acceptance of personal risk and the determination to be seen and heard were all tactics developed by civil and human rights campaigns throughout the West. These were tactics which West German Greens shared with their East German counterparts. The spread of such repertoires of resistance has always been encouraged by underground networks relying upon traditional printed forms of *samizdat* such as the illegal poster, handbill and newsletter (Skilling, 1989). The opening up of the media magnified these channels of communication, allowing for a significant increase in movement solidarity and praxis across the entire eastern bloc. As the communist governments of the region lost legitimacy these tactics proved devastatingly potent forms of protest, illustrating the contingent nature of formal political power.

Whilst the role of the electronic media is highly visible it is more difficult to evaluate the significance of the print medium in relation to the 1989 revolutions. Immediately prior to the revolutions there was a steady increase in clandestine independent newspapers dealing with peace, ecology and human rights issues. This was part of the usually implicit activist strategy of '*glasnost* from below' in many countries of eastern Europe (Kux, 1991: 106). Such newspapers play a crucial role in creating movement cohesion and solidarity and represent one of the key means through which diffuse social movements negotiate a sense of identity and purpose whilst identifying the object of their opposition (Melucci, 1989, 1992, 1996). Such latency periods can be of a considerable duration and give rise to a diverse range of social movements.

CHARACTERIZING THE ENVIRONMENTAL MOVEMENTS?

The emergence of environmental activists, and environmental movements more generally, as significant political forces during the revolutions of 1989 and the subsequent transition period raises a series of issues about the available social scientific models which might be expected to explain such events. The variety of models is exceedingly diverse and a comprehensive review of these is beyond our present scope. For our present purposes we wish to argue for the central importance of social movement theory, however. Properly conceived, social movement activity belongs in the sphere of informal networks embedded firmly in civil society and enunciating a systemic challenge to society based upon an essentially conflictual relationship (Melucci, 1989, 1996; Touraine, 1992). Whilst there is a minimal consensus about this definition there is considerably less agreement about how such conflicts are conducted, at what point a movement comes into being or the point at which a movement ceases to exist or is transformed into another type of social solidarity or even institutionalized. An appreciation of these areas of disagreement is vital to any consideration of the mobilizations around the environment in the FSU and central and eastern Europe between the mid-/late 1980s and the present day.

We are painfully aware that the empirical work necessary to confirm or refute the theoretical and analytical argument advanced here is largely incomplete. Accordingly, what is offered should be read as an initial conceptual mapping based on a deep familiarity with a theoretical literature on new social movements, an exhaustive reading of available accounts and research in this area, many lengthy conversations with academics from eastern Europe and first-hand experience of the transition in many countries in the region. The need for generalizable theory in this area is both urgent and important but should always be set within the context of Rudiger Schmitt-Beck's (1992) argument that the theorization of social movements is inevitably shaped by national social, cultural and political characteristics.

Given this, it is important to outline the main features of social movement activity which assume analytical importance for our present purposes. First and perhaps foremost we would re-emphasize the importance of recognizing environmentalism within eastern Europe as a movement with a long history (Yanitsky, 1993 and various authors in this volume). This is particularly important to counteract the still widespread view that environmentalism is something peculiar to 'modern times'. The historical durability of conservation movements which steadily expand their remit to include increasingly social objectives is a feature of environmentalism in both the West and the East. For our present purposes this is a crucial part of the processes by which the environment became sedimented in the interstices of the party-state. The official recognition of conservation following a narrow, scientific conception of ecology provided a key channel granting legitimacy to environmentalism as the contingent forces aligned around these issues, such as the need to maintain a Cold War dialogue, changed.

It is perhaps useful to draw a distinction here between the existence of formal conservation networks and informal environmentalist networks. Whilst the membership of these organizations may enjoy considerable overlap, their formal functions are often quite distinct. Informal networks typically engage in activities which do not enjoy the approval of formal bodies, such as the academies of science or the state. These activities inevitably tend to challenge existing frameworks, representing legitimation-stripping activities, such as the circulation of underground literature mentioned above.

The environmental movements which consolidated throughout the region during the 1970s and 1980s were typified by characteristically intense emotional commitments to both issues and fellow activists. The intensity of social bonding which occurs within such movements can be understood in terms of a number of factors. Frequently, social movement interventions act to 'declare the stakes' to a society and in this sense they inevitably question accepted wisdoms, which are frequently buttressed by considerable bodies of scientific knowledge and institutionalized scientific and political power. Within a system based on scientific socialism this kind of questioning is particularly courageous, given the proclivity of the party-state to silence critics by a variety of means. The issues around which the mobilizations occurred thus related to both dimensions of the environment identified previously – the natural and organic as well as the human and social. As we have noted, the courageous demonstration of political independence by environmental activists made them trusted figures once the revolutions were under way and rapidly precipitated key figures into government positions. Whilst some commentators (Flam, 1994) consider that social movements can continue to operate within 'state space', the transition to office inevitably introduces a range of structural constraints which preclude legitimation-stripping activities and the declaration of previously unperceived issues. The presence of sympathetic voices within 'state space' may significantly affect the potency of social movements but they should not be thought of as an extension of the movement. Whether this constitutes the entry of social movement activity into state space or signals the end of social movement and the transfer of support to new struggles undertaken by similar means is an area of complete disagreement amongst social scientists (Welsh, 1995).

An analogous though less clear-cut set of issues relates to the rise of formal environmental non-governmental organizations (ENGOs) throughout the region. Such organizations, typified internationally by groups such as Greenpeace, the World Wide Fund for Nature (WWF) and Friends of the Earth, represent a degree of movement formalization and consolidation. This brings advantages such as the mobilization of a range of resources including financial reserves, organizational capacities, technical and media sophistication and scientific expertise. Against these advantages have to be balanced certain costs such as the curtailment of spontaneity, increased respectability and responsibility.

As previously mentioned, events in 1989 precipitated key activists into positions of political office in an unexpectedly short space of time. This produced immense pressures on individuals who suddenly found themselves writing state policies in very compressed periods of time (see Vavroušek, 1993), although previously underground documents and political demands often formed a ready basis for new state policy. Other pressures were also exerted on the movement which had been unexpectedly swept to power. As the experts from western investment banks flooded the region with plans and blueprints for marketization, representatives of established western ENGOs also moved into the region with agendas of their own. The extent to which the ambitions of these international ENGOs matched the aspirations of environmentalists or the needs of the region's organic environment is an area of some debate. It can be suggested that the spread of western ENGOs tended to follow one of three patterns, which were generally related to their previous experience of environmental campaigning in eastern Europe.

First, a number of groups, such as Friends of the Earth International (FoE-I) and the Dutch group Milieukontakt Oosteuropa, were able to formalize their previous links with the region, which had principally been with the Greenway organization, the sole eastern European environmental network group. Prior to 1989 their joint activities had primarily focused on youth-oriented events and building networks such as Youth and Environment Europe (YEE) and European Youth Forest Action (EYFA). Interestingly, this reflects the increasing 'acceptability' of environmental issues and groups by the communist states in the mid- to late 1980s whereby indigenous environmental groups were able to make formal international links, a possibility still largely denied to human rights activists. After 1989 such contacts continued and expanded (albeit at a fairly low level of activity because of resource constraints), often focusing on pan-national problems such as acid rain and the European transport network. In addition, some of the native environmental groups jostled for the privilege of country partner status with Friends of the Earth International, thus allowing them to rename themselves after the international group, if they so wished.

If this first model of involvement could be described as *networking*, then the second would be *capacity building* (although a number of activities within each model would be common). This was best exemplified by work undertaken by the Swedish NGO Secretariat on Acid Rain, a Scandinavian umbrella group of nature conservationists and amenity users opposed to acid rain, which (in the context of central and eastern Europe) focused on the distribution of financial and other resources (largely state-sourced) to selected groups in eastern Europe. Thus between 1988 and 1991 nearly one million Swedish kroner was given on a largely untied basis to improve the effectiveness of extant activists and groups.

The third and starkest model was that of '*imperialism*', best exemplified by Greenpeace International. Greenpeace had been interested in the region for a number of years because of its role in transboundary pollution of air and water; however, unlike other groups, it had not worked closely with comparable eastern groups or individuals. Despite this, Greenpeace went on to stage the first western-inspired environmental direct action in eastern Europe in April 1984, when a small number of activists climbed a factory chimney in Karlovy Vary (Czechoslovakia) to hang a banner protesting against emissions causing acid rain (this was part of the renowned 'STOP' action carried out simultaneously in seven other countries).[16] Unsurprisingly, given the state's intolerance of public protest, Czechoslovak reaction to the action was fierce: initially the climbers were fired at and later arrested and deported. Three years later, another banner was hung in Czechoslovakia – on the National Museum at the head of Prague's Wenceslas Square, this time by Austrian Greenpeace activists campaigning against the Czechoslovak nuclear power programme. Once again the participants were arrested, taken forcibly to the Austrian border and deported.

In the same years, Greenpeace (principally through its East/West Project) had also established working relationships in the Soviet Union, aimed at establishing a long-term influence in the country. This had begun slowly but, with Gorbachev's rise to power and the associated policies of *glasnost* and *perestroika*, the development of Greenpeace USSR accelerated, and it was formally established as a legal entity at the end of June 1989. This was an historic achievement – the first western environmental group to be officially permitted in the communist bloc – and a minor, yet clear, signal of the political changes taking place throughout the region.

Greenpeace's official attitude to the satellite states of the Soviet Union was, at this time, viewed principally through the 'lens' of the East/West Project. Attitudes from this project appear to be based strongly on the North American culture of the Cold War, albeit with the moral imperative (through global environmental values) of breaking down such artifical constructs. Mirroring the political centralism of the communist bloc, Greenpeace saw Moscow as the 'capital' of eastern Europe and as a starting point for activities in the other countries. It was envisaged therefore that the Moscow centre, in addition to its Soviet activities, would service requests from other eastern European countries and also invite appropriate personnel from the satellite states to serve on the Greenpeace USSR Board as a method of widening representation and exploring campaigning needs and opportunities in those countries.

In hindsight, this 'Russocentric' approach to eastern Europe would have been unlikely to increase Greenpeace's standing with independent environmentalists in other central and eastern European countries. Luckily for Greenpeace, history – in the form of the 1989 revolutions – intervened before the Moscow-based model of development was implemented. The fall of the Berlin Wall precipitated a rapid response from Greenpeace International, with the East German office being created almost immediately – as much by public demand as by Greenpeace planning.

Although Greenpeace's 'expansion' to the east was primarily driven by the desire to address the former communist countries' significant environmental problems, much of Greenpeace's early activity was reactive and pre-emptive. One political and corporate concern was the establishment of legal Greenpeace entities before rogue groups could appropriate the name, another was the need to satisfy 'market' demand for Greenpeace's 'products'. This was best exemplified in relation to the former Czechoslovakia (see Tickle and Vavroušek, this volume), where a new organization was established, compared to Hungary and Poland, where the main model of engagement was co-operation with existing NGOs, both directly and through international networks and coalitions.

More generally, the rapid incorporation of the more prominent exponents of environmentalism within the emergent state and party political structures left western ENGOs in something of an impasse. Their most natural allies were part of government and the priorities of the wider movement were not necessarily congruent with their own. Civil society, the sphere which organizations like Greenpeace had become accustomed to occupying, was still being formalized. The major options were co-operation with new governments or the time-consuming and painstaking task of building a sophisticated environmental movement along familiar western lines. Either way the ability of imported ENGOs to shape the environmental agenda was to be subject to the same forces of displacement discussed above, although the level of resources available to them often gave them a significant advantage in operational ability (Dawson, 1996: 165).

CONCLUSIONS

This introductory chapter has argued that environmentalism in eastern and central Europe has to be seen as a key feature in the transition to democracy from the late 1980s onwards. The argument is advanced through several inter-related stages emphasizing a range of structural, political and contingent elements.

Structurally, we have argued that the party-state in its various national guises granted the environment and ecology a sphere of legitimacy both internally and externally over a very long period of time. This permitted the consolidation of widespread networks of a conservationist and environmentalist nature which laid the foundation of more politicized movements. During the post-war period the tensions between this officially sanctioned environmentalism and the environmental impacts of Soviet industrialism produced a significant discourse through which the supremacy of scientific socialism and the legitimacy of Marxism–Leninism as an organizing ideology became increasingly undermined. The promulgation of the environment as an arena within which a discourse could be maintained with the West throughout the Cold War further intensified these contradictions.

Politically, Gorbachev's attempt to modernize the CMEA, along lines adopted within the USA and the EU, intensified these tensions as activists embarked upon successful '*glasnost* from below' initiatives. Throughout this period, and since, the necessary financial aid to achieve stable economic and social transformation has not been forthcoming from the West. As political and economic legitimacy became increasingly fragile, the submerged environmentalist networks emerged in many countries as a key part of the political opposition, offering an alternative vision of society. Once these groupings became visible they quickly accreted wider movements for democracy and freedom, thus becoming the substantive opposition.

The revolutions of 1989 have been seen by some (e.g. Dahrendorf, 1990) as peculiar in that they did not enunciate a set of demands for something wholly new; rather they are portrayed as demanding the substitution of one system for another. Once the revolutions were consolidated into formally elected governments it is easy to come to this view. By this time the radicalism of the environmentalist agenda as espoused by Vavroušek was already being emasculated by the combined pressures of internal and external forces pursuing particular forms of capitalist free enterprise. To resurrect some sublimely unfashionable Marxist idiom, events were then 'structured in dominance' (Althusser) by a range of institutions including the IMF, the World Bank and the EU – a claim we will return to in the final chapter.

In successfully sweeping aside the environmental and social aspirations of the velvet revolutions these forces successfully subverted the first green revolutions in history. The contingent phenomena which aided this process are not to be overlooked here. Central elements have been the extent to which past traditions from previous civil societies have contributed to the (re)subordination of women and the silencing of their voices within the revolutionary moment. This process is enhanced by elements of the mass media in depicting women in a wide range of subordinate positions within capitalism, ranging from domestic soap operas to TV pornography.

Following Hobsbawm (1994), we acknowledge that we are too close (temporally and figuratively) to these events to produce anything other than a partial account. Intellectually there can be no such thing as objective history and here we have marshalled material and arguments to produce a considered position which will inevitably be modified by the passage of time. We believe firmly that market solutions to environmental problems are a chimera; to work they require forms of intervention which render classical market principles inoperable. The promise of market solutions in both East and West will lose legitimacy over time as social and political pressures for action mount. As we have hinted throughout this chapter, and go on to outline more fully in the conclusions, the discernible alignment of environmental issues and concerns over social justice will lay the foundation for new sets of demands, which can be fulfilled only through more fully fledged green revolutions which will prove less easy to displace. In this sense we would agree with

Lipietz (1995) that the future of political ecology lies in constituting a systemic challenge to both free market orthodoxy and the now discredited central planning of ex-actual socialism.

NOTES

1. Oleg Yanitsky, personal communication, June 1992; for a more extensive consideration see Filippov (1993).
2. Elections in 1997 removed the communists from power in Poland, reinstating a coalition built around Solidarity.
3. Prins (1983) cites Pentagon papers outlining tactics of pursuing war by economic means such as denial of technologies via trade policies and procurement of weapons systems which impose disproportionate costs, opening new spheres of military competition and rendering existing Soviet capacities obsolete. The Star Wars programme became the ultimate expression of this strategy.
4. See note 6, below.
5. At the Political Studies Association annual conference in 1988 senior American defence analysts were 'terrified' that they would soon see television pictures of the Soviet missile submarine fleet being cut up in their home ports. They considered that Gorbachev had out-manoeuvred the West through successive arms-cutting moves undermining the credibility of the West's declaratory posture.
6. This dialogue dates from the Khrushchev and Brezhnev eras when it was prioritized as an arena where collaboration within overall hostility remained possible, most notably within the Helsinki/CSCE talks of the mid-1970s. This led eventually to the adoption of environmental issues as part of the diplomatic ambit of the United Nations Economic Commission for Europe (UN ECE), starting with negotiations on transboundary air pollution problems in Europe.
7. This is not to say that urban environments do not create new habitats or niches for existing species, the urban fox being a prime example. The advent of urban civilization is widely regarded as playing a key part in the separation of human society from 'nature'. In Marx's view the end of the practice of moving night soil from Victorian cities heralded the severing of the last organic link, a divide which has been widely regarded as having major implications for the nature of human society (see for example Simmel, 1971).
8. Electronic miniaturization is one area (as with the insertion of miniature cameras to replace eyes) and the prospect of genetic manipulation and control represents a biological basis for artificial enhancement and repair. On cyborgism see Donna Haraway (1997).
9. The accident at Chernobyl and its aftermath have been widely dealt with (e.g. Gould, 1990). The full consequences are still not known. Soviet estimates indicate that 6000 children received thyroid doses over 200 rem, a level of irradiation with very serious consequences. Large tracts of Ukraine remain uninhabitable with 100,000 people permanently relocated, 275,000 people temporarily relocated and a further 600,000 people undergoing continuing monitoring. Over nine billion roubles was spent dealing with the immediate consequences of the accident, with a further 6.5 billion committed to ongoing medical and social costs (based on Congdon, 1992: 150–165). It is highly likely that the areas requiring permanent evacuation and the toll in human lives will continue to rise.

10. The International Atomic Energy Agency (IAEA) and EU have allocated at least US$4.7 million for these purposes (DeBardeleben and Hannigan, 1995: 51). Countries immediately threatened by specific plants have also contributed. Norway donated US$2.6 million and Finland US$1.5 million in 1993 (Feshbach, 1995: 89) In Belarus the cost of Chernobyl has been estimated as equivalent to ten national annual expenditure budgets and Ukraine continues to spend 28 per cent of the annual budget on remedial measures (Feshbach, 1995: 31–32).

11. One estimate put the replacement costs for the remaining sixteen RBMK reactors at US$45 billion. The cost of installing modern safety systems was estimated at between US$8.88 and $25 billion.

12. This view was expressed by various academics from Russia at an International Sociology Association conference held at Woudschoten, the Netherlands, in June 1992.

13. There are exceptions to this general displacement. Whilst the environment remained on the agenda in Czechoslovakia due to the prominence of key advocates, the establishment of policy and its execution diverged markedly.

14. The almost universal use of 'reading' within this mode of analysis is problematic and inadequately addresses significant differences between modes of reception of media products. Reading is completely different from visual incorporation, leading some commentators to identify a 'spectral' form of post-modernity.

15. See *East European Reporter* 2(3–4) 1987 for commentaries on cultural represssion in Czechoslovakia.

16. Each action had a banner with a single giant letter 'S', 'T', 'O', 'P' on it. When photographs of the various banners were placed in a row, they spelt 'STOP' (see Brown and May, 1991: 104–105).

REFERENCES

Adomeit, H. (1990) Gorbachev and German unification: revision of thinking, realignment of power. *Problems of Communism* XXXIX, 1–23.

Arizpe, L. (1991) The global cube. *International Social Science Journal* 130, 599–608.

Becher, T. (1989) *Academic Tribes and Territories*. Open University Press, Milton Keynes.

Benton, T. (1989) Marxism and natural limits: an ecological critique and reconstruction. *New Left Review* 178, 51–86.

Bhaskar, R. (1975) *A Realist Theory of Science*. Harvester, Sussex.

Brown, M. and May, J. (1991) *The Greenpeace Story*. Dorling Kindersley, London.

Carter, F.W. and Turnock, D., eds (1993) *Environmental Problems in Eastern Europe*. Routledge, London.

Congdon, J. (1992) US–USSR nuclear safety co-operation: prospects for health and environmental collaboration. In *The Soviet Environment: Problems, Policies and Politics* (ed. J. Massey Stewart). Cambridge University Press, Cambridge.

Dahrendorf, R. (1990) *Reflections on the Revolution in Europe*. Chatto & Windus, London.

Dawson, J.I. (1996) *Eco-nationalism: Anti-nuclear Activism and National Identity in Russia, Lithuania and Ukraine*. Duke University Press, London.

DeBardeleben, J. (1985) *The Environment and Marxism–Leninism: The Soviet and East German Experience*. Westview, Boulder, CO.

DeBardeleben, J. and Hannigan, J., eds (1995) *Environmental Security and Quality after Communism: Eastern Europe and the Soviet Successor States*. Westview, Boulder, CO.

Devall, B. and Sessions, G. (1985) *Deep Ecology*. Peregrine Smith, Salt Lake City, UT.

Dolling, I. (1991) Shock therapy: GDR women in transition from a socialist welfare State to a social market. *Signs* 17(1), 129–151.

Eckersley, R. (1992) Green versus ecosocialist economic programmes: the market rules OK? *Political Studies* XL, 315–333.

Einhorn, B. (1993) *Cinderella Goes to Market: Citizenship, Gender and Women's Movements in East and Central Europe*. Verso, London.

Enloe, C. (1989) *Bananas, Beaches and Bases*. Pandora, London.

Enzensberger, H.M. (1974) Critique of Political Ecology. *New Left Review* 84, 3–31.

Feshbach, M. (1995) *Ecological Disaster: Cleaning up the Hidden Legacy of the Soviet Regime*. Twentieth Century Funds Press, New York.

Filippov, A.F. (1993) A final look back at Soviet sociology. *International Sociology* 8(3), 355–373.

Fisher, D. (1993a) The emergence of the environmental movement in eastern Europe and its role in the revolutions of 1989. In *Environmental Action in Eastern Europe: Response to Crisis* (ed. B. Jancar-Webster). M.E. Sharpe, Armonk, NY.

Fisher, D., ed. (1993b) *Paradise Deferred: Environmental Policy Making in Central and Eastern Europe*. RIIA, London.

Flam, H., ed. (1994) *States and Anti-Nuclear Movements*. Edinburgh University Press, Edinburgh.

Fox, W. (1990) *Towards a Transpersonal Ecology*. Shambala, London.

Frankland, E.G. and Cox, R.H. (1995) The legitimation problems of new democracies: postcommunist dilemmas in Czechoslovakia and Hungary. *Environment and Planning C* 13, 141–158.

Friendly, A. and Feshbach, M. (1992) *Ecocide in the USSR*. Basic Books, New York.

Fukuyama, F. (1989) The End of History. *The National Interest* (Summer).

Gare A. (1993) Marxism and ecology: Soviet environmentalism – the path not taken. *Capitalism, Nature, Socialism* 4(4), 69–88.

Glasman, M. (1994) The great deformation: Polyani, Poland and the terrors of planned spontaneity. *New Left Review* 205, 59–86.

Goldman, M.I. (1992) Environmentalism and nationalism: an unlikely twist in an unlikely direction. In *The Soviet Environment: Problems, Policies and Politics* (ed. J. Massey Stewart). Cambridge University Press, Cambridge.

Gould, P. (1990) *Fire in the Rain*. Polity, Oxford.

Gowan, P. (1995) Neo-liberal theory and practice in eastern Europe. *New Left Review* 213, 3–60.

Hamilton, D. (1992) Germany after unification. *Problems of Communism* XLI, 1–18.

Hannigan, J.A. (1995) *Environmental Sociology: A Social Constructionist Perspective*. Routledge, London.

Haraway, D. (1992) *Primate Visions*. Verso, London.

Haraway, D. (1997) *Modest Witness@Second Millennium. FemaleMan Meets Oncomouse*™. Routledge, London.

Hicks, B. (1996) *Environmental Politics in Poland: A Social Movement Between Regime and Opposition*. Columbia University Press, New York.

Hobsbawm, E. (1994) *Age of Extremes: The Short Twentieth Century 1914–1991*. Michael Joseph, London.

Jackson, C. (1995) Radical environmental myths: a gender perspective. *New Left Review* 210, 124–140.

Jancar, B. (1985) Women in the opposition in Poland and Czechoslovakia in the 1970s. In *Women, State and Party in Eastern Europe* (eds S.L. Wolchik and A.G. Meyer) Duke University Press, Durham, NC.

Jancar, B. (1987) *Environmental Management in the Soviet Union and Yugoslavia*. Duke University Press, Durham, NC.

Jancar-Webster, B., ed. (1993) *Environmental Action in Eastern Europe: Response to Crisis*. M.E. Sharpe, Armonk, NY.

Joppke, C. (1995) *East German Dissidents and the Revolution of 1989: Social Movement in a Leninist Regime*. Macmillan, London.

Kabele, J. (1993) The dynamics of social problems and transformation of Czechoslovak society. *Social Research* 60(4), 763–785.

Kramer, J.M. (1986) Chernobyl and Eastern Europe. *Problems of Communism* XXV, 40–58.

Kusin, V.K. (1986) Gorbachev and Eastern Europe. *Problems of Communism* XXXV, 39–53.

Kux, E. (1991) Revolution in Eastern Europe – revolution in the West. *Problems of Communism* XL, 1–13.

Lash, S. (1990) Learning from Leipzig – or politics in the semiotic society. *Theory, Culture and Society* 7, 145–158.

Lipietz, A. (1995) *Green Hopes: The Future of Political Ecology*. Polity, Oxford.

Massey Stewart, J., ed. (1992) *The Soviet Environment: Problems, Policies and Politics*. Cambridge University Press, Cambridge.

Melucci, A. (1989) *Nomads of the Present*. Radius Hutchinson, London.

Melucci, A. (1992) Liberation or meaning? Social movements, culture and democracy. *Development and Change* 23(3), 43–77.

Melucci, A. (1996) *Challenging Codes: Collective Action in the Information Age*. Cambridge University Press, Cambridge.

Merchant, C. (1983) *The Death of Nature: Women, Ecology and the Scientific Revolution*. Harper & Row, San Francisco, CA.

Merchant, C. (1992) *Radical Ecology*. Routledge, London.

Mieczkowski, B. (1985) Social services for women and childcare facilities in eastern Europe. In *Women, State and Party in Eastern Europe* (eds S. Wolchik and A.G. Meyer). Duke University Press, Durham, NC, 257–269.

Mies, M. and Shiva, V. (1993) *Ecofeminism*. Routledge, London.

Molyneux, M. (1900) The woman question in the age of *perestroika*. *New Left Review* 183, 23–49.

Mulberg, J. (1992) Who rules the market? Green versus ecosocialist economic programmes: a response to Eckersley. *Political Studies* XL, 334–341.

O'Neill, J.F. (1993) *Ecology, Policy and Politics: Human Wellbeing and the Natural World*. Routledge, London.

Polyani, K. (1944) *The Great Transformation*. Beacon Press, Boston, MA.

Prins G., ed. (1983) *Defended to Death*. Penguin, Harmondsworth.

Prins, G., ed. (1990) *Spring in Winter: The 1989 Revolutions*. Manchester University Press, Manchester.

Pryde, P.R. (1992) The environmental basis for ethnic unrest in the Baltic republics. In *The Soviet Environment: Problems, Policies and Politics* (ed. J. Massey Stewart). Cambridge University Press, Cambridge.

Pryde, P.R., ed. (1995) *Environmental Resources and Constraints in the Former Soviet Republics*. Westview, Boulder, CO.

Ramet, S.P. (1994) *Rocking the State: Rock Music and Politics in Eastern Europe and Russia*. Westview, Boulder, CO.

Ross, A. (1994) *The Chicago Gangster Theory of Life: Nature's Debt to Society*. Verso, London.

Sachs, J. (1990) What is to be done? *The Economist* 13 January.

Schmitt-Beck, R. (1992) A myth institutionalized: theory and research on new social movements in Germany. *European Journal of Political Research* 21(2), 357–383.

Senkevich, V.M. (1991) Ecological education: integration of scientific knowledge and figurative representations. *Soviet Education* 33(1), 47–54.

Simmel, G. (1971) The metropolis and mental life. In *George Simmel on Individuality and Social Forms* (ed. D.N. Levine). University of Chicago Press, London.

Skilling, G. (1989) *Samizdat and an Independent Society in Central and Eastern Europe.* Macmillan, London.

Smoker, P.L. and Bradley, M., eds (1988) Accidental Nuclear War. *Current Research on Peace and Violence* 1–2, esp. 2–13.

Stokes, G. (1991) Lessons of the east European revolutions. *Problems of Communism* XL, 17–22.

Tismaneanu, V. (1989) Nascent civil society in the GDR. *Problems of Communism* XXXVIII, 90–111.

Touraine, A. (1992) Beyond social movements. *Theory, Culture and Society* 9, 125–145.

Vavroušek, J. (1993) Institutions for environmental security. In *Threat Without Enemies* (ed. G. Prins). Earthscan, London.

Volgyes, I. (1974) *Environmental Deterioration in the Soviet Union and Eastern Europe.* Praeger, New York.

Walby, S. (1994) Is citizenship gendered? *Sociology* 28(2), 379–395.

Watson, P. (1993a) Eastern Europe's silent revolution: Gender. *Sociology* 27(3), 471–487.

Watson, P. (1993b) The rise of masculinism in eastern Europe. *New Left Review* 198, 71–82.

Weeks, J., ed. (1994) *The Lesser Evil and the Greater Good: The Theory and Practice of Diversity.* Rivers Oram Press, London.

Welsh, H.A. (1994) Political transition processes in central and eastern Europe. *Comparative Politics* 26(4), 379–394.

Welsh, I. (1987) *Deterrence or Defence?* Richardson Institute, University of Lancaster.

Welsh. I. (1988) Technological Imperatives, Human Fallibility and C³I. *Current Research on Peace and Violence* 1–2, 40–47.

Welsh, I. (1995) *Risk, Reflexivity and the Globalisation of Environmental Politics.* SEPEG Working Paper No. 1, University of the West of England, Bristol.

Wilson, E. (1977) *Women and the Welfare State.* Tavistock, London.

Wolfson, Z. (1994) *The Geography of Survival: Ecology in the Post-Soviet Era.* Sharpe, London.

Wolchik, S.L. and Meyer, A.G., eds (1985) *Women, State and Party in Eastern Europe.* Duke University Press, Durham, NC.

World Commission on Environment and Development (1987) *Our Common Future.* Oxford University Press, Oxford.

Yanitsky O. (1993) *Russian Environmentalism.* Mezhdunarodnyje Otnoshenija, Moscow.

Yearly, S. (1994) Social movements and environmental change. In *Social Theory and the Global Environment* (eds M. Redclift and T. Benton). Westview, Boulder, CO.

Young, M.J. and Launer, M.K. (1991) Redefining *glasnost* in the Soviet media: the recontextualisation of Chernobyl. *Journal of Communication* 41(2), 102–124.

Ziegler, C. (1987) *Environmental Policy in the USSR.* University of Massachusetts Press, Amherst, MA.

Zizek, S. (1990) Eastern Europe's republics of Gilead. *New Left Review* 183, 50–62.

CHAPTER 2

THE ENVIRONMENTAL MOVEMENT IN THE FORMER SOVIET UNION
Natalia Mirovitskaya

INTRODUCTION

A progressive, politically visible 'green' movement is a relatively new factor in the socio-political arena of the former Soviet Union (FSU). By 1992 such a movement had grown on an unprecedented scale to number more than 840 non-governmental environmental organizations in the Russian Federation alone – operating at local, regional, inter-regional and international levels. Many organizations dealing with the urban environment and the preservation of cultural and historical heritage were not included in this total. In addition, women's movements, labour and youth groups also addressed environmental issues along with other concerns. These numerous grass-roots initiatives, based in the cultural tradition of social and political self-organization, form the basis of the widespread civic movement. This civic movement enjoys considerable significance and holds the potential to exercise an enormous influence over the state of the environment in eastern Europe and former Soviet Asia.

During the last decade the activities of environmental and pro-environmental NGOs have spread from the traditional functions of the preservation of historic monuments and nature to the protection of the animal rights, environmental monitoring, enforcement of environmental legislation and the defence of consumer rights. Environmental movements have also become sources of environmental expertise and education within civil society.

The rapid increase in size and political influence of environmental groups shortly before the collapse of the Soviet Union was once defined in the Russian parliament as an 'orgy of ecologists'. Indeed, some authors give the Greens credit for bringing down the Soviet empire (Peterson, 1993). On the other hand, most national experts in the sphere of environmental management (72.8 per cent of poll respondents) did not regard this movement as having major significance (Gosudarstvenyi Doklad, 1993). Perhaps now, several years after the peak of vigorous growth of environmentalism in the country, it is easier to assess adequately the movement's strength and potential, to summarize the initial victories and the reasons for the subsequent failures.

Such an attempt is interesting not only for historical and analytical reasons but also because the environmental security of the former Soviet Union – a massive geopolitical entity with a unique variety of landscapes and resources – has important regional and global dimensions. The 1986 nuclear disaster at Chernobyl clearly demonstrated the importance of global ecological interdependence. The Siberian forests are even more important for the planetary production of oxygen than Amazonia and the large-scale exploitation of these resources by transnational corporations would jeopardize international environmental security. In the struggle for Siberian forests Russian Greens unite with their western counterparts, being dependent upon international rather than domestic support. The ongoing environmental situation in Russia/CIS (Commonwealth of Independent States) in the 1990s makes the NGOs a major source of hope.

Despite massive popular interest in the environment, writings on this subject are limited and have mainly been carried out by American scholars (Jancar, 1987; Ziegler, 1987; Weiner, 1988a, 1988b; Peterson, 1993). In Russian, most works have been primarily descriptive with the notable exception of Yanitsky's sociological analyses (1991, 1993, 1994). Whilst some explanations for the emergence of environmentalism are almost universal, such as the crisis experienced by industrialized societies at a certain level of development, each country has specifically national characteristics which are also crucial. This is certainly the case for Russian/Soviet environmentalism, which cannot be understood separately from, first, its internal historical traditions and, second, the social and political context of the former Soviet and contemporary Russian society. These factors determine not only the contemporary role of environmentalism in each society but also the significance of the environment during the post-1989 transition process.

In Russia there is a strong 'ecological' tradition, which has become part of the social conscience through literature, philosophy and common ethics. In historical terms, the predominantly peasant population practised ancient pagan cults of nature until comparatively recently. These cults were quaintly intertwined with the culture of the Eastern Orthodox Church, which sanctified water, prayed for harvests, and decreed the desecration of bread a sin, and environmental education taught in schools. On the other side, the creation of totalitarian mechanisms under Stalinism turned most Soviet people into small parts of the great machine of socialist transformation and suppressed their individual behaviour and conscience. Environmentalism in Russia/Soviet Union has a long tradition and range of achievements. During its century-long existence environmentalism has been both patronized and manipulated by the state. The demolition of totalitarian society has seemingly broken this tradition of communist manipulation; however, environmental concerns quickly became the stock in trade of new political games. The traditional 'ecological' conscience of the Russian people, the country's long history of environmentalism and established tradition of political manipulation, combined with the political challenges mounted by the movement against ecological, economic and political problems of the FSU, both defines Soviet/Russian environmentalism and explains its differences from its western counterparts.

In this chapter I describe the main phases of the environmental movement in Russia–Soviet Union–CIS, define its main forms and methods, identify key controversial factors and the results of its politicization, whilst attempting to analyse the social basis of the movement and the ideological differences within it. My assessment of the past development, current stage and prospects of Russian environmentalism are certainly shaped by personal perceptions and practical experience gained whilst conducting research and practical environmental projects in this country. These perceptions and experiences might well differ from those of other analysts and practitioners and there might also be different interpretations of the facts and phenomena described below.

ORIGINS AND DEVELOPMENT

Despite the common belief that environmentalism developed rapidly during the last few years of the Soviet Union's existence, the environment has a long and uneven history as a focus of citizens' initiatives. An excellent analysis of the early phases of Russian environmentalism, starting with the first stirrings of public conservation in the 1850s, has been presented (Jancar, 1987; Weiner, 1988a, 1988b; Jancar-Webster, 1993). Using extensive original data, these studies demonstrated the decades-long struggle between Soviet environmental and economic interests, a struggle which offers both striking parallels and notable divergences from the history of western conservation movements.

There are three major periods when environmentalism was most articulated in the FSU/Russia: 1910–20, 1950–60 and the second half of the 1980s. All three periods coincided with the late stages of periods of economic expansion heralding radical political changes and rising social tension and activism. Membership of environmental groups grew rapidly; people from different social strata joined to express their general discontent with the state of the system and/or the limited technocratic values of its leadership. The environmental cause became a key catalyst for social change. Prior to this, the environmental movement in the country was dominated by professional scientists, and its development was closely connected with progress in ecology and other areas of environmental studies.

Phase one: 1910–20

The beginning of Russian environmentalism dates back as far as the late nineteenth century. From then until the 1930s, surprisingly, Russia was at the cutting edge of conservation theory and practice (Weiner, 1988a). Russian scientists established the then unique system of *zapovedniks* and other types of protected areas,[1] introduced regional land use planning, and developed phytosociology and several other major concepts making fundamental contributions to both ecology and conservation practice. These formal scientific contributions were accompanied by a considerable growth in informal associations dealing directly or indirectly with the environment towards the turn of the century. Among these organizations were special groups for the protection of nature, organizations for the study of local traditions and landscapes and geographical societies.[2] Most of the informal groups were concentrated around the established universities (Moscow, St Petersburg, Khar'kov), which became increasingly active in promoting new environmental values and initiating conservation activities. Though the number of environmental activists in the Russian empire prior to the 1917 revolution could have hardly exceeded a thousand, their influence on the public mood and governmental policy was out of all proportion to their size (Weiner, 1988b).

There are several historical reasons why early Russian environmentalism faded to relative obscurity. Russian nationalists,[3] as well as some western authors (Mafia, 1994), argue that from 1917 onwards the Bolsheviks deliberately undertook the destruction of both Russian nature and the Russian nation. Whilst the question of whether Lenin or Stalin was the originator of the Soviet totalitarian system is beyond the scope of this chapter, the differing perceptions of these leaders and their policies towards the environment play an important part in shaping contemporary views.

Indeed, the first government of socialist Russia was friendly to the environmental cause. Early communist leaders of Russia (V.I. Lenin, A.V. Lunacharsky, P.G. Smidovich) came from a segment of the intellectual community that regarded socialism's mission to be enlightenment, and the rational organization of social and economic life. This view gave strong backing to basic research into the structure of nature, which 'in order to be commanded, had to be obeyed', as well as specific attention to environmental and resource policy. By providing a materialist, scientific explanation for complex natural phenomena, ecological science would work for the enlightenment of a backward, predominantly peasant Russia. By establishing parameters of economic activity for specific natural regions, ecologists would help promote a rational and self-sustaining economy.

Under Lenin's political leadership, rational exploitation and conservation of nature was defined as a vital component of the radical socio-economic transformation that was undertaken in the 1920s (Mirovitskaya and Soroos, 1995). The successes of the first stage of state policy on resources and the environment in Russia included a radical improvement in urban cleanliness, the creation of national medical and sanitary–hygienic systems, the establishment of the nationwide system of forest economy, and setting aside protected territories for the study of ecological communities. Lenin's Draft Plan of Scientific and Technical Work laid a basis for pioneering integrated research into the natural environment and resource utilization. These academic concerns were applied through the creation of a National System of Environmental Monitoring and the elaboration of the first principles of nature conservation. Under favourable political leadership, environmental theory in Russia flourished (Weiner, 1988a), while ecologists and other scientists enjoyed a growing influence over decision-making (Weiner, 1988b).

The political climate was also favourable to civic environmentalism. After the 1917 revolution, and until the 1930s, most of the relevant public institutions not only remained intact but even received governmental support.[4] The pace of conservation activities stepped up and, in an attempt to build a national unified environmental movement, an All-Russian Society for Conservation (VOOP) was created in 1924 with an initial membership of a thousand (Vinogradov, 1982). The first years of this organization were marked by a rapidly expanding membership, a diversification of activities (encompassing research, education, public propaganda) and the development of extensive contacts with foreign counterparts. VOOP was by no means the only environmental organization in post-revolutionary Russia, however.

Various conservation issues were addressed by an All-Ukrainian Union for the Defence of Living Nature, the Union of Young Naturalists with its 45,000 membership, the Moscow-based Central Bureau for the Study of Local Lore, Petrograd/ Leningrad's group 'Old St Petersburg', and the Krasnoyarsk Branch of the Geographical Society. Another organization which played a surprisingly strong (relative to its size and aims) role in the development of environmentalism in the country was a Club of Young Biologists of the Moscow Zoo (KUbZ), created in 1924 by P.A. Manteifel. This small organization was particularly effective in promoting traditions of free thought and love of nature among Moscow youth.

The list of descendants from this environmentalists' 'nursery' includes Nikolai Vorontsov (the last Soviet Minister of Environment), Alexei Yablokov (the former Counsellor to the President of the Russian Federation on Environment and Public Health), Dmitry Kavtaradze (the author of the Ecopolis programme), Maria Cherkasova (one of the leaders of the Socio-Ecological Union) and other central figures in contemporary environmental policy and civil movements. Youth emerged as the most militant actor of the post-revolutionary phase of Russian environmentalism, demonstrating annually for nature conservation on Arbor Day, celebrating Bird Day, and actively participating in the preservation and restoration of the historical heritage and natural environment of Petrograd, Moscow and other cities.

Early Russian environmentalism did not survive Stalin's rise to power in 1928, which has been called the Second Russian Revolution. Failing to appreciate the ways in which Lenin's co-operative strategy of the NEP was gradually 'constructing' the basis for socialism, Stalin preferred socialism to be 'conveyed' to all realms of the nation's life regardless of the costs. All society's resources, natural and human, were taken under direct control of the state and manipulated by political leadership in the name of the national interest. The task was to ensure the speediest industrialization by all means, including the productive refashioning of both the natural environment and the people. Nature would be made more efficient through, amongst other means, the creation of an integrated nationwide water system necessitating the construction of gigantic canals and the diversion of rivers. Vast areas of virgin grasslands were converted to agriculture, by changing local ecosystems through the introduction of non-native and hybrid species (Mirovitskaya and Soroos, 1995). The labour-intensive nature of these projects simultaneously created a disciplined proletariat, provided tasks suitable for forced labour camps, and created projects portraying the symbolic unity and superiority of the Soviet system.

The consequences of the 'great transformation' were ruinous for the existing system of nature conservation, which was practically abandoned during these years. The twin missions of enlightenment and the scientific organization of economic life were derided as elitist and reformist (Weiner, 1988b). Proponents of these missions were attacked for creating 'artificial' limits to the successful transformation of human and non-human nature and were phased out of policy-making and academic circles. The emphasis on conservation pursued by early Russian environmentalists was displaced by the severe utilitarian view of nature as a spatial resource. The new pseudo-Marxist conception of human domination over nature was declared central to the survival of socialist society, which must transform nature's handiwork, displaying a boundless confidence in the inventive capacities of socialism.

The move to 'patriarchal and authoritarian communism' produced an official cessation of the civic environmental movement by the late 1930s. The legislation permitting informal associations was altered and many prominent organizations were persecuted. The influential pro-environmental Society for the Study of Local Lore, with more than 1,000,000 members, was abolished. The once highly visible VOOP, with its relatively high membership (15,000 in 1932), extensive foreign contacts and popular publications, practically disappeared from the public arena. While VOOP's publications ceased to appear, its membership did not become completely moribund, but their activities became restricted to informal associations through pastimes such as gardening and urban beautification. The few attempts by militant activists to raise public protests against the closure of *zapovedniks* and reckless industrial expansion were unsuccessful, leading to official sanctions and the organization's liquidation. So, VOOP and the wider environmental organizations entered a period of forced hibernation.

The costs of the 'Second Russian Revolution' were both human and environmental. On one side, in a twelve-year period the Russian economy was transformed from a predominantly rural agricultural base to an urban industrial one. In the West the same economic transformation had taken fifty to a hundred years (Kuznets, 1963). The creation of a huge professional cadre of engineers and trained workers, capable of designing, operating and maintaining complex equipment, and the numerical growth of scientists and other professionals with higher education from a previously backward and predominantly illiterate society, was an impressive accomplishment.[5] These new social strata represented an enormous recruiting ground for the environmental cause, though not for its pure preservationist perspective. Later on, the emergence of this urban-educated stratum was followed by a rapid growth in the membership and influence of the numerous scientific and technical societies with environmental concerns. These concerns included the impact of pollution, low-waste technology and the efficient use of resources, and contributed to a striking expansion of scientific literature, which in turn influenced the level of educational awareness within Russian society.

On the down side of the 'great leap' lay enormous wasted resources, effort and lives: loss of human lives numbered in the millions. The immense natural resources of the country were plundered, the large industrial centres created on the peripheries of the Soviet empire under the programmes of nationwide industrialization are now among the areas of most critical environmental concern. The pseudo-Marxist perception of nature as an infinite and free resource to be used and transformed for the benefit of economic growth became embedded in the conscience of Soviet people for decades to come. The initial 'great leap' produced long-term projects with high environmental impacts, including rapid industrial expansion in the Arctic, Siberia and the Far East. Later projects such as the Virgin Lands Exploitation and the construction of the Baikal–Amur Mainline railway added to these impacts. Irrespective of the environmental and human consequences, millions of enthusiasts engaged in these 'great projects of communism' sincerely believed in the enormous potential and necessity of collective effort to remould nature for the benefit of the people. The extreme application of this anthropocentrism became a key characteristic of the whole Soviet nation and is amongst the major factors that brought the FSU to the brink of environmental crisis.

However, despite all the attempts to turn Soviet society into a totalitarian regime devoid of free thought and independent activity, the traditions of Russian environmentalism never vanished completely. Small groups, unions and collectives of like-minded people concerned with the conservation of nature and the preservation of cultural traditions managed to survive. A set of nature reserves and other protected areas, as well as experimental field stations, continued to function. Scientists exiled from the universities to far-away settlements created 'oases' of environmental education and research (Yanitsky, 1993). Starting from the mid-1950s with the so-called 'thaw' following Khrushchev's period of political liberalization, these cells of restricted civic activity became field stations for university natural science departments. In a broader sense, they served as a 'fermenting' source for the social rebirth of the environmental cause.

Phase two: 1950–60

During the 1950s the human–nature conflicts and contradictions implicit in earlier social and political commitments to progress began to assert themselves. The consequences of the 'great leap' combined with the wartime relocation of industrial complexes to militarily secure but environmentally fragile areas started to become apparent. In addition, unique natural landscapes and historic habitats had been destroyed by war. The demands of a rapidly rising urban population, combined with the post-war policy of the wholesale resettlement of entire ethnic groups, led to the increasing settlement of virgin lands and an enormous rise in human resource pressure. The most populated areas were doomed to suffer the so-called 'spot' pollution and resource degradation associated with this intense industrialization. Meanwhile, Soviet society, practically frozen by fear for twenty years, experienced the emergence of various groups expressing their own interests and values, groups that were eager to influence policy and sometimes able to succeed in this.

The limited political liberalization of the 1950s made it possible for these groups to bring the intensifying human–nature problems to the attention of the leadership of the Communist Party. Within the limits of official ideology it became possible to propose remedial measures. The Academy of Sciences re-started the campaign against the closure of *zapovedniks* and was able to restore many of the liquidated reserves. By the 1960s, changes in technology policy intended to produce enhanced environmental sensitivity were promoted. The new concept of the 'ecologization of production', though not challenging the basic societal goal of economic growth, was meant to adapt the Soviet productive structure through new technology (such as closed-cycle or low-waste production) to the ecological demands of the new age (DeBardeleben, 1992).

By the 1980s social scientists had brought to the attention of both public and scientific communities the reality of global environmental problems.[6] Whilst much of this literature either criticized western environmental alarmism or addressed problems relevant to capitalist society, it also created a public awareness of global and local environmental problems, thus creating the theoretical basis of environmental responsibility. In the sphere of civic environmentalism, the oldest groups, such as VOOP, resumed their activities with increased memberships and newly acquired energy. VOOP, in particular, launched several massive campaigns: more than 1,000,000 people participated in public inspections to identify environmental malpractice and to campaign for the clean-up of small rivers.

Regretfully, this organization paid a high price for its huge numbers and the political tolerance of its activities. A process of bureaucratic incorporation turned VOOP into a mechanism ensuring conformity with regime priorities.[7] Currently, few experts list VOOP among viable actors of contemporary environmentalism. In parallel with this semi-official stream, more vibrant and militant social forces emerged. The Baikal controversy (which has been described in detail by practically all eco-sovietologists[8]) could be cited as evidence of the breadth of the Soviet environmental movement during its second phase. The largest reservoir of fresh water on Earth, Lake Baikal has always been a national symbol to Russians. In the late 1950s, plans for the intensive development of the area, including changes in water flow and the creation of pulp-and-paper plants on the shores of the lake, unleashed a thirty-year-long public movement to defend Baikal.

The origin of this movement was a round-robin letter of protest against clearance works at Angara signed by prominent scientists, doctors, writers and publicists (*Literaturnaya Gazeta*, 28 October 1958). The tactics of the movement – which united members of the Academy of Science and several scientific societies, prominent Russian writers and artists, students and journalists – included campaigns, appeals, civic expert commissions and protests.

Though the movement did not succeed in having the plants dismantled, its activities did result in significant investment in pollution abatement facilities. More recently, two national parks and a nature reserve have been planned in the area. Among other campaigns were vigorous attempts to save the last cedar forests of Siberia, to ensure rational water use in the Volga basin, and to prevent the Siberian river diversion.

The most militant and durable of the environmental groups of the second phase has proved to be the 'students' movement. The so-called Students' Nature Protection Corps started with the founding of the Tartu Young People Nature Protection Organization in Estonia during 1958. The same year also saw the formation of a students' section within the Moscow Society of Naturalists, and the creation of a self-governing student organization within the Department of Biology of Moscow State University quickly followed. These organizations gave an impetus to the development of the Nature Protection Corps, which acquired the status of a movement in 1968, throughout the country. When the statutes of the Corps were reformulated, removing age, social or professional restrictions, the movement became a haven for liberal intellectuals seeking autonomy from state oppression.

Having begun as a small, almost insignificant organization, VOOP membership exceeded 37 million by the mid-1980s, making it the largest environmental organization in the world, but its co-opted status blunted its impact (Vinogradov, 1982). Instead, the Nature Protection Corps played a similar role to that of VOOP in the pre-war period, becoming the home for a wide range of independent thinkers and radicals.

By the late 1980s, the total number of affiliated Students' Corps exceeded 100, with a membership of 3500. Having combined the enthusiasm of youth and the legitimacy of a university milieu it soon became a prominent actor within Soviet environmentalism. The most visible of the Corps' activities was Operation 'Vystrel' aimed at poaching and other breaches of legislation in the protected areas. At the time every tenth poacher was a member of the Party, military or administrative elite (Shvarts and Prozorova, 1993), and this campaign was certainly an act of political courage, symbolizing the emergence of social control over the Soviet patriciate. Other Corps' programmes were aimed at spotting nesting sites of rare and endangered species (Operation 'Fauna'), locating endangered biotic communities (Operation 'Flora') and identifying ecosystems and landscapes in need of protection (Operation 'Tribune Reserves'). Students' associations exercised control over the existing nature reserves, participated in the creation of new ones, and organized ecological expeditions and joint (inter-corps) programmes. Most were also engaged in environmental education and propaganda. For instance, the Corps of the Moscow State University during 1961–81 detained over 5000 violators of nature preservation legislation, established twelve local-level nature reserves, and organized over a thousand lectures and ecological excursions (Tikhomirov, 1982).

Quite soon, however, it was understood that environmental concerns could not be limited to the preservation of wildlife. Even politically sound campaigns such as Operation 'Vystrel' addressed only the symptoms of the national environmental problem, not the underlying causes. Exposing the activities of poachers had no major impact on the character of the system of production and management, which was becoming more and more environmentally destructive. Under these circumstances, purely conservationist and politically neutral actions were not sufficient.

Phase three: the 1980s

The second and third phases of Russian/Soviet environmentalism had a lot in common. They both emerged in periods of political liberalization but still had to operate in the extra-monopolized industrial system with overwhelming state control over social activities. Under strong state paternalism the environmental activities of scientists, writers, students and the urban-educated stratum were doomed to be mainly conservationist and politically neutral. The main reason for joining the environmental movement during the 1960s–80s was to protest against industrial monopoly and assert intellectual autonomy against an increasingly intrusive regime. The protest, however, was largely silent and autonomy remained illusive. The regime tolerated the movement and considered that it represented no particular threat to its existence. Irrespective of this, it was only on the basis of these groups that a powerful, politically vigorous environmental movement could have emerged in the 1980s.

The third phase of Soviet environmentalism differs from its 'conservationist' predecessors in several ways. First, it coincided with significant state environmental reforms, secondly, it reflected widespread concerns linking environment and health issues, and thirdly, the social bases of environmental concern had assumed historically significant proportions. The most important difference came about as linkages were increasingly established between environmental degradation, human health problems and the practices of the communist regime. This resulted in the emergence of mass political opposition with sufficient support to make public demonstrations viable.

The sphere of environmental protection was one of the main targets of Gorbachev's *perestroika*. From 1987, the Soviet authorities issued a number of important environmental documents and regulations. These included the 1987 decree on Lake Baikal, the 1988 decree on the Aral Sea and the Resolution on the Radical Perestroika of Nature Conservation. By 1989, increasingly pressing environmental problems produced a decree 'On the Emergency Measures to Improve the Environmental Situation'. An All-Union Committee on Environmental Protection (*Goskompriroda*) was also hurriedly brought into being. The urgent need to demonstrate the independence of such bodies saw the appointment of non-Party chairs, such as Nikolai Vorontsov, who had direct access to the Kremlin. Vorontsov was influential in shaping and securing the first Soviet State Environmental Programme, which was adopted in 1990. This promoted a number of radical changes in Soviet environmental and resource management regimes.

A new Committee on Ecology and Natural Resources of the USSR Supreme Soviet became packed with radically oriented deputies. The new leadership put forward important initiatives in the realm of international environmental co-operation; however, in the domestic arena progress was more modest.[9] The notion of eco-*glasnost* was perhaps the most significant feature of this period, beginning the process of declassifying environmentally sensitive information and making it available to the public for the first time.[10]

The release of this information banished for ever the propagandist claims of communism revolving around a harmonious development of human–nature relations. The 1989 national survey revealed that 83.5 per cent of the population were 'strongly' or 'rather strongly' disturbed by the state of their environment. The emergence of environmental consciousness in the former Soviet society was accompanied by the rapid development of a potent green movement which coalesced with both anti-military and nationalist movements to produce a complex political situation.

Official declarations of support for the environmental cause further fuelled this mobilization phase. The steady release of information into the public domain reinvigorated earlier upsurges, such as those around Chernobyl in 1986, and created new ones as data on other 'hot spots' were released. By 1990 there were around a thousand registered environmental groups with a wide range of memberships, declared goals, tactics and political orientations (Anon., 1991).

The majority of environmental groups were small organizations at regional or city level dealing with specifically local problems, which often included community and development issues. Examples included the Moscow-based 'Bitza Environmental Union', which campaigned against the relocation of Moscow Zoo, and the Brateevo Committee of Social Self-Management, which worked for the cancellation of further redevelopment work. Others such as 'Women of Nizhnii Novgorod Against the Construction of Nuclear Power Plant' campaigned within a more widely recognized environmental agenda. The concentration of environmental health hazards in specific areas tended to produce an emphasis on immediate and tangible measures. This in turn gave environmentalism a pronounced NIMBY ('Not in My Back Yard') appearance.

The main forms of intervention included public protests, petitions, meetings, picketing and strikes. Starting in one local area, these often spread to involve whole cities, sometimes reaching regional or republic-wide proportions. One example of this kind of mobilization will suffice for illustrative purposes, though there were many more.

In Kirishi, ten residents started a campaign to secure the closure of a plant producing artificial protein concentrate (BVK) from paraffin oil. This small group was joined by others from Tomsk, Volgograd and Kremenchug, leading to the collection of signatures from all over the country. In 1988 the groups were able to hold a demonstration in which 10,000–15,000 people participated. Following this the Supreme Soviet of the USSR announced the cancellation of the production of BVK throughout the country from 1991 onwards (Social'no-Ecologicheskii Soyuz, 1994). In total over a thousand of these plants were closed down or had production severely curtailed as a result of protests. The chemical, pharmaceutical and metallurgical industries were also besieged by the wave of environmental and political activism.[11]

The most coherent campaigns amongst Soviet civic groups during the 1980s were, however, anti-nuclear. In the aftermath of the accident at Chernobyl, revelations about nuclear dumping, combined with suspicions that even more grave data remained in military archives, created widespread anti-nuclear sentiments. The horror of the Chernobyl catastrophe, the hesitancy and visible weakness of the government in dealing with it, and the secrecy and distortion in the subsequent treatment of events, produced widespread 'radiophobia' and rising mistrust of the authorities. This widespread disquiet did not, however, become focused until almost two years after the accident. Then, a vigorous public debate on the safety and future of nuclear power suddenly erupted in the mass media and scientific circles.[12] Academician Sakharov proposed the immediate suspension of all nuclear construction projects. Publication of the memoirs of Academician Legasov, one of the founding fathers of the Soviet nuclear programme, who had personally supervised the clean-up operations at Chernobyl, confirmed public suspicions about the unreliability of the Soviet nuclear power sector.

The flood of letters and petitions to the Central Committee of the CPSU, government and mass media were overwhelming. In 1988 civic groups of the Nikolaev area collected 210,000 signatures in support of demands for an environmental impact assessment of the regional nuclear station and succeeded in having the operating capacity of the South-Ukranian nuclear complex halved (Social'no-Ekologicheskii Soyuz, 1994). More impressive still was the tide of cancellation orders. In 1988 alone, state authorities announced the cessation of work at the Krasnodar, Minsk, Ignalina, Odessa, Vitebsk and Chigrin nuclear plants. Other projects were cancelled whilst still in the planning stage (*Boston Globe*, 24 December 1988). By the beginning of 1991 a total of sixty projects had been cancelled totalling 160,000 MW of capacity (*Izvestiia*, 26 January 1991).

In a country where nuclear power supplied one-tenth of all electricity generated, the loss of so many orders was a major blow. Anti-nuclear protests were not confined to power reactors, however. The Nevada-Semipalatinsk movement was created in 1989 through the initiative of the Kazakh writer Olszhas Suleimenov to stop the nuclear weapons testing programme. Between the early 1950s and 1990, 468 nuclear tests were conducted by the military, as well as numerous tests for 'peaceful purposes' (Atakhanova, 1994).

Though it has never been admitted by former Soviet officials, it is widely believed that these tests produced an increased incidence of genetic disease and heightened mortality amongst both local residents and site workers. Nevada-Semipalatinsk mobilized independent expertise on the health effects of nuclear testing, staged public demonstrations, conducted letter-writing campaigns, and used the mass media and international contacts to gain the maximum political exposure for the issue. In 1990 one million signatures were gathered on a petition calling for the closure of the site. The disintegration of the Soviet empire eventually enabled the Kazakh government to comply with the demand.

Other targets of the green groups included areas in the Urals and Siberia heavily contaminated with radioactivity from weapons production and waste dumping. The secrecy surrounding all nuclear issues only intensified speculation and the public demand for information.[13] From the end of the 1980s one of the pinnacles of big Soviet science became the focus of green groups determined to reveal the damage done to the area and its residents. Groups organized public hearings, referendums and scientific conferences on the issue of nuclear safety whilst attempting to stop the importation of nuclear waste from other countries and to catalogue the effects of the nuclear industry on the environment and health.[14]

In 1989 the scope for public demonstrations and collective organizations expressing opposition views expanded immensely. Mass demonstrations, strikes and other civic actions became a regular feature of Soviet political life. At least 4 per cent of all strikes during 1989 were called to oppose environmental conditions (*Vestnik-Statistiki*, 1991, No. 4). The expanding scale of actions brought into being a number of 'umbrella' groups which attempted to co-ordinate the movement on a regional and national level. An example of the successful co-ordination of activities can be seen in the Socio-ecological Union (SEU) campaign against the construction of the 'Volga–Chograi' canal. This in turn was part of a huge project to divert the northern rivers. Meetings and demonstrations were held in over a hundred cities with at least 500,000 people in attendance, while over one million signatures were gathered. The day before construction was due to start the Soviet government took a decision to cancel it (Social'no-Ekologocheskii Soyuz, 1994).

Despite such victories the effectiveness of protest movements declined rapidly over time and environmental problems intensified as a result of economic 'shock therapy'. An alternative to negative campaigning was sought by many as a means of influencing policy-making. Policy relevance increased the politicization of Soviet environmentalism. The emergence of organizations with a broad social base and strong nationalistic tendencies, such as the Lithuanian Green Party or the Moldavian Green Movement, brought a new dimension to Soviet environmentalism during the 1980s.[15] In the Baltic and Caucasian republics, where environmentalism was conjoined with the idea of national revival and independence, the politicization of the movement was particularly rapid. The idea of internal colonialism[16] placed the blame for environmental problems on central government and Russian domination. This quickly became a unifying concept forging previously diverse civic groups into integrated political movements, not only in the Baltic states of Lithuania, Estonia and Latvia but also Georgia, Armenia, Moldova and, surprisingly to many, the Ukraine.

In previous phases of Russian environmentalism the Baltic republics had championed the creation of national parks and conservation zones (Weiner, 1988b); now they championed popular demands against the FSU. The radical nature of their response can be accounted for by a number of factors. Latvia, Estonia and Lithuania were amongst the most modern of the industrialized Soviet republics and had well-developed political cultures derived in part from their period of self-governance between the two world wars. They also had particularly intense environmental concerns, ranging from contamination by industrial wastes to polluted groundwater and depleted fish stocks. The strategic goal of the Baltic greens was the preservation of national culture and identity through the restoration of statehood.

In the Baltic case environmental concerns served as a marshalling point for nationalism. Controversy over oil-shale and phosphate mining gave an impetus to the formation of the Popular Front of Estonia in 1988. The Lithunania Green Party was established in 1989 following a vigorous campaign against the Ignalina nuclear power station. The statutes of the party included the establishment of an independent, ecologically healthy and secure, neutral and demilitarized Lithuania (Vebra, 1993). Latvian environmentalism was activated by debates over the Daugava hydroelectric station in 1986, which resulted in the formation of the Green Party of Latvia in 1990. In effect there were two mobilizations in the region, though the linkages between them were considerable. The Baltic greens expressed a desire to cleanse not only the natural environment but also the political, mental and ethnic environment of their republics. These ecological concerns became part of the arsenal of issues deployed by the Popular Fronts, which became the most powerful social movements in the Baltic region and were central in the organization of massive demonstrations against the Moscow administration.[17]

Believing that coalition-building would accelerate their withdrawal from the Union, the Baltic greens actively sought support in other republics. Close contacts were developed with the Uzbek 'Birlik' movement, which called for the revival of nature and a return to a traditional economy. Links were also formed with the Popular Fronts in Georgia, Armenia and Azerbaijan, as well as the Moldavian green movement. This combination of voices accused the central leadership of bringing the country to the verge of environmental crisis and demanded full control over their indigenous natural resources (Ziegler, 1991). Whilst these movements constituted a considerable political challenge, the most formidable challenge came from the Ukraine in the form of the 'Zelenyi Svit' movement.

The Ukraine suffered some of the most severe industrial pollution in the USSR, a problem aggravated by reckless irrigation schemes undertaken by the infamous All-Union Ministry of Land Reclamation and Irrigation. The latent resentment over the imposition of centrally planned projects was triggered by the Chernobyl accident of 1986, prompting a small environmental club of writers and cinematographers to found Zelenyi Svit in 1987. Within two years, Zelenyi Svit had become an umbrella organization with 300 affiliated groups throughout the Ukraine. The heart of the campaign was opposition to nuclear power and this led to mass demonstrations and petitions. In 1989 the chair of Zelenyi Svit became head of the Parliamentary Sub-committee on Nuclear Ecology. This influential position enabled the movement to accomplish some of its objectives quickly.

The authorities cancelled several nuclear power stations and a range of other environmentally harmful initiatives. It was agreed that information about the Chernobyl accident would be declassified and that serious medical research into the correlation between human health and pollution would be undertaken. Zelenyi Svit drafted environmental proposals for the Ukrainian Supreme Soviet which were instrumental in the move to declare the entire Ukraine an 'environmental disaster area' and gained support for a costly environmental rehabilitation programme.[18]

In Russia the politicization of environmentalism has been slower than in other republics of the FSU. This can be understood in terms of several factors. First, the role played by nationalism in areas like the Baltic was largely absent in Russia, where it was difficult to formulate a simple unifying 'us' and 'them' agenda. Secondly, the immense scale of the Russian Federation and the geography of the environmental crisis, which produced widely dispersed 'black spots',[19] militated against identifying common causes. Thirdly, the absence of effective communications also militated against the formation of national movements, a problem compounded by the vastly uneven development of political culture. Moreover, the specifically Russian environmental movement deliberately shunned formal political intervention, regarding its role as being a generator of new values through education and grass-roots initiatives (Shubin, 1992). Russia was not completely devoid of a nationalist wing to the environmental movement, with 'Pamyat', founded in the mid-1980s, declaring its intention to cleanse the ethnic and mental climate of the country.[20]

Towards the end of the 1980s Russian environmentalism became characterized by two main approaches. On one side was an environmental vanguard striving for participation in the decision-making process, which was quickly accommodated within the political echelons. On the other hand, established politicians, such as Anatoly Sobchak and Yegor Gaidar, quickly incorporated environmental concerns within their programmes. The newly formed Bloc of Russian Patriotic Movements and 'Democratic Russia'[21] also played the green card as 'democratic' elections loomed. This phase of political incorporation divided the sympathies of the civic groups but the majority chose to support 'Democratic Russia' with its abstract democratic principles and 'green-plus-market' slogans.

In the political climate of the time both eco-activists and politicians with 'green' credentials were doomed to electoral success, easily winning seats in the elections for the Congress of People's Deputies of the USSR in 1989 and the 1990 republican and local elections. Following the elections it was estimated that 12 per cent, or 300, deputies were 'environmentally oriented' (Yanitsky, 1993). Thirty-nine were environmental leaders such as Alexei Yablokov, Nikolai Vorontsov and Alexei Kazannik from the Omsk 'Green City' group. Eco-activists were also elected, becoming members of the executive within the Ministries of Environment and Natural Resources of the USSR as well as finding representative status in the republics and local committees. Whilst in power the former members of civic groups maintained close contacts with their organizations, using them as reliable sources of information, expertise and public support. Alexei Yablokov, for example, used his position as state counsellor on environment and health issues to appoint the SEU leader Sviatoslav Zabelin as his assistant. This made the SEU an effective channel of communication between legislators, the executive and the wider environmental movement, though this is a position which has attracted much criticism.[22]

The election of greens to such prominent positions and the commitment of 'Democratic Russia' to economic liberalization within the context of environmental sustainability held out the promise of radical environmental legislation. The 1990 State Environmental Programme of the USSR and the 1992 Environmental Law of the Russian Federation, combined with similar acts within the sovereign states of the FSU, created a framework for progress in this direction. The devolution of authority to the regions also offered communities greater control over natural resources and economic development.

Despite this the environmental reforms have failed to meet the aspirations of the civic movement during the mobilization phase. The political promises of the 'green-plus-market' democrats were quickly swept aside by the shock therapy of economic liberalization required by the IMF and World Bank. The efforts of greens within the Soviet parliament of 1990 to win support for a resolution entitled 'On Urgent Measures to Improve the State of the Environment' produced a stillborn act which was never implemented at the local level. In the republican parliaments environmental issues were also subordinated to debates on economic recession imposed from above by the Union. Economic imperatives quickly asserted themselves even at this level. The Estonian parliament, which had an effective green bloc within it, did not even include the issue of assistance to zones of environmental disaster within its agenda (Yanitsky, 1993). In Lithuania, the government which came to power on the back of the campaign against the Ignalina nuclear power station voted to re-open it several months later. In Georgia, individuals who had challenged the Trans-Caucasian Railway and energy complexes as leaders of national environmental movements championed the same projects as essential to national development and independence (Peterson, 1993). The Kazakh groups 'Ecological International' and 'Ecology and Public Opinion' supported several candidates in the 1994 parliamentary elections in order to develop links with policy-makers. The successful parliamentary candidates quickly ceased regular contacts with their grass-roots supporters once elected (Solyanik, 1994a). In Russia, Gaidar's green-and-market government adopted a national programme of nuclear energy development without a proper environmental impact assessment. The tensions between economic expediency and political and expert authority have produced contradictory legislative initiatives which leave the position of the environment unclear. For example, despite concerted opposition from the Ministry of the Environment, the Inter-Agency Commission on Environmental Security and the Committee on Science and Public Protests, the State Duma continued its intention of adopting laws 'On State Policy in Dealing with Radioactive Wastes'.

The highly optimistic phase of environmentalism was rapidly swept aside by a tide of pragmatic accommodation which intensified the rate of environmental degradation in Russia. Industrial enterprises formerly closed for environmental reasons have been re-opened,[23] forests in protected areas are being logged, nature reserves are being closed, and rare species of wildlife are sold for profit on foreign markets.[24] Despite the protests of local greens, the Ukrainian parliament, facing an extreme energy shortage and the crippling costs of imported fuel, voted to end the moratorium on new nuclear stations and to continue to operate the remaining reactors at Chernobyl. In Kazakhstan, environmental and technical programmes, including those aimed at restoring the Aral and Caspian Seas, were discarded and forgotten (Baitulin, 1994).

At the local level the desire to attract foreign investment as a means of reinforcing independence from Moscow overshadowed concerns for the environment. Western firms were exempted from a range of taxes and charges relating to resource use and pollution in order to acquire western technologies whilst securing jobs and income.

The rapid transformation of the 'green-plus-market' democrats to overtly anti-environmental positions aroused strong protests from environmentally conscious people, some of whom joined the ranks of the opposition. In the 1993 elections for the Russian Federation, the former 'green-plus-market' democrats practically excluded environmental and resource issues from their manifestos. Such concerns became the preserve of the Liberal Democratic, Communist and Agrarian parties. The environment thus moved from the centrepiece of the elected parties' political programme to become a weapon of the opposition movement. This had disastrous consequences for the credibility of those environmental activists who had sought direct involvement in the political struggle in the late 1980s (Yanitsky, 1993). Having been politically outmanoeuvred by much more powerful and experienced political actors, their credibility as both politicians and activists was irreparably tarnished.

Whilst the notion of a 'new environmental paradigm' remains embedded in the programmes of many political parties, it is an empty slogan. The absence of meaningful solutions to existing environmental problems and the lack of commitment to effective environmental impact assessments for new measures bears testimony to this. The environmental movement was precipitated into a period of bitter recrimination and infighting by these events, with charges of corruption, money laundering and idleness proving damaging to previously successful movements like Nevada-Semipalatinsk.

Discredited as openly green candidates, most environmental leaders in Kazakhstan chose to stand as affiliates of the LAD (Slavic Cultural Party) in 1994, despite the widespread perception that it was closely associated with Russian ultra-nationalism. Though this move was politically expedient under the prevailing conditions, it has weakened the prospects of the emergent multi-ethnic green movement in central Asia even further. In Russia, mutual accusations between green parliamentarians Mikhail Lemeshev, Anatoly Schramchenko and Tamara Zlotnikova (*Spasenie*, 1994, Nos 31–34) and Victor Danilov-Danilian (Yablokov, 1993), based on political preferences, ambitions and personal interests have prevailed over 'environmental causes'. This has severely shaken public trust, a process fuelled by numerous revelations about politicians' personal benefits from playing the 'green card'.[25]

In Russia, the failure of 'democratic' governments, including environmentalists, to prevent the continuing destruction of nature contributed to the creation of core/periphery, 'them and us' cleavages within the federation. Chechnya proclaimed its independence, and other autonomous republics such as Tataria, Bashkiria, Byriatia and Tyva demanded exclusive control over their resources and the right to independent economic development in protest against being treated like internal colonies. The subsequent military response to Chechen independence has placed major question marks over the reform process with the federation. The cost of the initial operation has been put at US$5 billion, with continuing costs of US$30 million a day (*The Salt Lake Tribune*, 9 January 1995). Within a devastated economy there is little left in the coffers for environmental rehabilitation.[26]

The politicization of the environment in the third phase has been instrumental in fragmenting the Soviet empire. The leaders of the greens had unprecedented opportunities to participate in the decision-making process and create progressive laws and legislative initiatives. Despite this, actual improvements in the environmental situation in Russia remain poor. Enforcement of environmental regulation has declined from sporadic under the Soviet system to virtually non-existent. These developments provoked a crisis in the environmental movement accompanied by an acute decline in its activities and the loss of support amidst the ensuing ideological discord. Whilst lacking a coherent platform prior to the revolutions of 1989, environmentalists remained united by their sense of silent opposition and assumed role as bearers of a new environmental paradigm. The subsequent politicization of the movement has largely weakened this sense of unity and, along with the economic factors briefly touched on here, has devalued the environment as a unifying cause within the public arena. For the time being the environment can no longer be seen as a major independent element in the political agenda of the FSU.

CONTOURS OF THE SOVIET ENVIRONMENTAL MOVEMENT

In comparison with the uniformity imposed by the totalitarianism of the Communist Party, the informal groups of the FSU are surprisingly diverse in their goals, aims and tactics, membership, structures, ideology and relationship with the authorities. The contemporary geography of environmentalism in the area is rather uneven. By 1989 the pro-environmental movement seemed to encompass virtually the whole country, although currently it does not have a national character in the former Soviet states. On the map of the FSU, environmental activities are located in areas of relatively sophisticated political culture and zones with particularly intense environmental degradation. Spatially there is thus a concentration in the western and north-western areas. Initially the most comprehensive environmental networks were created in the Baltic republics, Ukraine and Georgia, but here the recent decline in the visibility of environmentalism is most noticeable. Within the Russian Federation, both the emergence and decline of an integrated environmental movement have been more gradual.

Currently, Russia leads the former Soviet bloc in terms of environmental activity, the number of groups, their joint membership and scale of activities. The urban centres of Moscow and St Petersburg have been prominent nodes of activity, as have zones with high environmental impacts and high concentrations of industrial labour. These include the Volga Basin, the Kola Peninsula and some towns in Siberia and the Far East.

As environmentalism spread throughout Russian the incandescence of the movement during its initial phase of mobilization vanished. In several regions with particularly serious environmental conditions social reaction has been very limited. Environmentalism is practically unknown in rural areas and small autonomous republics and districts of the Russian Federation. In the republics of central Asia, the first green groups appeared during the late 1980s, yet the movement is still at its nascent stage. The first organizational meeting of representatives from Kazakhstan, Turkmenistan and Uzbekistan took place in 1993. However, since then meetings between greens in central Asia have been infrequent and irregular and their activities are still not co-ordinated. Typically, central Asian organizations have more contacts with their Russian and western colleagues than with their compatriots in the area. In terms of membership, contemporary environmental groups vary from the micro with several members, to the small with several dozen participants, the large comprising up to a thousand members, and the mass, encompassing several thousand people. Despite impressive numbers and several campaigns accomplished by mass organizations, there is a substantial gap between the enlisted membership and activists. These tensions are heightened by the quasi-non-governmental character of some of the organizations.[28] The majority of green groups in the NIS (New Independent States) are of a small size, poorly organized, and often short-lived.

Despite this apparent fragmentation the ultimate goal of the movement can be defined as the preservation of the richness and diversity of the environment in its broadest sense – both natural and social. With this ultimate goal in common, informal organizations enjoy significant differences in both value priorities and practical aims. It is noteworthy that different attitudes towards the same general goal do, to a major extent, reflect the three main trends of early Russian environmentalism: utilitarian, cultural–aesthetic and scientific.[29]

By their extreme anthropocentrism, the majority of environmentalists in the FSU could be regarded as successors of the 'scientific' or 'ecological' trend. Historically, adherents of this world view emphasized nature's fragility and the disruptive impact of industrial civilization upon the delicate equilibrium between the various biotic components of the environment. Natural scientists who most exclusively held this view at the beginning of the century were, however, concerned not with the integrity of nature itself but primarily with the consequences of the envisioned ecological collapse for human civilization. They claimed a policy-making role in economic matters and resource use, arguing that only scientific expertise could ensure that growth would remain within the possibilities afforded by a healthy nature (Weiner, 1988a). There are several historical, social and geographical reasons why the anthropocentric approach continues to prevail in Russian/Soviet culture. Currently, the majority of the NIS environmentalists regard the preservation of nature exclusively within the context of human survival and quality of life. The core of this trend consists of natural scientists striving to influence policy-making (like Alexei Yablokov, Nikolai Vorontsov, Sviatoslav Zabelin and Oleg Khabarov[30]), and leaders of local protest groups and political activists (e.g. Yury Shcherbak). Around this core group are assembled a broad periphery drawn from a very diverse range of social groups. These range from retired engineers promoting the ideas of alternative energy sources or environmentally safe cemeteries (*Spasenie*, 1994, No. 34) to unemployed women and radical youth picketing environmentally sensitive sites such as the Balakovo and Rostov nuclear stations and the chemical plants at Svetloyarsk and Cheboksary. A primary concern of these groups is the health impact of environmental pollution in the densely populated industrial centres.

Concrete aims include a struggle for the closure of polluting industries, energy and transportation complexes,[31] participation in environmental restoration, and the provision of expertise to reconstruct economic activities. Another stream within the movement might be presented as an historical succession of the pastoralist trend of the 1900s focused on the cultural, aesthetic and ethical aspects of nature protection. Like their predecessors, contemporary 'ecocentric' groups emphasize that nature is valuable in itself, irrespective of its utility to humans, and that other living things have an equal right to exist. The primary task of 'ecocentric environmentalists' is to preserve the maximum biotic diversity through the protection of the few remaining oases of pristine nature and the creation of large protected territories throughout the country. The most prominent organizations within this stream are probably the Students' Corps and a few groups of the SEU.

The statutes of the SEU, for example, include the objective of enlarging the system of protected territories to comprise 50 per cent of the total area of the country (Social'no-ekologicheskii Soyuz, 1994). Despite the general trend of massive closure of nature reserves all over the FSU in the 1990s, SEU affiliates were instrumental in planning and creating the Big Arctic (Taimyr), Katunskii (Altai) and Kerzhenskii (Volga Basin) *zapovedniks*, Anayarvi (Karelia), Us't-Koksinskii (Altai), Shirkent (Tadjikistan) and Lukomor'e (Ukraine) national parks, several nature parks and *zakazniks* (Social'no-ekologicheskii Soyuz, 1994). Some ecological clubs and associations of that stream ('*Vstrechnoye Dvizhenie*' Ecological Patriotic Association from Magnitogorsk, Goodwill from Yalta and Kiev, and Noosphere Ecocultural Association, to name a few) champion historical and cultural issues. The ecocentric trend of the movement was strengthened with the creation in the former Soviet states of affiliates of international environmental organizations such as Greenpeace, Sacred Earth, Friends of the Earth and Ekologiia, whose methods of work were adapted (with varying degrees of success) to post-Soviet conditions.

A link between two main streams is a trend towards creating environmentally balanced human settlements. The idea of Ecopolis, initiated by Dmitry Kavtaradze and developed by several teams of scientists and activists, is to ensure balance between the carrying capacity of environmental sites and different kinds of human pressure. The Ecopolis programme consists of several stages. The first comprises an environmental impact assessment of the settlement and its population and outlines possible reconstruction projects. A second phase includes the creation of urban nature and game reserves alongside the conservation and restoration of historical and cultural landmarks. The third phase concentrates on environmental education through local environmental clubs and children's programmes (Serebrovskaya, 1994). An attempt to create Ecopolis was first tried in Puschino (a small residential town of the Academy of Sciences), then in the Moscow suburb of Kosino, and later in suburbs of St Petersburg.

Both 'anthropocentric' and 'ecocentric' environmentalists doubt that the ultimate goal of the movement can be achieved within the existing industrial system. They see the problems rooted in the very character of the system and neither the creation of new *zapovedniks* nor closure of the polluting industries could change it. To remedy the environmental predicament a new social system of values compatible with a pro-environmental mentality is needed. Accordingly, public environmental education is recognized by all groups within the movement as amongst the most important and immediate task. This function is carried by the environmental newspapers *Spasenie* and *Zelenyi Mir* (both supported by the Ministry of Environment and foreign grants), *Nabat* (published by several 'Chernobyl' societies and the Nevada-Semipalatinsk movement), *Bereginia* (published in Nizhnii Novgorod by Ecocenter 'Dront'), and *Zelenyi Luch* (Russian Green Party). These newspapers are supplemented by recently founded specialist magazines such as *Ecos* and *Evrasia*. Information agencies Ecodefence (Kaliningrad), Soceco Agency (Moscow) and Severo-Zapad (St Petersburg) make effective use of electronic communications to disperse relevant reports and news. Confronted with the rapidly escalating costs imposed by marketization and privatization, most of these media organs have come near to closing and are now heavily dependent upon support from kindred western organizations.

Another aspect of environmental education is conducted through centres of children's ecologo-aesthetic education, such as those created by Elena Sedletskaya in Moscow, by Viktor Grebennikov in Novosibirsk, and Club Eco-Orbis in Smolensk. Original methods used by these centres are meant not only to teach children the basics of environmental knowledge and skills but primarily to develop self-expression and the inner feeling of being a part of nature (Sedletskaya, 1994).

Finally, some contemporary organizations with environmentally friendly titles follow a utilitarian approach (also known as 'wise-use'). Growth-oriented and state-oriented versions of wise-use sought to introduce the principle of sustained yield wherever applicable and to make resource use generally more efficient (Weiner, 1988a). Wise-use is guided by two central beliefs: first, that nature has only a narrowly economic, instrumental value, and secondly, that environmental components can be divided into 'useful' and 'harmful' for humans. These are the guiding axioms of environmental management as pursued by this stream. The mass of engineers and natural scientists in the former Soviet society were structurally destined to follow this pragmatic perspective. Currently, employees of the poverty-stricken research institutes, laboratories and industrial enterprises also regard the environment as a potential source of contracts, additional income or material benefits.[32] The emergence of environmental co-operatives, exchanges and small environmental consultancies signals the adaptation of this social stratum to the new market system. These small consultancies are very practical and often effective in filling existing gaps in public needs, being familiar with both the technical detail of environmental problems and the social and cultural milieu within which solutions must be brokered.[33]

What differentiates this stream is its technocratic orientation, emphasizing the efficient utilization of resources and technology, acceptance of the traditional paradigm of development and the lack of political ambitions. Development of the wise-use stream of contemporary environmentalism was initially supported by a few economic actors, usually referred to as anti-environmental. Some ministries have formed their own 'green' organizations. The Ecological Foundation, which in the last few years has sponsored several highly advertised public initiatives and contests, was reportedly created under the initiative of the Ministries of Oil and Chemical Production. Another organization reportedly connected with industrial interests is the environmental movement KEDR, which is officially headed by Victor Danilov-Danilian (Minister of Environment) and recently has announced the creation of the Environmental Party of Russia (*Spasenie*, 1994, No. 22).

Numerous environmental funds also seem to pursue the interests of local authorities under the cover of benevolent activities.[34] The newly formed environmental consultancies have found it difficult to stay in business through *bona fide* work, with major western development agencies prioritizing western consultants over local ones. There are numerous examples of environmental businesses being engaged in all kinds of un-ecological affairs, including trade in endangered species and assisting industries in avoiding environmental regulations.

Despite all the differences between agendas, values and priorities, most of the groups claim similar basic principles – ecological *glasnost*, comprehensive monitoring and public-participatory environmental assessments. A strong emphasis is placed on the availability of reliable data as most of the information has been classified in the past. In the political realm traditional democratic practices and institutions such as referendums, public opinion polling, public hearings and fund-raising remain tentatively welcome. These new-found democratic freedoms also explain the similarities in the tactics of the green groups. The lawsuit, however, has not yet become a realistic option in a country where a plethora of laws is not combined with feasible enforcement.[35]

Consequently, in the late 1980s the most popular tactics of the green groups were organizing mass demonstrations and petitions. In the 1990s diminishing public support saw a turn to pickets, public declarations of limited dissemination and, what is most promising, practical work of professional quality. Substantial changes also occurred in the ideological status of the movement. Until the late 1980s, most environmentalists (though always in silent opposition to the government) avoided taking an ideologically critical position, preferring a stance grounded in a technical neutrality. Currently, groups span the whole ideological spectrum, ranging from fiercely nationalist organizations and eco-anarchists to apolitical environmental businesses and societies of naturalists. *Sovetskaya Rossiia*, the most conservative Russian newspaper, sponsored the Committee to Save the Volga, whereas the Committee to Save the Ob has been based in the liberal-minded scientific research centre of Novosibirsk. In St Petersburg, Krasnoyarsk, Novosibirsk and Chelyabinsk, there are environmental movements with extremely nationalistic programmes, including ideas of 'ethnocracy' and, in the meantime, the green parties from these cities are adherents of liberal democratic ideology (Shubin, 1992). Many of the recently politicized groups have taken an anarcho-socialist position.[36] The ideological eclecticism of the contemporary environmental movement is reflected in the so-called 'Green Politics' – a programme statement of the Green Party of Russia which combines specific environmental measures with thoroughgoing social and political reforms. The Russian Green Party thus campaigns for the cancellation of all nuclear energy projects, automatic compliance with environmental regulations, and reforestation to the level of the 1900s. Constitutionally it demands direct democracy through governmental accountability before parliament and supports social self-management and cultural–national autonomy (*Spasenie*, 1994, No. 22).

It should be noted that the ideological positions occupied by greens in the FSU, whilst sharing the same nomenclature as their western counterparts, translate into different praxis. The democrats' environmental policy, until recently supported by most Soviet environmentalists, for example, represents a conservative and environmentally deficient approach heavily criticized by greens in the West. At the same time, those who in Russia are on the 'right' wing of the ideological spectrum support ideas of communal, decentralized and putatively natural life-styles, which by western political definitions belong to anarcho-communist or eco-socialist positions well to the left of centre.

Whilst contemporary environmentalism in the NIS countries is not mature enough to generate a unifying ideology, more than any other movement, environmentalism represents a broad vision of an alternative paradigm of development. Despite all the inconsistencies between different groups, both in their visions of an alternative order and the practical politics needed to reach such an order,[37] the greens continue to share a concern with human survival and societal development widely seen as lacking amongst the major political parties struggling for power in Russia and other NIS countries.

The divergence between environmentalists in the FSU makes the gap between them and their western counterparts profound, despite rapidly growing contacts. The differing historical development of the movements in their respective social, economic, ideological and information realms helps explain the differences in goals, values, priorities and methods. Perhaps the most striking difference is the domination of the anthropocentric stream of environmentalism within the FSU, combined with the search for political influence amongst the professional and pragmatic reformers. In contradistinction the western green movement can be characterized by the prevalence of an ecocentric stream and a sizeable number of ecological 'radicals'.

Expressed simply, most Soviet citizens are convinced that westerners have far fewer problems in the environmental sphere and therefore can afford to care about biodiversity and to oppose consumerism. Westerners are bewildered that ex-Soviets have so many environmental problems but concentrate mainly on health problems whilst weakening the movement by playing political games.

Another nuanced difference between the former Soviet and western environmentalists noted by Weiner (1988b) is the targets of the movements. Historically, American preservationists have opposed what they saw as the tyrannizing, philistine majority. To preservationists in the FSU the principal adversary has always been the state or local administration. Besides, in the totalitarian Soviet society and the politically indefinable post-Soviet system the stakes have always been substantially higher than in the West, including as they have the struggle over intellectual freedom.

The status of the environmental movement as a politicized force of opposition in the post-*perestroika* period has been closely tied to 'market–environment' dualism. People who joined the movement in the political and ideological turbulence of the late 1980s did so under the illusion that the West did not have environmental problems. Accordingly, 'green plus market' was seen as a viable strategy to remedy the numerous environmental disasters engendered by the communist regime. It was widely thought that the introduction of western technology and institutions, along with the expected flow of aid, would cure the disasters. However, western environmental groups were certainly aware that the introduction of capitalism into Russia would not work environmental miracles. The market euphoria of Soviet/Russian environmentalists was short-lived, but still few of them have a realistic picture of the difficulties ahead.

The mainstay of western environmentalism, which functions within the system of established democratic institutions, is the rule of law. In the post-Soviet system, the plethora of laws has not ensured the creation of a civic, law-abiding society. All the actors in the environmental realm (government, industry, citizens and informal groups themselves) violate existing legislation and prefer to use other methods (mostly direct political actions and the media) to pursue their goals.

The relative independence of western groups also contrasts sharply with a growing subordination of environmental activities in the FSU to the interests of funding sources. Western groups enjoy access to different sources of potential support: numerous foundations, government grants, membership subscriptions and volunteer work. They thus enjoy a greater diversity of funding sources, enabling them to pursue their specific projects through specialized work. In Russia and other CIS states, access to financial and other kinds of support for environmental causes is extremely limited. Empty government coffers, the absence of private foundations and the reluctance of newly rich economic actors such as banks and businesses to make open-ended contributions have resulted in a very hostile resourcing climate for environmental groups.

Western foundations, NGOs and businesses currently appear to be the only feasible source of support for post-Soviet environmentalism. But the number of foundations is limited, their support is largely defined by the perceptions of western experts and granted to pre-selected and frequently western partners. The ability of indigenous groups to formulate their own environmental agendas and work towards their fulfilment using local methods and knowledge is thus heavily compromised. This phenomenon, in turn, further fragments the movement, creating cut-throat competition, growing animosity and political accusations among former colleagues, leading to further declines in public support.[38]

Dependence on foreign funding sources, with their specific demands and perceptions, explains the broad spectrum of activities claimed by most environmental groups. Claims to expert status usually exceed the actual professional capacity of the group, but without the claims to over-extended expertise potential sources of funding would be lost. The pursuit of funding thus threatens the credibility and legitimacy of such groups. The pursuit of legitimacy and public support through the gathering and dissemination of information represents another area of difference between eastern and western groups.

While western groups disseminate their information in a search for public support, in the FSU environmental information is regarded as an asset. Particularly sensitive information, such as 'hot' data on nuclear contamination or illegal whaling, is more likely to be sold to a foreign wire service than to be freely distributed. Competition for information, grants and governmental support has been destructive to the former unity of the Russian/Soviet environmental movement. Finally, the environmental movement in the West is still a powerful actor in terms of public influence. In contrast, despite its long history and the political successes of the late 1980s, the environmental movement in the post-socialist system currently has much less public and political impact. Whilst the outburst of environmental activities in the 1980s and their subsequent politicization cradled the democratic movement in Russia, the movement literally depleted its own reserves in the process.

THE SOCIAL BASIS OF ENVIRONMENTALISM

Social support for environmentalism can be gauged through a variety of means, including the number and composition of environmental groups, their level of support within society and by public perceptions of the urgency of environmental problems and value priorities. During the uneven history of Soviet/Russian environmentalism, public support for the environmental cause has fluctuated from a few hundred liberal intellectuals to millions of militant citizens.

During the initial phase, the movement was limited to a scientific milieu with support provided by representatives of the well-educated and better-off strata of society. The period 1917–26 witnessed a dramatic rise in civic activism amongst all strata of the urban population of the new, socialist Russia. Organizations of the second phase comprised primarily university students and graduates in biology, zoology and geography. Through their field studies and analytical work these people were able to gain more data on the state of the environment, which enabled them to assess the damage caused by anthropogenic pressure. Scientists as a group, however, along with the creative intelligentsia, were excluded from decision-making both in the Russian empire and in the former Soviet system. For these groups, environment-alism became a means to challenge the power base of society through the prism of their professions. After *perestroika*, the vitality and the social basis of the move-ment were changed.

Since 1986, between 5 and 8 per cent of the adult population of the country has become involved in different civic activities (Yanitsky, 1993). In Russia alone there were more than 500 environmental groups by 1992, uniting several thousand citizens. In addition, many informal organizations of that time (anti-nuclear and anti-military groups, women's and labour associations, as well as nationalist and radical youth organizations) swelled the ranks of the environmental movement as environmental objectives constituted a prominent goal. Indeed, in the late 1980s, nationalist, youth and labour support for environmental clean-up was the strongest in the history of these movements. Environmental issues had emerged from being the concern of a highly educated and devoted minority to what political scientists refer to as a 'valence' issue. Currently, practically all the participants of the movement live in towns and cities. Intellectuals of lower ranks and modest incomes comprise the core of the movement. Besides natural scientists, two other professional affili-ations are represented most prominently: engineers and writers and journalists. It is the substantial involvement of engineers that differentiates the NIS movement from its western counterparts, reflecting their dominance in the economically active population and their privileged access to environment-related information and technology. The active participation of journalists and writers can be explained, first, by their better information-handling skills, secondly, by their professional commitment to civic activities, and thirdly, by their flexible working schedules. The creation of organizations such as the Committees to Save the Volga, Lake Baikal, the Dnepr and Pridneprovie, the Aral Sea, Balkhash, Ladoga and the Black Sea are all the initiatives of writers and journalists. The potency of the media as a means of fighting secrecy and bureaucracy has enabled such individuals as Sergei Zalygin (Campaign against Diverting the Siberian Rivers), Yury Shcherbak (anti-nuclear campaign in Ukraine) and Olszhas Suleimenov (Nevada-Semipalatinsk movement) to bring their initiatives to success.

Markedly absent from the movement are managers and administrators, polit-ical and trade-union functionaries, the military and businessmen (Yanitsky, 1993). Sociological research on industrial centres in Russia also showed the absence of industrial, agricultural and service workers, as well as most people with low levels of education (Khalyi, 1993). Social scientists are also a scarce category. Thus, the profile of Soviet/Russian environmentalism differs from that in the West, where the majority of participants are radically minded service-sector professionals or humanities majors (Weiner, 1988b). There are also substantial differences in terms of age, gender and social status. In western Europe (Poguntke, 1989), the USA and other western countries (Papadakis, 1993), the young, the fairly affluent and the well-educated are the strongest supporters of environmental causes. The history of these countries attests that environmentalism is often at root a protest by the young against the values and philosophies of the older generation. In contrast, among the Russian/CIS environmentalists there are very few young people. The backbone of the movement comprises baby-boomers – those who were once active in the Students' Corps and nature-protection campaigns of the 1970s. There is also a high representation of recently retired people. For the elderly, the environmental movement is an avenue through which to keep in touch with the community, making use of their broad knowledge and bringing to the surface their long-tolerated indignation with the authorities and the system (either former or contemporary).

The substantial contribution of women to the creation and continued existence of the environmental movement in Russia/CIS is another feature worthy of comment. Women comprise one-third of the Green Party membership and 50 per cent of the membership and 40 per cent of the leadership in the Blue Movement for Social Ecology of Human Beings. Women as a social group tend to approach environmental issues differently from men (their positions on matters of public policy, in contrast to those of men, are more likely to be compassionate than 'tough', communitarian than individualistic, and public-interested than self-interested). Their presence at leadership levels would shape Soviet/Russian environmentalism in a more humanitarian way. However, the general trend towards a mono-gendered system of male societal governance which became evident in Russia in 1991–5 is also reflected at the informal level. The leaders of large environmental groups and movements are even less likely to include women at the decision-making levels than were the old Soviet-era elites. The need to address specifically women's issues or introduce distinct women's perspectives is largely denied by the male leadership. In response to this, women have created independent organizations dealing mainly with environmental health, environmental education and legislation. In the last few years, women's environmental groups have increased in numbers although not yet in political influence (Mirovitskaya, 1993). We can thus talk of the emergence of a distinctive female environmentalism, which has separate dynamics, addresses more specific issues and is largely reinforced by the wider women's movement.

Another feature of Soviet/Russian environmentalism is the marginalization of its participants within wider society. With very few exceptions, most of the contemporary greens have not been very successful in their professional careers, material well-being or political activities. There is a dual process in operation whereby the system denies access to people with good leadership qualities whilst others eschew official careers to work independently. As Yanitsky's (1993) extensive research reveals, environmental groups become an adaptive niche for people who have fallen out of the normal social or professional life or who are affected by broken personal relationships. Questionnaires distributed by the Russian Association of University Women in Moscow among well-educated women who had recently lost their jobs revealed that most of them specified environmentalism as the realm they would like to exist in, either in a professional or a social capacity (Mirovitskaya, unpublished data). Personal acquaintance with the leaders of several groups gives the firm impression that for most of them societal marginalization goes hand in hand with the best qualities of the Russian intelligentsia: comprehensive education, professionalism, and a well-developed sense of the collective good.

In 1990, a poll of Muscovites revealed that the green movement in the USSR was second only to the Church in terms of public trust (*Moscow News*, 1990, No. 22). Several environmental campaigns brought over a million participants each. In the late 1980s, by organizing popular protests environmental groups have influenced both political processes and economic performance. It should be mentioned, however, that such mobilization power did not result exclusively from popular trust in the green leadership. In the early years of *perestroika*, when a party-state monopoly still made open attacks against political leadership impossible, environmentalism provided a political space where people could organize against the regime. In a few years the thinly veiled anti-governmental character of environmental slogans was replaced by openly nationalistic and anti-communist declarations. Another factor which appeared to bolster mass support for environmentalism in the late 1980s was the struggle amongst ordinary people to maintain their sense of identity. When socialist ideals, which throughout the decades of propaganda were driven into the public conscience, suddenly came under severe attack, people felt a need for some basic linkages which would exist under any political regime, a necessity to belong to some particular space (national, cultural, social, geographical) – and environmentalism provided these feelings.

Yet, along with the economic decline and political discord, public support for the environmental cause has diminished. A 1992 poll of professional environmental experts showed that 19.4 per cent of them were of the opinion that the green movement in Russia did not exist at all, while 72.8 per cent did not consider it to be of any socio-political importance (Gosudarstvenyi Doklad, 1993). Only one-third of experts supported the movement in general while another third supported only some of its actions. Only dozens (instead of the hundreds expected) showed up at the 1993 and 1994 celebrations of Earth Day in Moscow. The current public attitude can be defined as environmental mobilization fatigue.

The dynamics of public support for environmentalism over the last decade were to a major extent a variable of societal environmental perceptions and economic interests. Environmental perceptions of '*Homo sovieticus*' depend upon several factors (most of them unique to Soviet society) and deserve a special study.[39] Our ability to address this issue is limited by the incompleteness and the non-systematic character of the data: media campaigns, limited public surveys, letters of citizens to authorities and to the periodicals. First of all, images of the environment in such a complex society as Russia (or the FSU) could not be something uniform. Historically, the environmental perceptions of the scientific community, political elite and public differed, though these differences had not always been reflected at the level of policy-making.

The diversity of approaches and comprehensive policy of the early stage of Russian/Soviet environmentalism was replaced in the 1930s by the necessity of the 'great transformation of nature' in the interests of rapid economic growth. Nature was generally perceived as a limitless spatial resource without any intrinsic value. Only a few individuals chose to challenge this approach and their fate was not enviable. This underlying principle of 'nature for the benefit of socialism' was to some extent questioned during the 'thaw'. Since the 1960s, discussions in the mass media and professional publications have exhibited a great diversity of ideas and informed debate on environmental issues (Ziegler, 1987).

The public was not silent either. During the discussion of the 1977 draft constitution, the editors of two leading Soviet newspapers – *Pravda* and *Izvestiia* – received numerous letters expressing support for environmental efforts. Similarly, thousands of letters commenting on environmental protection were sent to Moscow prior to the twenty-fourth Party Congress. After Chernobyl, ecological issues became the subject of the most intensive polemics in the mass media for several months. Environmental newspapers, magazines, newsletters and e-mail conferences mushroomed. Several anthologies of prominent writers and politicians were published, most of them unequivocally linking the state of the environment with the issue of national dignity and even survival (for instance, *Alternativy niet*, Moscow, 1989). The destruction of nature was epitomized as a symbol of societal decay and the impending doom of the system. Following the media, public indignation with the system (or sometimes its changes imposed from above) was channelled through environmental causes.

A 1990 poll of Muscovites revealed that environmental pollution was perceived as the number one concern, even more urgent than social issues such as growing crime, food shortages and ethnic conflicts (*Moscow News*, 1990, No. 22). The 1990 Goskomstat official survey confirmed that practically every second urban dweller in the FSU defined environmental conditions in the neighbourhood as 'unsatisfactory' (*Vestnik Statistiki*, 1991, No. 4). Annual letters and collective petitions to newspapers and authorities ran into millions. All these phenomena testified to the emergence of pro-environmental values in Soviet society. Regretably, environmentalism became used as a negotiating card in political manoeuvres. In the 1993 elections, the market-oriented parties practically excluded environmental and resource issues from their programmes, while opposition forces, including the Liberal Democratic, Communist and Agrarian parties, have paid considerable attention to them. Environmental concerns have been largely moved form the 'democratic' to the 'opposition' media. The very pattern of transition to the market system turned out to be anti-environmental in its essence (Mirovitskaya and Soroos, 1995). This effectively fragmented the development of pro-environmental consciousness in post-Soviet society. The economic recession made many people (including the relatively affluent and educated middle class, which has always been the backbone of the movement) preoccupied literally with where their food and shelter were to come from. Though national polls indicate that 50 per cent of Russians believe that the environment has grown substantially worse (Doktorov *et al.*, 1992), this is only a small fraction of what once seemed to be a strong tidal wave. Due to rocketing costs, environmental newspapers have closed their headquarters. Mass environmental mobilizations have been unheard of since 1991. In 1992, the Ministry of Environment received only 16,000 letters, a quarter of which came from Moscow and St Petersburg; the others were mainly from the Urals, Kuzbass and Tataria (Gosudarstvenyi Doklad, 1993).[40]

By 1991, the all-Russian random opinion poll revealed that the environment has dropped to fifth place among citizens' concerns (after growing prices, food shortages, mounting crime and weakness of state authority) (*Moscow News*, 1991, No. 38).[41] Moreover, when asked to name the dominant feelings characterizing society, 48 per cent of respondents mentioned 'tiredness and indifference', 25 per cent 'cruelty and aggression' and 19 per cent 'confusion and despair'.

Such feelings hardly go along with environmental consciousness. Among those who still have the strongest concerns are the so-called 'residents' – those who are specifically dependent on the quality of their immediate environment such as elderly people and mothers with young children. The list of anti-environmental opposition, however, is longer. The decrease in general public support coincided with the open rise of tension between the greens and their various adversaries. Despite their proclaimed adherence to universal human values in general and environmental causes in particular, the governments of the transformed former Soviet republics are still the major anti-environmental force.

In Russia, changing the national flag from red to the tricolour did not change the essence and value orientation of environmental policy, which remained anthropocentric and growth-oriented. While in power, former 'green-plus-market' democrats decided that under the menace of economic collapse and political chaos the environment could wait. Environmental programmes were not only under-financed during these years, but in 1992 no money at all was allocated for environmental purposes by the government, and a national programme of nuclear energy development was adopted without a proper environmental assessment. Environmental opposition to the government now ranges from anarchist rejection of any centralized government at all (society should be fully self-governed by the local labour communities) to the ideological and practical critique from both right and left wings of the movement.

Government reluctance to embark upon meaningful environmental reform has been reinforced by the influence exerted by the new *nomenklatura* – the top echelons of the groups exercising economic interests. Market reforms in Russia were pursued in such a way that, even though the model of societal co-ordination has been changed (or at least change has been attempted), the basic structure of resource management remained virtually the same (Mirovitskaya and Soroos, 1995). As the result of 'privatization', the new economic *nomenklatura* became the sole owners of major resource-using and industrial enterprises in many cases. Thus, former monopolies of resource-use agencies in Russia have been replaced by monopolies of the business groups. These business groups have become the most powerful lobby in the government and a further anti-environmental force.

The most influential and environmentally destructive of these bodies, which represent the military and energy complexes, have been able to claim official exemption from environmental regulations (Mirovitskaya and Soroos, 1995). Thus economic networks have an interest in the rapacious use of resources and in the evasion of pollution abatement standards in order to deliver the maximum profits to the top echelons. The network of elites with a vested interest in the continued exploitation of the environment is far-reaching.

Besides elites within the various ministries, members of numerous committees and the 'areopagus' of in-house scientists form networks which extend to include all those who enjoy material and social benefits from environmentally risky enterprises. These networks extend far into the so-called 'state discipline' (military personnel and defence workers), to include residents of centrally planned towns with limited and environmentally degrading employment possibilities. The anti-environmental front also includes workers fearful of losing their jobs. In the late 1980s, the improvement of working and residential environments was one of the demands of the re-emerging independent labour movement. Such demands were quickly dropped when new legislation made industrial enterprises financially responsible for environmental performance and imposed fees and fines for failure to comply. The imposition of environmental fines and taxes compounded the poor economic performance in many industries and both were used as reasons for cutting wages and social benefits for workers.

Several large labour strikes of the 1990s were organized, *inter alia*, to lift pollution fines from enterprises (Peterson, 1993). Studies indicate that workers in industries with higher levels of environmental risk are quite aware of the risks. However, they discount personal and familial health impacts to hold jobs that are either their only source of subsistence or offer favourable wages and other benefits. Current labour–environmentalism relations can be summarized by reference to the once popular American car slogan: 'If you are hungry and out of work, go eat an environmentalist'.

Most of the new businesses are also among anti-environmentalist forces. In the atmosphere of economic chaos and flourishing corruption, the so-called 'new Russians' not only lack any incentive to follow environmental regulations, but are inclined to exploit loopholes to gain profits.[42] Maybe the most outrageous examples are the private businesses which through their connections with corrupt authorities are literally plundering natural resources,[43] often in conjunction with western corporations.

The list above, though incomplete, shows the main reasons why public support for environmentalism has declined so rapidly in the 1990s. In a society where traditional patterns of growth-oriented industrial development became reinforced by the newly introduced elements of a primitive, bureaucratized form of monopolistic capitalism, the immediate interests of most socio-economic groups and individuals are inevitably reproduced as anti-environmental. The prospects of smooth progress for environmentalism in such an alien socio-economic climate are unfavourable.

Yet environmental issues do not disappear from the political agenda. Throughout an extremely difficult period, environmentalism has not only survived but has, if anything, diversified its activities. From being confined to a few central and local organizations the movement has experienced a period of professionalization and increasing links to state and local authorities. The transition has marked a shift from a position of negative criticism to a proactive phase often based in practical initiatives. Despite the absence of mass mobilizations, environmentalism continues to evolve. This, combined with the introduction of environmental issues to the platforms of opposition parties, provides some hopes that social controls can still be put in place to stop the environmental degradation of the country.

NOTES

1. The Russian/Soviet system of nature preservation is somewhat different from that of other countries and includes several types of protected areas. *Zapovedniks* are nature reserves aimed at the protection of what are believed to be pristine, integral ecosystems, with no recreation or resource extraction allowed and human activity being minimized to long-term ecological studies. *Zakazniks* are less stringently protected reserves, usually established for periods of five to ten years for the propagation of particular species of protected wildlife (and not the protection of the entire natural complex) or preservation of specific kind of landscape. *Pamiatnik*, the smallest of the protected territories, usually include unique botanical or geological curiosities. There are also other types of protected nature areas such as People's Parks, Cultural Monuments, Forest Reserves and National Parks.

2. The first group specifically defined as a nature conservation organization was the Khortitsa Association for the Protection of Nature, created in 1910. Examples of other types of pro-environmental associations are the Amur Area Research Society, founded in 1884, and the semi-governmental Permanent Conservation Commission of the Russian Geographical Society.

3. Film director Stanislav Govorukhin, and writers Vladimir Soloukhin and Valentin Rasputin are among the most talented and influential proponents of this world view.

4. For instance, the Moscow Society of Naturalists and the Geographical Association.

5. The numeric growth of engineers over the period from 1950 to 1972 was the most dramatic, from 400,200 to 2,820,000 (Weiner, 1988b). The interest of the rapidly growing urban-educated stratum in environmental issues was reflected by high circulation of specialized academic magazines and public monthly periodicals such as *Priroda, Nauka i Zhizn'*, *Khimia i Zhizn'* and *Chelovek i Priroda*.

6. Such publications as 'Nauka i global'nye problemy sovremennosti' (round table discussion) in *Voprosy Filosofii*, 1974, 9–11; *Global'nye Problemy Sovremennosti* (Nauka, Moscow, 1973); *Ekologicheskaya Problema v Sovremennom Mire* (Nauka, Moscow, 1981); Shakhnazarov, G., *Griadushchyi Miroporiadok* (Politizdat, Moscow, 1981); Kravchenko, M., *Ekologicheskaya Problema v Sovremennikh Teoriiakh Obshestvennogo Razvitiia* (Nauka, Moscow, 1982) presented human–nature interaction as a global problem.

7. The Chairman of the VOOP was no longer a prominent scholar elected by members, as the position had been in the first years of VOOP's existence, but a spokesman for industry 'strongly recommended' by the Party authorities. For more than a decade, a VOOP branch in the Russian Federation was directed by N. Ovsyannikov, first deputy minister of land reclamation (*Ekonomicheskaya Gazeta*, 4 January 1967). The Ministry of Land Reclamation is fairly cited as the most powerful anti-environmental lobby in the country.

8. See Pryde (1972); Feshbach and Friendly (1992); Ziegler (1987).

9. In the second half of the 1980s, the Soviet leadership came out with a long-term and pragmatic programme of international environmental co-operation which included the concept of international environmental security; proposals for international conservation and protection regimes for unique natural regions, such as Antarctica; suggestions for international mechanisms to facilitate the exchange of environment-saving technologies and networks for environmental monitoring; proposals for national reporting on nature conservation activities and environmental accidents, as well as for mutual assistance in emergencies.

10. In 1989, two official documents were released which contained a wealth of declassified environmental data: *Sostoyanie Prirodnoy Sredy v SSSR v 1988 godu: Gosudarstvennyi*

Doklad (USSR Committee for the Protection of Nature, Moscow, 1989) and *Okhrana Okruzhayushchei Sredy i Racional' noe Ispol' zovani Prirodnykh Resursov v SSSR. Statisticheskii Sbornik* (Goskomstat, Moscow, 1989). Though mass media started to tackle environmental issues long before that, most of the information until then was limited and unreliable.

11. At the beginning of the 1990s, the domestic production of medicines fell to 30 per cent of demand. Under the pressure of the greens, the Armenian government closed some basic industrial units: the Alaverdskyi copper plant, a chemical complex in Kirovakan, the caoutchouk plant 'Nairit' (the largest in the country) and a nuclear power station. The closing of the latter resulted in a deep energy crisis causing three-quarters of the republic's enterprises to cease production (*Pravda* 20 October 1994).

12. Publication of the two counter-attacking opinions in the most popular Moscow newspaper (*Moscow News* 1988, No. 2) and the appearance of the memoirs of Valery Legasov (*Pravda* 20 May 1988) finally triggered intensive speculation in Soviet mass media.

13. The 1957 release of large amounts of radioactive wastes at Chelyabinsk-65 has never been acknowledged by Soviet officials, though 10,200 people were relocated from the affected territory (Solyanik, 1994b). This accident, as well as the 1959 nuclear tests at Totsk, when 44,000 soldiers became victims of a military experiment (*Spasenie* 1994, No. 22), were a sort of 'secret of Polishinel'. Local inhabitants knew about accidents and suffered from their consequences but were persistently told by officials that they never happened.

14. For an expanded description of social activism in the regions of nuclear facilities see Solyanik (1994b).

15. Some data about the origin and goals of the Lithuanian green movement are presented by Vebra (1993) and Yanitsky (1993). Information on the emergence of the Moldavian green movement can be found in Socor (1989). For analysis of green nationalism in the former Soviet Union see Ziegler (1991) and Peterson (1993).

16. The worldwide phenomena first defined by Michael Hechtor. With internal colonialism the national government is the metropole and dominates peripheral regions or groups within its borders for exploitative purposes. More often this exploitation is to fuel the core's industrial growth with the burdensome costs assumed by the peripheral population whose resources and culture are degraded.

17. For instance, in August 1989, a living chain with slogans against 'Soviet occupying forces' and 'Moscow environmental colonialism' extended 370 miles from Tallin to Vilnius.

18. For detailed description and analysis of the Ukrainian environmentalism see Marples (1991) and Dawson (1993).

19. In Russia, a number of heavily industrialized regions such as the southern Urals, western Siberia, central Russia and the Kola Peninsula bear the load of so-called national 'spot' pollution. By contrast, approximately 60 per cent of the land area of the country (the highest share in the world) is hardly affected by human impact (Danilov-Danilian, 1993).

20. Another example of the early politicization of Russian environmentalism is the 1988 split of the Baikal movement, initially set up as an environmental club, into conservation (Society to Defend Baikal) and political (Baikal Defence Movement) groups. The final goal of the latter is non-industrial Baikal, i.e. the transformation of the area into a single world-ranking national park (Yanitsky, 1993).

21. Bloc of Russian Patriotic movements, which united twelve cultural, religious and political groups, was one of the most influential in the 1989 convocation of the USSR

Congress of People's Deputies. 'Democratic Russia' was a radical caucus in the former Soviet and Russian parliaments with Boris Yeltsin as *de facto* leader.

22. There has been much bitter criticism of the SEU's leadership by other environmental groups for its monopolization of access to national and foreign funding sources, holding back information received from government contacts and practical phasing-out of other groups. With all respect for the substantial work accomplished by SEU affiliates in the last few years, I would argue that criticism of its leadership is not groundless.

23. In view of the state of economic emergency, enterprises shut down for environmental reasons in 1989 were re-opened in late 1990 by presidential decree (*Pravda* 28 September 1990).

24. In Turkmenistan, which led the *zapovedniks* movement in the 1970 and 1980s, much land has been turned over to state farms and private interests. Recently, Turkmenistan announced an ambitious new programme of hunting tourism in which virtually everything in *zapovedniks* literally becomes 'fair game', including the extremely endangered Near Eastern leopard and other rare species. See 'Protected lands', *Ecostan News* 1994, 2(5).

25. President Karimov of Uzbekistan and President Nazarbaev of Kazakhstan publicize themselves as 'Green Presidents' and special patrons of the Aral. Strident in urging the world community to recognize the ills imposed on central Asia by the Soviet government and to render financial help for its cure, they, however, pave the same roads of development as before the disintegration. Moreover, both presidents set up special funds (Ecosan in Uzbekistan and International Fund for the Salvation of the Aral Sea in Kazakhstan) to administer foreign donations independently, and separately from their respective environmental ministries. According to environmental activists from central Asia, these funds are widely observed to serve as political machines for acquiring foreign donations, whilst actually providing petty cash funds for the government (Tzaruk, 1993).

26. It should be noted that several members of the SEU put forward a declaration condemning the military adventure of Russian authorities in Chechnya and asked Russian people to raise their voices in protest against it. See 'The Declaration of the Socio-Ecological Union on the Military Actions in Chechen Republic', transmitted electronically by env.cis, 6 January 1995.

27. For instance, the Moscow-based organization Women for Environmental Protection or Irkutsk's Society to Defend Baikal might be classified as micro-organizations, the Moscow Green Party or the Tomsk Ecological Initiative are regarded as small, the Green Movement of Russia and Ecology of the North Association are examples of large organizations, while VOOP or the Ukrainian Zelenyi Svit should be called mass groups. Despite small membership, most micro-organizations have a good record of concrete and successful projects.

28. Overwhelming bureaucratization and co-option of VOOP for the last two decades is one of the examples. The practical transformation of the Nevada-Semipalatinsk movement into a political party for Olszhas Suleimenov, with a corresponding financial and organizational basis and political goals which extend far beyond environmentalism, is another.

29. It does not mean, of course, that new environmentalists think and act exactly the same way as their predecessors of several decades ago. Besides, the agendas of most groups are quite eclectic and statute declarations and speeches of leaders do not often reflect exactly the character of groups' activities. Yet the main perceptions and reasonings of the early Russian environmentalists are surprisingly reflected in the general approaches to human–nature interaction of the contemporary greens.

30. The name of Oleg Khabarov, one of the most controversial (and thus typical for the movement in general) figures, has not been mentioned previously. An engineer by training, he is the head of the Aero-Cosmic Consortium 'Interozone', president of the public organization Ecological International of the Green Cross and the Green Crescent, chairman of the Russian Environmental Exchange and the Hetman of the Moscow Cossack Hundred. He was going to join the presidential campaign of 1996 with a programme based on the notion 'Russia as an Ecological Power' (*Spasenie* 1994, Nos 32, 34, etc.; pers. comm., 23 July 1994). Yury Shcherbak, Ukrainian doctor and writer, became a prominent politician and government leader through his struggle to reveal the consequences of the Chernobyl accident.

31. For instance, in June 1992, the Association of Anarchist Movements organized a protest camp near the St Petersburg nuclear power station. The same year, together with 'Rainbow Keepers' and the League of Green Parties, they launched a campaign against the Russian–Swedish joint venture Viking-Raps. Picketing, call-in strikes, organizing petitions and intrusions to the administrative offices resulted in the cancellation of the project. In 1993–4, the same coalition organized protest camps around Cherepovets plant (*Spasenie* 1994, No. 33).

32. The 'foreign card' phenomena, noted with bitter irony by Shvarts and Prozorova (1993), is certainly one powerful factor in the creation of several green organizations, whose leaders prefer to protect nature abroad by giving tearful interviews and angry presentations at international conferences on the 'genocide' crimes of the Soviet regime but apply much less effort to concrete activities on the national scene.

33. For instance, one environmental group in Smolensk is involved solely in inventorizing and recycling industrial wastes, tasks left undone by the appropriate authorities.

34. A concrete example of such a liaison is the quasi-environmental group Navin from Kazakhstan, which made substantial efforts to declare the Kapustin Yar site a national area of environmental disaster. However, it was discovered that this 'non-governmental' organization was totally financed by the local administration and several large farms that were interested in financial compensation following such a classification of the area. See 'The nuclear lands of central Asia, courtesy of Lenin and Mao: a continuing tragedy', *Ecostan News* 1993, No. 2.

35. The first and until recently the only public interest environmental organization in Russia was Ecojuris-WLED, which provides a broad spectrum of legal services in the sphere of environmental protection, ecological safety and resource use. It has only eight lawyers (all of them women). Ecojuris has been engaged in several litigations, representing citizens of Butovo against the Moscow authorities, Moscow citizens against the Moscow Regional Administration, a former soldier injured in a 1954 nuclear test against the Ministry of Defence, etc. However, until now only one case has been won. The President of Ecojuris, Vera Mishenko, explains this by reference to the numerous loopholes in environmental legislation, lack of enforcement mechanisms and concentration of real power in the hands of economic actors (pers. comm., 25 February 1995, Chicago, USA).

36. For instance, the Green Party in 1992 split into a Russian Green Party with an anarcho-syndicalist programme and the League of Green Parties, which follows ideas of eco-socialism.

37. Russian Ecological Power from O. Khabarov's electoral campaign, based on the principles of state patriotism and introduction of 'mental-environmental dictatorship' (*Spasenie* 1994, No. 34), and eco-villages of the Anarchist Movement are certainly elements of different social orders.

38. It is worth noting that the low level of political culture in society, for many decades dominated by one-party ideology, has its reflections in the green milieu also. It is common to find environmental newspapers accusing other organizations of non-professionalism, shameful connections with the Communist Party, or the KGB, or the industrial sector, and of holding ideologically incorrect positions.

39. Attempts to define and analyse such perceptions have been made by Ziegler (1987) and Yanitsky (1994).

40. Collective petitions continued to come from the inhabitants of Krasnoyarsk Krai and Chelyabinsk area (in relation to nuclear contamination) and from the residents of the Volga Basin, who protested against the drowning of agricultural land through another project of the ill-famed Ministry of Land Reclamation. The total number of petitions was, however, considerably lower than a few years before.

41. Broadly speaking, public concern has been shifted to the highest point in the hierarchy of national goals depicted by O'Riordan (1981), which include economic growth, employment and 'national security'. At times when these are threatened, they displace concerns further down the hierarchy – including environmental quality and ecological harmony.

42. Though there are tens of thousands of private so-called 'environmental businesses', in practice most of them pursue venal activities that assist industrial enterprises to elude regulations (see Moszhin *et al.*, 1993).

43. The fact that the natural resources of Russia are now, in effect, being stolen can no longer be doubted. Hundreds of thousands of tons of non-ferrous and rare metals, large quantities of oil, diamonds and nuclear materials have been flowing to the West since 1991. Moreover, even the environmental authorities in some of the former Soviet republics do not abstain from making profit from the resources they are supposed to guard. In central Asia, highly placed bureaucrats make business by selling rare species of wildlife abroad, and by selling wealthy foreigners licences to hunt endangered species.

REFERENCES

Anon. (1991) *Spravochnik Ekologicheskich Obshestvennych Ob'edinenyi na Territorii SSSR 1991* [Inventory of the Environmental Public Organizations in the Territory of the USSR]. VNIIC 'Ecologia,' Moscow.

Atakhanova, K. (1994) The monster of Semipalatinsk. *Surviving Together* 37, 32–35.

Baitulin, I. (1994) Tortoise and butterfly hunts. *Ecostan News* 2(3).

Danilov-Danilian, V., ed. (1993) *Problemy Ekologii Rossii* [Problems of Ecology in Russia]. Moscow.

Dawson, J. (1993) Intellectuals and anti-nuclear protest in the USSR. In *Beyond Sovietology: Essays in Politics and History* (ed. S. Solomon). M.E. Sharpe, Armonk, NY. 94–124.

DeBardeleben, J. (1992) Ecology and technology in the USSR. In *Technology, Culture, and Development: The Experience of the Soviet Model* (ed. J. Scanlan). M.E. Sharpe, Armonk, NY.

Doktorov, B. *et al.* (1992) Uroven' osoznaniia ekologicheskikh problem: profil' obshchestvennogo mneniia [The level of apprehension of the environmental problems: profile of public opinion]. *Sociologicheskie Issledovaniia* 4, 51–57.

Feshbach, M. and Friendly, A. (1992) *Ecocide in the USSR*. Basic Books, New York.

Gosudarstvenyi Doklad (1993) *Sostoyanie Prirodnoy Sredy i Resursov v 1992 godu* [State Report on the State of the Environment in the USSR in 1992]. USSR State Committee for the Protection of Nature, Moscow.

Jancar, B. (1987) *Environmental Management in the Soviet Union and Yugoslavia: Structure and Regulation in Federal Communist States.* Duke University Press, Durham, NC.

Jancar-Webster, B., ed. (1993) *Environmental Action in Eastern Europe: Responses to Crisis.* M.E. Sharpe, Armonk, NY.

Kuznets, S. (1963) A comparative analysis. In *Economic Trends in the Soviet Union* (eds A. Bergson and S. Kuznets). Harvard University Press, Cambridge, MA.

Mafia, M. (1994) *The Soviet Tragedy: A History of Socialism in Russia, 1917–1991.* Macmillan, New York.

Marples, D. (1991) The greening of Ukraine: ecology and emergence of Zelenyi svit, 1986–1990. In *Perestroika from Below: Social Movements in the Soviet Union* (eds J. Sedaitis and J. Butterfield). Westview, Boulder, CO, 133–144.

Mirovitskaya, N. (1993) Women, nature and society: changing the Soviet paradigm. *Surviving Together* 11(4).

Mirovitskaya, N. and Soroos, M. (1995) Socialism and the tragedy of the commons: reflections on environmental practice in the Soviet Union and Russia. *Journal of Environment and Development* 4(1), 77–110.

Moszhin V., Belkin, V. and Storoszhenko, V. (1993) Ob ekologicheskoi politike Rossii [On the environmental policy of Russia]. *Svobodnaya Mysl* 4, 88–96.

O'Riordan, T. (1981) *Environmentalism.* Pion, London.

Papadakis, E. (1993) *Politics and the Environment: the Australian Experience.* Allen & Unwin, St Leonards.

Peterson, D.J. (1993) *Troubled Lands: The Legacy of Soviet Environmental Destruction.* Westview, Boulder, CO.

Poguntke, T. (1989) The 'new politics dimension' in European Green Parties. In *New Politics in Western Europe: The Rise and Success of Green Parties and Alternative Lists* (ed. F. Muller-Rommel). Westview, Boulder, CO.

Pryde, P.R. (1972) *Conservation in the Soviet Union.* Cambridge University Press, Cambridge.

Sedletskaya, E. (1994) Pers. comm., 21 June, Suzdal.

Serebrovskaya, K. (1994) Ecopolis-Kosino. Pers. comm., 16 February, Moscow.

Shubin, A. (1992) Ekologicheskoe dviszhenie v SSSR i vyshedshikh iz nego stranakh [Environmental movement in the USSR and the states which quit it]. In *Ekologicheskie Organizacii na Territorii byvshego SSSR* [Environmental Organizations in the Territory of the Former USSR]. Moscow.

Shvarts, E. and Prozorova, I. (1993) Soviet Greens: who are they? The view from inside. In *Environmental Action in Eastern Europe: Responses to Crisis* (ed. B. Jancar-Webster). M.E. Sharpe, Armonk, NY.

Social'no-ekologicheskii Soyuz (1994) Social'no-ekologicheskii Soyuz: Istoria i Real'nost' [Socio-Ecological Union: History and Reality]. SEU, Moscow.

Socor, V. (1989) The Moldavian Greens: an independent ecological association. *Report on the USSR*, 17 March, 1–11.

Solyanik, S. (1994a) The ecology movement in Kazakhstan: problems and perspectives. *Ecostan News* 2(12).

Solyanik, S. (1994b) Spotlight on nuclear sites. *Surviving Together* 37, 25–36.

Tikhomirov, V.V. (1982) *Studentchestvo i Okhrara Prirody* [Students and Nature Conservation]. MGU, Moscow.

Tzaruk, O. (1993) Dam the cascades, full speed ahead: Uzbekistan's hydroelectric plans. *Ecostan News* 1(1).

Vebra, E. (1993) Environmental protection in Baltic States. In *Environmental Action in Eastern Europe: Responses to Crisis* (ed. B. Jancar-Webster). M.E. Sharpe, Armonk, NY.

Vinogradov, V.N. (1982) Vserossiiskoye Obshchestvo Okhrany Prirody otmechaet svoyu 60 godovshchinu [The All-Russia Nature Conservation Society marks its 60th anniversary]. In *Environmental Management in the USSR*. Nauka, Moscow.

Weiner D. (1988a) *Models of Nature: Conservation, Ecology, and Cultural Revolution in Soviet Russia*. Indiana University Press, Bloomington, IN.

Weiner D. (1988b) The changing face of Soviet conservation. In *The Ends of the Earth* (ed. D.E. Worster). Cambridge University Press, Cambridge, 252–273.

Yablokov, A. (1993) An open letter to the Minister of the Environment V. Danilov-Danilian, 13 May. Distributed by SEU through mailing lists and e-mail.

Yanitsky, O. (1991) Environmental movements: some conceptual issues in east–west comparisons. *International Journal of Urban and Regional Research* 15, 524–541.

Yanitsky, O. (1993) *Russian Environmentalism: Leading Figures, Facts, Opinions*. Mezhdunarodnyie Otnoshenija Publishing House, Moscow.

Yanitsky, O. (1994) Industrialism i environmentalism: Rossiia narubeszhe kul'tur [Industrialism and environmentalism: Russia at the edge of cultures]. *SOCIS* 1994(3), 3–14.

Ziegler, C. (1987) *Environmental Policy in the USSR*. University of Massachusetts Press, Amherst, MA.

Ziegler, C. (1991) Environmental politics and policy under *perestroika*. In *Perestroika from Below: Social Movements in the Soviet Union* (eds J. Sedaitis and J. Butterfield). Westview, Boulder, CO, 113–132.

CHAPTER 3

ENVIRONMENT-FRIENDLY DEINDUSTRIALIZATION: IMPACTS OF UNIFICATION ON EAST GERMANY

Sonja Boehmer-Christiansen

CONTEXT AND BACKGROUND

Before the implications of the case study presented here can be fully appreciated it is necessary to outline a range of background themes and issues. Without this, the wider social and theoretical questions raised here and throughout this volume cannot be appreciated. Of prime importance are the geographical, regulatory and environmental features of East Germany within the context of an expanding German and European framework.

The German Democratic Republic (GDR) ceased to exist formally in 1990; its effective economic collapse occurred long before this, being determined by a combination of West German policies and ambitions and events in the former Soviet Union during the late 1980s. Despite these ambitions, unification made people in the 'two' Germanies more aware of their separateness and differences than ever before. In the East, many experienced unification as a self-interested take-over by West German enterprises in a bargaining process within which they had no representation. The analysis of changes within the energy sector offers a particularly direct appreciation of the difficulties associated with unification.

ENVIRONMENTAL PERCEPTIONS AND REALITIES

Both parts of Germany are heavily industrialized with about one-third of the total area covered by commercially exploited forests, many privately owned and used for wood production and leisure. Coal was the foundation of German industrialization and remains an important and valued fuel with protected status. Declining reserves of hard coal, particularly in the East, has led to intensified exploitation of brown coal deposits in both parts of Germany, with major impacts on landscape, emission problems, the location of electricity generation and employment prospects.

Prior to 1990 East Germany appeared to be an environmental contradiction. Those relying on West German media stories and government documents perceived East Germany as an ecological disaster zone where air, water and soil were so terribly polluted that human health was impaired and communism stood condemned.

To others, less interested in proving the superiority of the 'market economy' and possessing more historical knowledge, large parts of the GDR seemed pristine compared to the environmental disasters of the West. Peace and quiet still prevailed in forests and along lakes and beaches, roads were empty and wildlife prospered in many areas where access was restricted to the genuine hiker. 'Disaster areas' were found less in rural areas than in crumbling inner cities and industrial regions, from which rising outputs were demanded with declining investment.

The energy supply system in the GDR was 'rationally' organized and a planner's dream. Monopolistic and centrally directed, it linked three types of fuel-based energy combines (brown coal, nuclear and gas) to fifteen district energy combines, which generated electricity and supplied it to customers at very low prices. The blackness and grime of East German urban centres and monuments still bear witness to decades of brown coal use in homes and factories. Significant deposits of uranium ore were found only in the East, where the ore was mined, washed and prepared for use in the former USSR.

Germany as a whole suffers from episodic poor air quality and transboundary air pollution and therefore experiences considerable acid deposition. In the East, air quality improved little if at all during the 1980s, while West Germany cleaned up its 'acid rain' thoroughly, reducing total output from stationary sources from about 5 million tonnes to below 1 million.[1] For sulphur dioxide pollution one is therefore comparing the very best in the world with a typical early twentieth-century developed economy or an industrializing country. High sulphur and carbon dioxide emissions in East Germany do, however, have to be balanced against comparatively low emission levels for nitrogen oxides, arising from dependence on lower-temperature combustion processes and two-stroke engines.[2]

German society as a whole values mobility highly, but this had been severely curtailed in the East, largely for financial reasons. Both German societies are culturally impregnated with the idea that nature is 'a good thing' and that natural products are somehow healthier than synthetic ones. Combining this with other 'loves', especially those of technology and industry as expressed in German engineering prowess, produced an emphasis on technical progress which did not constitute a threat to 'the environment'. Instead, the art and science of engineering was applied to imitating nature more closely, seeking to co-operate with biological processes rather than dominate them. These cultural biases are important elements of the overall policy paradigm.

Ecological restructuring, *ökologischer Umbau*, or ecological modernization, became prominent ideas deployed by all political parties during the late 1980s as they competed in their claims to be able to implement this vision.[3] The German concept could be translated as achieving sustainability (a word the Germans had much difficulty in translating) through technological progress.[4] The close tie, in official German thinking, between technology and environmental protection is not understood in Britain but explains Germany's comparative neglect of environmental science in policy formation.

East Germans could not but compare their environmental problems with those of West Germany, and were encouraged to do so by the virtuous West. This encouraged the political 'destabilization' process preceding unification and led to a highly negative evaluation of East German assets. The picture of environmental disaster 'over there' was promoted nationally and internationally by environmentalists. Water and air pollution were (and remain) indeed more serious in the East than in West, due to reliance on poorly maintained and outdated technology, resulting from under-investment and resource misallocation rather than socialism *per se*. Comparable industrial pollution had been commonplace only a few decades earlier in the indus-trial areas of the Ruhr and in Great Britain.

Examples of the exaggeration of environmental catastrophes include the asser-tion that a slightly lower life expectancy was caused by pollution (rather than diet, available health care, etc.) and the claim that the entire East German housing stock would need rebuilding because of asbestos problems. Other examples more closely related to energy are mentioned below, but the dominant West German perspect-ive is well summarized in the claims of a former BMWi (Federal Ministry for Economic Affairs) minister that 'the energy industries of the GDR are examples of what centralism and strict planning do to an energy supply system which has no concern for environmental protection and secure competitive supply'. The positive environmental achievements of the former GDR, such as its household waste recyc-ling system and small, slow cars, became completely overshadowed by the domin-ance of negative images, such as those associated with deforestation.

The dominance of production to meet direct needs rather than wider consumer wants resulted in little packaging; one bought only what was available and recycled almost everything. Love of nature and *Heimat* (homeland) were taught at school as a socialist virtue. To many 'greens' the GDR of the late 1980s was attractive, repres-enting a prime opportunity for transformation into a region where environment-friendly decentralization and technological modernization could become reality. The East German reply, given hastily and with imperfect knowledge, was to decline – 'we do not want to be your guinea pig'.[5]

In fact, in response to the worldwide interest in matters environmental, East Germany had developed its own approach to environmental regulation. Had it been able to implement only part of it in the industrial sphere, the GDR might not have deserved the bad press it received.

APPROACHES TO REGULATION IN EAST AND WEST

Environmental regulation, apart from claiming to protect environmental 'goods', is also a potent tool of commercial and technological competition. Selectively, it can be expected to attract more attention in capitalist than socialist economies. For example, regulations to achieve reductions in acid or greenhouse gas emissions can be aimed at encouraging fuel substitution between fossil fuels (in order of decreas-ing costs regulation will weaken demand for coal, oil and gas), or at fuel cleaning (removing sulphur from coal or diesel). Environmental regulations produce im-provements in safety, for example to prevent methane leaks, nuclear explosions or radioactive discharges, or the containment of long-lasting pollutants (radionuclides in nuclear waste storage). Tough regulatory regimes lead to significant investments, significantly alter the economics of fuel use and hence influence fuel competition and technology choice. By comparison, taxes have quite different, less predictable effects on energy use and investment strategies.

Reducing acid and greenhouse gas emission strategies have been a major boon to natural gas and its owners, the oil companies, as well as to existing nuclear power facilities. Both can produce 'cleaner' energy, as long as 'clean' remains defined purely in terms of atmospheric emissions. Clean energy policies have thus contributed towards numerous 'global environmental' goals perceived as solutions to global problems. The vendors of gas could promote their wares, as could the fast-breeder reactor and renewable energy lobbies. However, national environmental problems created by global solutions could be ignored within global intergovernmental bargaining. Secondary impacts, ranging from inventing new technologies, the closure of mines, the transport of vast quantities of limestone and disposal options for sludge produced by acid emission cleaning, all remain with local communities. In order to save the planet, we may be reducing the quality of local environments; by improving our competitiveness in the global market place we may be destroying jobs.

In West Germany, environmental regulation increases the power of the state over industry, and the economy may be guided in a 'social' direction as defined by the political process. If this power is used wisely it ensures investments vital to future prosperity are not displaced by short-term profit-taking. In the East, a more British perception prevailed; regulation was seen as something to be avoided as it would increase the costs of production.

In West Germany, environmental awareness promoted the social acceptability of certain technical options, acting as a rallying point, especially at the local planning level, against the forces of 'rampant' capitalism or corrupt government. 'The environment', or rather *Umweltschutz* (environmental protection) played a major role in both the promotion of development and in resisting its excesses, a process requiring active politics rather than technocratic decisions. Environmental regulations are thus made in a relatively open, pluralist manner involving government ministries, civil servants, the media and NGOs which have their power bases at regional levels. A very complex decision-making system operates which trades off a host of interrelated objectives and resolves conflicts with reference to a highly developed legal framework within a political context which allows considerable access for lobbies. Policy in general is best perceived as the outcome of a policy-formation process based on informed bargaining. Bargaining takes place at several interacting levels, involving varying degrees of competition for market shares and sites, official research and development (R&D) funding, co-operative efforts to maintain public good will and protect preferred relationships with public authorities. The regulatory powers in the hands of three layers of public administration (communal, regional and federal) have been much amended by environmental regulations since the early 1970s and are sufficient to define and implement overriding public goals. Economics tends to serve politics and hence the 'social will', rather than vice versa. It is an expensive system and not suited to poor countries, unless one could show that a cheap decision-making system leads to overall weakness and eventual collapse. The GDR system appears to have been very cheap indeed.

In the East, a more 'British' model prevailed. Regulations were made in a highly technocratic manner, by experts subject to a perpetual political veto by a small group of ageing Party leaders, the 'Council of the Gods'.[6] The planners were devoted to science and rationality. Great plans were formulated and debated behind closed doors, but rarely adopted for fear of increasing public spending. Increases in consumer prices were felt to be politically unsustainable under socialism. Failure followed but was not reported.[7] Western talk of a planned economy is a misrepresentation; whilst imaginary targets were set at the 'top', lack of systematic investment resulted in stagnation at plant level. This turned a planned economy into an unplanned short-term struggle for survival.

Environmentalism did not bypass the GDR but again resembled developments in Britain. A ministry for environmental protection and water economy was set up in 1971. The *Landeskulturgesetz* of 1970 has been described by western analysts as a good, all-embracing piece of environmental legislation based on the 1968 constitution. Article 15 of the 1974 constitution stated that:

> In the interest of the well-being of citizens, state and society care for the protection of nature. Maintaining clean air and water, as well as protecting plants and animals and the beauty of our *Heimat*, is guaranteed by the competent authorities and a task for every citizen.

An enthusiastic environmental programme concentrating on the chemical industry and air pollution was initiated in the early 1970s. It was not implemented for fear of economic impacts. As with industrial pollution control in the UK during the 1970s and 1980s, perceived economic and political necessity did not free the necessary investment. Enforcement was neglected, although heavy fines could be levied if breaches of regulations were discovered. The energy economy inherited from the Nazi regime could not invest in modernization as its products had to remain cheap. It had been unable to replace plant for over a decade and was therefore rapidly deteriorating physically. Declining investment and technological stagnation had become obvious to the observant by the mid-1980s.[8] As in the West, this neglect or implementation deficit led to a political response in which the environment proved to be particularly attractive to small parties,[9] academic economists and lawyers.[10]

The East German environment became a focus for social protest, forcing the Honecker government to attempt reconciliation by requiring the environmental inspection of industrial premises and increasing fines in 1985. This apparently served to increase state revenue but had little effect on pollution levels. The struggle for peace, felt to be ideologically inseparable from environmental protection, had probably absorbed so many resources that environmental protection measures could not be implemented. Elsewhere, the political need to buy votes may have had a similar effect on investment. None of this had been predicted by Marxist theory and left the communist leadership helpless.

Marxism–Leninism gave no guidelines on how to deal with the environment. Air and water pollution were not, as sometimes alleged in the West, a necessary by-product of socialism. They were certainly not intended by the economic planners and their masters. Rather they were unavoidable outcomes of an inflexible social policy combined with economic stagnation, that is, a fixed price policy for consumer goods combined with little real economic growth.[11] In theory, planned economic growth under socialism should be stable and continuous, satisfying no more 'than the material and cultural needs of human beings'. Part of this was a living and working environment which was burdened as little as possible by noise, dust and waste gases. Environmental protection was not, party ideologues insisted, a source of profit as it was under capitalism. The implication was that socialism could afford to be a little dirtier. Since environmental degradation and pollution should not have existed, but had nevertheless attracted criticism and protest at home and abroad, excuses were needed. The old men in Berlin adopted a familiar strategy and blamed their problems on predecessors – capitalism, fascism and, with some justification, the last war. They could not really blame another political party.

East and West did not disagree on everything. East Berlin firmly believed that the 'unfolding of economic potentials is the decisive precondition for releasing resources to limit and repair environmental problems' and that 'continuously high economic growth rates' were the condition for environmental protection.[12] Both German states agreed that 'technological progress is the best path towards a caring approach to our natural resources'.[13] Liberal and Marxist economists also shared the theoretical neglect of valuing nature or 'land'. Academic growth was therefore stimulated by the environment in both East and West. Complex formulae were developed in the East for calculating fines for breaching environmental standards but the two Germanies could not agree over the axiomatic East German assumption that effective environmental protection was predicated on state ownership of natural resources. To West Germany the example of the GDR's industrial and agricultural pollution control did little to support this claim.

ENVIRONMENTAL AND OTHER CONSEQUENCES OF ENERGY POLICIES

The environmental consequences of pollution or declining biodiversity are notoriously difficult to predict. The complexity of environmental science is such that these consequences (from forest decline and global warming to human and ecosystem health) invite large research agendas but provide 'uncertain' policy advice. The consequences of pollution control, however, are often more readily predicted if victims and beneficiaries can be consulted. Scientific uncertainty allows 'other' constituencies to participate strongly in the definition of environmental threats and hence the objectives of environmental policy.

If society is perceived as part of nature, change caused by human beings in their use of the Earth need not by definition be negative or exploitative, but requires very complex assessments. If humans are distinct from nature, and the assessment of their impact is left to the natural sciences, only change from a baseline without humans can be measured objectively. This leads to an almost automatic definition of all human impacts as 'impairment' or pollution. The perception of human action as negative and the assertion that 'authority' must prevent such harm is the basis of a fundamentalist green position. In Germany, the strong association between environmental harm and the natural sciences which exists in the Anglo-Saxon world is, however, largely absent. From the outside it may thus appear that German policy (East and West) is irrational, prioritizing broader goals defined in the political process and giving less weight to science.

Energy policies provide an excellent illustration of these complexities. Social theory about the interactions between society, environment and economy under different ideological and organizational systems may be tested. In virtually all countries, including Germany, energy policy has not been 'left to the market' but remains based on a complex societal bargain struck with reference to many 'stakes' and objectives. Environmental protection is one new ingredient in a complex recipe; it may drive as well as respond to energy policy. Social, political and security considerations have always played a major role in defining energy policy in Germany, with the private, semi-private and public energy actors accepting the duty of the state to determine the energy mix in the national interest. This duty has only recently been challenged by the spread of neo-liberal economic theory. This neo-liberal turn serves the ambitions of the European Commission and the globalization of the energy business.

The transitional phase

This phase began before formal unification was achieved and was particularly exploited by energy interests. The East German energy sector sought to redress its political weakness by simultaneously offering a ready profit stream to western utilities and using the prospect of co-operation and modernization to strengthen its position with public authorities. With the full imposition of West German law (and its implementation), unification has been achieved and its short-term consequences can be assessed.

In particular, the rhetoric that the East would be the first to experience 'ecological modernization' and 'leap-frog' over the West can be tested. This involved the imposition of a new regulatory regime based on a competing ideology on a crumbling planned economy in the context of an assumed common culture.

Unification and the promise of marketization

In June 1990 the GDR parliament passed legislation enabling the privatization and reorganization of publicly owned property. This Communal Property Act (CPA) was one of the last sovereign acts of the GDR. At the same time the troubled Treuhandanstalt (Treuhand for short), a state-owned trust organization, became the legal owner of all East German enterprises and of most agricultural land. It was put in charge of privatization, a process which proved to be slower and more frustrating than had been expected. The West German legal system formally spread to the East after 1990, enabled not only by the unification treaty of 1990 but also by privatization. The privatization of electricity resulted in a major dispute between the large western utilities and small regional generators owned by municipalities, which was only resolved in July 1993.

The implementation of West German and EC legislation in the five new federal states (*länder*), including completion of the privatization process, also began in 1990. In October the Treuhand became responsible to the Federal Finance Ministry, which expected privatization to be completed by 1994, a target which has largely been kept. By the end of 1991, as federal structures in the East began to reconstitute themselves, the approach of regional government towards energy supply began to make an impact on policy. A new, complex planning system based on broad, regional consultations between regional and local government, experts and industry was beginning to take shape.

Privatization proved difficult and painful, frustrated by problems of liability and ownership disputes. Implementation was also deeply affected by administrative reform, which involved a return to the federal system and hence five new *länder* and bureaucracies. Complex bargaining rather than the technocratic policy-making behind tightly closed doors, so typical of the GDR, now prevailed in both parts of Germany. Yet the old ways were not so readily replaced in practice, something revealed by an examination of the legal base.

The Unification Treaty of October 1990 imposed a 'duty of solidarity' on all the parties involved. Some adjustments have been negotiated with the European Union (EU), but clean air legislation now applies with only minor exceptions. The united Germany has not yet reached agreement on a new legislative framework for the energy sector; it remains torn between 'coal' and 'nuclear power', and all this implies, as the West was during the late 1970s.

A major revision of the Energy Management Act of 1935 is still in preparation, aimed at strengthening environmental regulation and easing adjustments to Europe. The expansion of gas use was to be encouraged, but also resisted. Further attempts to reform, or liberalize, German energy law by creating an 'energy consensus' (*Energiekonsens*) failed in late 1993 and again in May 1994. A major source of contention remains the subsidy of German coal, with industry opposed to the further impositions of an energy/carbon tax. In fact, the status quo is largely maintained, which seems to serve society best.

The Treuhand has not been a popular organization: it inherited large debts and became the employer of most East Germans, the majority of whom were sacked to provide efficiency gains. Faced with ecological modernization via privatization, buyers had to be found for businesses and capital raised to meet new environmental legislation. Failure in either area resulted in the closure of factories.[14] Until 1993, the Treuhand owned the majority of energy resources and energy combines to be privatized. The electricity sector proved to be the first and most controversial privatization; completed by mid-1994, it left just one-third of companies to continue operating.

Given the legal and regulatory vacuum in the East during 1990–1, competition between western utilities expanding into the new market became particularly intense, even unscrupulous. Western utilities, accustomed to operating within mature, well-defined regulatory regimes subject to public scrutiny via NGOs and newspapers, adopted a more cavalier approach. Property and markets in the East were viewed as up for grabs in an environment with few rules, many innocents and few fast learners. Western energy industries were among the very first to make deals with eastern energy combines, even before the unification treaty had been signed. This was accompanied by much talk about environmental catastrophes which the West was 'at last' discovering and would clean up. The salience and politicization of environment problems was therefore high and explicitly linked to energy politics.

The market for fuels and technology

West German and foreign interest in the East German energy sector were purely commercial. With 5787 kilowatt hours (kWh) per capita consumption of electricity in 1987, and significantly lower ownership of consumer durables and cars, East Germany was seen as a buoyant futures market for electricity and petrol. The energy industries were considered among the few profitable enterprises in the East.[15] East Germans themselves saw (and still see) themselves as suffering from a large consumption deficit, something which the private sector was only too keen to satisfy, aided temporarily by the exchange rate. As coal gas and solid fuel were still dominating the space heating sector, West German coal producers had hoped that the East would need considerable amounts of hard coal for years to come. Gas companies were equally eager to extend and modernize the gas pipeline system and encourage industrial and domestic fuel switching. Oil companies anticipated rapid growth in petrol sales arising from a sharp increase in car ownership on a road system little changed since 1945. The nuclear industry was desperate to obtain new reactor orders.

Not all these hopes were fulfilled. The new owners of electricity utilities, whether private or municipal, faced the decision of whether to continue using domestic brown coal, to import hard coal, to switch to natural gas, or to operate nuclear power stations. The outcome has been a broader fuel mix available at considerably higher prices to consumers and the loss of direct control by the state. Non-German companies became important in both the gas distribution and oil-refining sectors, with some minor participation in electricity generation.

Large, cheap, brown coal deposits were the GDR's most valuable raw material. As the foundation of the East German economy, they were initially eagerly sought by the western enterprises. Whilst some mines were sold, most were in fact abandoned with heavy job losses. The interlocking, global nature of privatization was clearly revealed when an Anglo-American consortium consisting of PowerGen (UK) and NRG Energy (USA) finalized negotiations with the Treuhand for the sale of several mines, industrial power stations and a briquette factory in December 1993. This project entails mining 20 million tonnes of lignite per annum and the loss of 6900 jobs from a total labour force of 9000.

The sole owner of brown coal reserves in West Germany, Rheinisch-Westphalische Elektrizitatswerk (RWE), expressed a keen interest in buying into the GDR's reserves provided secure markets could be guaranteed. By early 1994, however, no sale had been completed, with the sale of lower sulphur deposits in the Lausitz to West German consortia being expected later in 1994. These negotiations apparently became protracted due to industry demands that no carbon taxes or restoration liabilities be imposed.[16] Brown coal output has more than halved since unification, but remains a significant proportion of the fuel mix for electricity generation. A massive slump in electricity sales is blamed for this demise of brown coal but it also reflects the emission problems its combustion creates.

Hard coal is no longer mined in East Germany, but the East was temporarily seen as a potential market for West German coal. This has proved unrealistic, for hard coal use in the West remains heavily subsidized until 2005. The government was not willing to extend these subsidies, preferring to contribute to retrofitting emission controls at power stations using brown coal. Utilities in West Germany received 'domestic' subsidies without which they claimed they could no longer bear the costs of environmental responsibilities in the East. Without coal subsidies, coal would have to be imported. There is much pressure from the EU to end these subsidies.

Oil and gas imports have long been subject to environmental regulation in West Germany. Industry has always responded, after some grumbling, with successful technical adjustments. Given the environmental virtues and current cheapness of natural gas,[17] and its ready availability, gas use was bound to expand, as was the consumption of transport fuels. East Germany had only small gas reserves (c. 175 billion cubic metres), with a high nitrogen content, and imported relatively little gas and oil. Priority is now given to the improvement and extension of the gas grid, as well as to the development of new gas technology; both were priorities of East–West co-operation before unification.

Gas use has expanded rapidly in the new *länder* using imports from Siberia by pipeline. Natural gas rapidly established itself as the preferred option of the utilities. In Dresden, Siemens built a 480 MW gas-fired combined heat and power (CHP) plant, which came on line in 1995. This delivered both large emission reductions and joint ownership between regional and communal utilities. In Leipzig, however, close to one major coalmining area, local government opted for base load supplies from a brown-coal-fired plant, supplemented by natural gas.

A US firm (Bourneville Pacific) broke the German monopoly over electricity supply, winning a contract to build a gas-fired power station at the Polish border for the city of Frankfurt. Its electricity is claimed to be very cheap, almost half the usual price. When the federal government wanted gas to replace the nuclear power station at Stade, its owner, Preussag, supported environmentalists' objections to gas being imported into Germany from Norway.[18]

Competition for ownership of the gas grid in East Germany led to particularly bitter competition between East and West German interests. The communes have claimed that a share had been promised to them, while West German companies, especially Ruhrgas and Wintershall, the energy subsidiary of the chemicals giant

BASF, were fighting over market shares until 1992. BASF alleged that Ruhrgas was orchestrating 'environmental' protests against its transmission projects. Owner-ship struggles over the supraregional gas transmission company seemed to be over in late 1991, but were delayed by the German Cartel Office's rejection of a deal between the companies and the communes as it represented a form of cheap credit to the latter. Non-German gas companies, all controlled by the oil companies, again participated in this struggle for market shares. British Gas (which buys gas from oil companies) competed for shares in the gas grid and regional companies. In mid-1992, the oil industry expressed concern about what it saw as excessive 'state intervention'. Government was resisting the building of a gas pipeline linked to the introduction of light fuel oil. The *länder* and municipalities wanted to reserve this market for themselves.

Demand for oil is still rising in the East but stagnating in the West. The oil companies (ARAL, BP, Shell, DEA), recognized the large appetite for cars and, in co-operation with the East German monopolist MINOL AG, are still expanding the net of petrol stations. Oil refining has now been sold to a consortium of European companies. Liabilities for inherited pollution and contamination stayed with the federal government. The East German EEG (Erdöl–Erdgas–Gommern) was bought by Veba Oil, Esso and Shell. Deminex, the German oil exploration company, declared record profits in 1990 and has negotiated joint ventures to develop and explore oil and gas resources in several areas of the former USSR. East German contacts and know-how are of great value as Soviet gas pipelines were built by East Germans.

The shut-down of some East German nuclear reactors began before unification by the now defunct Office for Atomic Safety and Radiation Protection on the basis of a West German safety assessment. Through these assessments Bonn gained know-ledge of VVER-440 type reactors, which might become useful in eastern Europe and the USSR.[19] The East Germans expected replacements to be built and plants under construction to be modernized. Before October 1990 West German utilities and Siemens had already made known their wish to built at least two new nuclear reactors of the Convoy type near Soviet ones on the Baltic coast.[20] The new reactors were to be operated with the French utility EDF. While a rational case for refurbish-ing or even replacing these reactors was forcefully made, western politicians decided otherwise.

The reasons are complex, but include the refusal of the utilities to accept full liability for the clean-up and safety improvements required at the existing plants. In June 1991 the chairman of RWE announced that there would be no new nuclear power stations without the support of the Social Democratic Party (SPD). This has not been forthcoming: there is no *Energiekonsens*. The reactor complex remains in the hands of the Treuhand; decommissioning and waste disposal will have to be paid for by German taxpayers.[21] Abandoning the nuclear option in the East has not come easily. While the environment ministry was suspicious of more nuclear power and associated public liabilities, the economics ministry would have preferred retrofitting, for reasons of employment and the protection of sunk investments.

A GREEN VISION AND RESTRUCTURING THE ENERGY SECTOR

In the view of West German environmental technologists, including the Environment Minister, Saxony's future was that of 'an international exhibition for waste management technology'.[22] The full application of German and EC environmental legislation, especially to the energy and mining sector, would ensure this.

As already noted, West German utilities had high expectations of enhanced profits in an expanding energy market in the GDR. This expectation clashed with the green visions attractive to East German planners and environmentalists in general. As East German society became frightened, it began pleading for special treatment.

The East was to become the place where the West should try out its 'green' concept of 'ecological restructuring' to the full. In early 1991, the former Institut für Energetik, now IfE Leipzig Ltd (Engineering and Service Company for Energy and Environment), recommended that the renewal of the energy system in the former GDR would require not only a great financial and material effort, but also 'offers the unique opportunity to develop energy supply structures which will point to the future, especially from the ecological perspective'.

Underlying these recommendations was the expectation that harmonization of German living standards would be achieved over a ten- to fifteen-year period. Following a downward slide, economic recovery would be extremely rapid, thus avoiding permanently depressed levels of productivity and welfare spending. Economic recovery would involve, IfE argued, the development of less-energy-intensive industries, resulting in a final energy demand roughly equivalent to that at unification, and envisaged much greater reliance on liquid and gaseous fuels. Primary energy demand was expected to fall by only 15 per cent during the period 1989–2000. (By late 1991 IfE had revised this to a 30 per cent drop for primary energy and 20 per cent for final energy.) Radical restructuring in the energy economy, IfE argued, would offer far greater opportunities than growth based on existing structures. The goal should not be to copy the structures existing in the old FRG, but to make full use of new opportunities. How precisely this was to be achieved could not yet be spelt out. Planning was now in the hands of new institutions – new regional authorities were gradually learning to work together with corporate interests.

Essential strategic policy decisions, IfE recommended, should be taken immediately in the following areas and in the interest of restructuring:

- the future of nuclear power and power station sites;
- implementation of the Single European Market for energy with its special impact on transmitted energy, that is, electricity and gas;
- ensuring security of supply, always a major concern in Germany, given its import dependence;
- strategies to reduce CO_2 emissions, now a major government goal which has largely replaced the objectives of acid emission abatement in the energy sector.

Outcomes would depend on the degree and nature of economic development not only in East Germany, but in the countries beyond the River Neisse.

What is the evidence that utilities and regulators have taken steps to 'restructure ecologically'? Can this be achieved given the nature of German and European energy politics? So far, events suggest that developments in the East have been mixed. Privatization has brought it nearer to the West, but some western taboos or restrictive practices have been weakened. Nuclear power has indeed been abandoned and the power of municipal utilities been restored.

Some renewables may have a chance of developing more rapidly in the East. Messerschmidt, Blöhm and Bölkov (MBB) plans a 4 MW photovoltaic pilot plant in the impoverished Thuringia hinterland, to occupy 32 hectares near the small town of Bad Langensalza. The site is apparently intended as a production centre for the building and marketing of solar cells. It is highly unlikely that any community in the West would have found this land use acceptable. The Thuringian community, however, is reported to be strongly supportive. Progress towards cleaning the air is under way, in addition to that achieved by 'deindustrialization'.

The 160 surviving large combustion plants had to comply with the Large Combustion Plant Regulation (GFAVo) by July 1996 and 6735 other plants must adjust to the tough air pollution norms of the TA(Luft) or shut down. To ensure compliance with the GFAVo, 8500 MW of capacity has already been closed down. Private investment of the order of DM115–130 billion is expected in the East German energy sector over the next two decades; most will serve to implement environmental regulation and thus modernize technology, products and services.

Economic, political and environmental imperatives have combined to produce major increases in energy efficiency in the East, already the main contributor to Germany's apparently impressive reduction in CO_2 emissions. Diversification and energy conservation are now official energy policy objectives in all the new *länder*. In June 1990, the Parliamentary Enquete Commission on the Protection of the Atmosphere recommended a reduction of 142 million tonnes of CO_2 (from 715 million tonnes in 1987) in the West, and of 72 million tonnes (from 352 million tonnes) in the East. Apart from R&D efforts organized by the research ministry, first decisions to guide the energy economy along this road were taken in mid-1991. The Saxon ministry for economics and labour adopted a directive in support of rational energy use and renewable energy sources which offers state subsidies of 20 per cent for the planning, capital and installation costs of investment into

- modernizing domestic space heating;
- use of waste heat;
- small-scale electricity generation (biomass, methane up to 100 kW; solar sources up to 200 kW and hydroelectric power up to 300 kW).

A number of directives to expand combined heat and power (CHP) were also adopted.

Deindustrialization is helping to achieve global greenhouse gas targets quite rapidly. In a report to the European Community (EC), Bonn estimated that CO_2 emissions in the new *länder* had already declined from 348 million tonnes (mT) in 1987 to 288 mT in 1990. The official target is to reduce the total (GDR plus FRG) 1987 figure by 30 per cent by 2005. The former GDR had achieved more than half of this by 1990 with an 18 per cent reduction, while in the western part of the country the reduction was only 1 per cent. The overall decline for the new Germany was 6.3 per cent.

The realities of unification

While political and financial problems have slowed down the implementation of the green visions, the objective remains. To ensure some employment, a future for brown coal use in East Germany had to be ensured, nuclear replacement became impossible and more advanced technological options had to be rejected or their application limited. New environmental costs likely to arise for the users of brown coal from Germany's proposed waste levy legislation as well as from any energy/carbon tax, were initially resisted.[23] A future for the nuclear industry in the West has to be ensured, with waste disposal remaining a fiercely contested subject, and the former GDR will remain a useful potential 'end store' depository area, especially if reprocessing is abandoned, as seems likely. The GDR will also provide a laboratory for the development of safety and decommissioning technology and techniques, with tremendous export potential even further east. Emphasis will therefore shift to nuclear waste management. The debate about the future of nuclear power thus continues and extends to the future of nuclear reactors in the CIS and Eastern European states.

By 1991 energy demand had fallen by one-third and energy prices had tripled; by mid-1994, electricity demand was down by 40 per cent. The following sections deal with the broader impacts of the transitions, the environmental legacies that have to be faced and a proposal of what 'ecological' modernization might mean for the energy industries.

MARKET-LED DEINDUSTRIALIZATION

While some of the problems East Germans have experienced since 1991 were predictable as a necessary part of the transformation of a 'real socialist' economy into a 'market' one, western observers and official sources agree that government had seriously underestimated the problems that would arise.[24] Deindustrialization in parts of Saxony, once the ancient industrial heartland of central Europe, is particularly serious as few new industries or retraining facilities have been attracted. Bonn, however, had been warned as early as November 1989 by the Council of Scientists advising the economics ministry (BMWi), which argued that only 'extraordinary transfers' of public money would enable modernization to take place. Without such transfers, the Council argued, even the best reforms in the GDR would not stop the outflow of people.

In essence, political unification was perceived by this Council as a political necessity for West Germany even before it happened. In mid-1992, even leading Christian Democrat (CDU) figures agreed that there had been no *Konzept* for unification. This is indeed an admission of fundamental failure in a country where acting without a concept, that is, acting pragmatically, is frowned upon (*Biedekopf*). Political opportunism had been the motivating force instead.[25]

The cost estimates of bringing the East 'up to standard' continued to rise.[26] The promised upturn in economic performance has still not happened. East Germans are still told by their much better paid '*Wessi*' (West German) advisers and regulators 'to roll up their sleeves', work harder, become assertive and entrepreneurial. Many of them wonder what they have been doing for the last forty years under imposed economic and political conditions less favourable than those imposed on West Germans after 1945. When unification came, the GDR was left with virtually no bargaining power to protect its own interests.

The threat to the former GDR arising from rapid political and especially monetary unification sprang from the capacity of the West German economy to supply virtually all the goods and services that the East might have wanted, and indeed did want. The much regretted monetary reform (undertaken against the advice of the Bundesbank) forced East German enterprises to compete in the world market virtually overnight. Many collapsed as their traditional markets further east disappeared and none emerged elsewhere. Initially, therefore, the East proved to be an immediate market for a large range of consumer goods, particularly foods, textiles and above all else, cars. Car ownership per capita soon reached that of the West in the early 1980s, causing terrible congestion on a totally inadequate road system.[27] However, the political context in which all environmental issues are now decided includes the urgent need of the united German state to cut public expenditure and raise its tax income in order to be able to support the East. Things will not become easier as the whole of Germany is now suffering a deep recession.

This raises the issue of how the new federal states can earn the income to pay for desired western 'imports' – which are often prioritized over domestic products for ephemeral reasons such as more attractive packaging. Imports compete with investment in their own future, for jobs in the private sector have largely disappeared. Mass unemployment continues. If part-time workers are included, unemployment in several industrial sectors is now 50 per cent and greater. Young people, the over fifties and women are the groups most severely affected. They are also the groups which had been particularly advantaged by the GDR regime. A huge wave of redundancies in the textile and chemical industries in late 1991 led to between 60 and 80 per cent unemployment in some areas.

Western entrepreneurs consider that a modernized enterprise requires only one-third of the previous workforce using outdated technology. For some industries the ratio is one to ten. Many energy-intensive industries, especially chemical and metal-lurgical plants, have been shut. In mid-1992, the Federal Labour Office expected the bottom of the trough to be reached at the end of the year, but this proved illusory. The slogan *Statt Ausbau im Westen lieber Aufbau im Osten* (Instead of more development in the West, rebuild the East) illustrates the politically dangerous choices now facing Germany. In 1990, the estimated difference of GNP per capita was DM54,700. By mid-1994, this difference had on average probably declined a little. Economic uncertainty, growing unemployment, new and more complex layers of bureaucracy and growing social unrest over guest workers spoilt the undoubted joys of freedom of speech and travel. Yet East Germans are incomparably better off, in purely financial terms, than their former socialist comrades in other states in eastern Europe. They tend to get little sympathy in the West, where they are perceived, to use a well-known British word, as scroungers.

It is now widely agreed that the speed of economic collapse in the East was intensified by hasty, ill-considered economic union based on unwise exchange rates. One conservative response to this problem is to send women back home and thus attain a level of employment similar to that in the West.[28] The prevailing right-wing ideology regards attracting private investment as the solution, a strategy which has worked in some sectors, such as property and retailing, but which so far has brought little general relief. For private investors in many other areas, such as manufacturing, there are far fewer attractions. Lower wages do not bring private enterprise into an area where the infrastructure is poor and property rights remain subject to legal challenges. These factors are compounded by the re-emergence of a culture suspicious of the motives of investors based on old teachings about the exploitative nature of capitalism.

Towards the end of 1991, observers described the socio-economic situation as *verheerend*, as if armies had devastated the land, and there has been only limited improvement since. East Germans report that western politicians, and visitors, have stopped coming and we hear and read less about the situation. Whole industrial suburbs of Leipzig were closed down by 1993, with satellite television keeping people at home – most of the sports and cultural facilities built under the GDR have closed down. All this ignores the small but prospering class of people with direct access to western incomes in the form of pensions or public service salaries or consultancies. They are able to shop in elegant boutiques in city centres that are being restored. The well-off, estimated to be as much as a third, tend to travel abroad as much as their funds permit. Little money stays inside the former GDR.

In sum, unification initiated a process of 'environment-friendly' deindustrialization and social disintegration caused by the loss of markets and import substitution, as well as the loss of certainties and orientation. This was well under way in the summer of 1991, when industrial output in the second half of the year was expected to shrink to a quarter of that of the first half year of 1990 and tax income was declining rapidly to about one-third of the level in the West. Table 3.1 indicates the extent of the economic collapse and also explains why local government was so determined to obtain a share from the profits to be made in the energy sector. Deindustrialization was expected to continue in eleven branches (including machines, office equipment, chemicals, optics) with export opportunities to eastern Europe still declining, without improving in the West. Energy demand fell accordingly. The further expansion of public investment in infrastructural development and environmental protection was therefore considered essential.

Fortunately for East Germany political unification did create considerable flows of money, many made palatable to western taxpayers as contributions to the protection of a shared environment. Three streams of funds can be identified: (i) public welfare payments, such as unemployment benefits and pensions; (ii) a host of grants and loans to East German firms and their export markets, including the

Table 3.1 The East German economy 1990–91: value added by economic sectors (percentage change)

Economic sector	Value added
Agriculture	−20.0
Small-scale industry	−43.3
Electricity, gas and water supply	−22.8
Mining and industrial processes	−53.8
Construction	−20.6
Trade	−20.2
Transport	−7.2
Government	−11.9
Total GNP	−23.9

Source: IAWC (Institute for Applied Economics), Berlin, October 1991.

former USSR; and most importantly here (iii) public and private money to ensure compliance with regulations, especially environmental standards.

The full size of the 'sacrifice' required by western taxpayers has only gradually been admitted by Bonn. The tasks requiring urgent investment and the transfer of money from West to East include environmental repair jobs. For example, uranium waste management and restoration work alone is estimated by some to eventually cost the public purse DM50 billion, although much lower figures have also been suggested (see below).

As new environmental disasters were discovered, they were used to promote public investment projects, though the prospect of further large transfers to the East has since led to political dissatisfaction in the West. The German state is running out of money and its indebtedness is growing. Taxes are likely to rise further, and attempts to reduce agricultural and coal subsidies, most commentators say, should be pursued in spite of the pain. One thing seems certain, however: 'industrial property owners in the East will transfer these costs (of environmental clean-up) to the public purse' (*Die Zeit*, No. 29, 10 July 1992: 18).

From a purely environmentalist point of view, this situation is less disturbing as there have been improvements. Healthier food is widely available and many chimney stacks and pipes have stopped emitting or discharging. Fewer people use public facilities other than roads. Trains are no longer crowded and many buildings are being restored by their former owners. The GDR begins to look much better despite huge traffic jams and parking difficulties in inner cities. The colourful flags and slogans of communism disappeared long ago, being replaced by the latest in western advertising and a new set of aesthetic registers.

Environment-friendly initiatives by Bonn

As early as July 1989 Bonn's environment minister, Professor Klaus Töpfer, and the then GDR environment minister, Dr Hans Reichelt, signed an international agreement to collaborate on six projects totalling DM940 million (East) and DM300 million (West). Before this was signed in December, the GDR promoted further projects worth billions of deutschmarks involving large amounts of East German investment, with technology being 'transferred' from the West. The projects covered air pollution control, water pollution and science and technology. Such agreements became irrelevant when the GDR ceased to exist in October 1990.

Bonn responded to its acquired problems by incorporating the GDR into its own legal and administrative structures. This included not just legal, monetary and economic union, but also an environmental one (the *Umweltunion*). This involved the provision of advice and, increasingly, flows of well-paid experts to the new *länder*, followed by public investment. The Environment Ministry (BMU) spent DM500 million by 1992 on over 600 environmental projects. This created 50,000 jobs in building the infrastructure for what the Germans aptly call *Sanierung von Altlasten* – the sanitizing of old burdens. First official steps involved the identification of over 12,000 contaminated sites in need of restoration.

The primary goal in Bonn shifted from environmental protection as a means of technology forcing to the legal transfer of public funds to the East in order to create employment and training opportunities. The main emphasis was on the development of plans and programmes for environmental 'sanitization' at the regional level. Urgent tasks included building water treatment plants, retrofitting combustion plants and ensuring compliance with a host of German and EU regulations. Revenue from environmental taxation, including DM5 billion from a carbon tax that still has not been agreed, would be spent on improving energy efficiency and promoting renewable forms of energy. A programme called 'National Solidarity Action Ecological Restructuring' was announced in February 1991.

In late 1991, however, environmental liabilities for new owners and investors were actually relaxed and in May 1992 the cabinet decided to grant 'administrative aid' to the East for the implementation of the Federal Air Quality Act (BImSchG) and for the delayed application of waste regulations. Serious shortages of qualified and experienced environmental administrators continued to hamper permit procedures. Land restoration and repairing pollution damage associated with opencast mining now provide most employment and the *Sanierung* of these eastern brown coal areas is by far the largest environmental protection project today from the perspective of employment, scope and finance required.

Large areas of the former GDR had already been declared nature parks by its last government and new 'set-aside' areas have followed rapidly. Six out of eight of Germany's terrestrial Biosphere Reserves are now found in the East. Regional plans have been developed which emphasize the provision of employment through 'gentle tourism', the German version of eco-tourism, though it is not clear that East Germans like earning their money by taking in curious visitors. The research programme of BMU has been altered to emphasize the needs of the East; its efforts must be 'planned and comprehensive'(*Umwelt*, No. 9, 1990: 424). As part of urgent ecological measures, funds of DM250 million were used to stage an international exhibition of waste management and clean-up technologies for the Halle/Leipzig region. The Research Ministry has switched funding from nuclear research to decommissioning. Most new employment is now provided by dealing with some of the legacies of the past.

ENVIRONMENTAL LEGACIES: A DIRTY ENERGY SECTOR AND THE IMPACT OF URANIUM MINING

The environmental situation facing the East German energy sector is best captured in a decision taken by the last GDR government in 1990, which decided to allocate more than half of the state budget (almost 3 per cent of GNP) to it, which was still considered insufficient in the West. This judgement may have helped to persuade East Berlin to give up the struggle for a degree of autonomy and agree to transfer its problems to Bonn. The energy-related inheritance of the GDR and the Cold War bequeathed to the 'old' FRG can be summarized as follows:

- almost 70 per cent of primary energy demand satisfied by brown coal, often of very low quality, but making the GDR much less dependent on energy imports than the old FRG (c. 78 per cent compared with 36 per cent);
- outdated and energy-inefficient technology typical of most energy-intensive industries, including electricity generation itself;
- specific energy demand in industrial processes on average 30 per cent higher compared with developed industrial countries;
- the virtual absence in all sectors of any incentives to reduce energy demand, hence the GDR's claim to being among the higher per capita consumers of primary energy (electricity demand increased by almost 20 terawatt hours between 1980 and 1989) and the third largest emitter of CO_2 per capita (after the USA and Canada);
- the lack of any technology in working order for reducing the emission of particulates and sulphur, which were among the highest in per capita and absolute terms in Europe;[29]
- one of the densest district heating networks in Europe, supplying 23 per cent of the heating market, with the rest falling almost exclusively to solid fuels, only 8 per cent to gas and 2 per cent to oil. The district heating network was poorly maintained and calls for investment of the order of DM15 billion were made in late 1990;[30]
- one of the densest and most heavily used railway networks in Europe, but with 70 per cent of capacity used for the transportation of brown coal;
- a large uranium mining company (Wismut), which had become redundant but left behind a multitude of environmental problems.

Transport and electricity generation in the East relied on a very different fuel mix from the West. Gas use for power had increased a little, but its contribution remained below that made by nuclear power from Soviet-designed reactors. These had been in constant use since 1980 and were a response to the oil shock, which hit the GDR much later than the West. According to former GDR officials, the Soviets had vetoed an ambitious programme to develop an earlier East German nuclear fuel cycle independent of the USSR. An offer, made in 1980, to build a reprocessing plant and Siemens PWR to operate from 1988/89 had also come to nothing, this time apparently because of US pressure.

The story of how the electricity sector is to be cleaned up by privatization and environmental regulation has largely been told. The uranium industry and the vision of an ecologically restructured energy industry remains to be outlined.

Cleaning-up radioactive contamination

Officially, uranium mining was viewed as a part of the German 'working-class' contribution to world peace. Officially beyond the knowledge of the energy planners in Leipzig, uranium mining for Soviet weapons and power generation began in 1950. The physical evidence of these activities occurs visibly throughout large areas of Saxony and Thuringia. The company in charge, Wismut AG, a German–Soviet (now German-owned) listed company, is still considered a state within a state. It possessed its own telephone network and *stasi* (secret police), and operated with extreme secrecy. Workers were well paid and the company's control over its property was absolute. While some environmentalists have claimed that the impacts of uranium mining have created a disaster area comparable to Chernobyl, environment minister Professor Klaus Töpfer has claimed that while the overall costs for the uranium mining clean-up will be around DM10 billion, there are no immediate and large-scale threats to public health.[31] Radon-affected homes were considered to be the main problem and experts from the whole world would be asked for advice.

Uranium mining ceased in mid-1991. The remaining labour force is now employed in decommissioning and reclamation. The big clean-up of several inherited problems had begun in 1991. For example, in Crossen, a dilapidated industrial site where a uranium preparation plant and loading station were situated, little evidence of serious decommissioning could be observed in June 1991. A vast, washed-out poster celebrating Soviet–German friendship remained visible above an assortment of disintegrating and rusting structures. The 15–20-year-long task of complete decommissioning was under way in 1994, with Wismut making strenuous efforts to win the trust of local people.

A large artificial 'mud lake' was created behind the picturesque village of Oberrothenbach near Crossen, north of Zwickau. Into this the radioactive materials from the uranium washing had been dumped. In 1992 the brook flowing through Oberrothenbach was being cleaned and old pipes taken away to add to the contaminated material in the lake. The site was by then accessible to those undaunted by prohibitory notices – the soldiers guarding a state secret had been withdrawn. Low-level nuclear waste had been pumped into the lake for many years. Fifty million tonnes of mud, said to contain 80 grammes of uranium ore per tonne, are held back by a dam about 60 metres tall. Cleaning this brook was part of a job-creation scheme in Zwickau during 1992, when many expert meetings on nuclear waste disposal were also held. More recent tasks have included determining the constituents of the mud and sealing the lake shores with uncontaminated earth in order to limit wind dispersion.

In August 1991 experts from eight European countries, Mexico and the USA met to discuss reclamation. They agreed that no final decisions could be reached for another four to five years due to lack of data. Information was most urgently needed on hydrological matters and health impacts. Most recent developments suggest that the lake will be filled in and concreted over, constituting a considerable burden on the taxpayer.

ELECTRICITY PRIVATIZATION AND THE CONSTITUTION

The transformation of the GDR's energy supply system and its integration into that of the West proved much more difficult and controversial than had been expected. Privatization was the most fundamental change, being based on sixteen electricity utility contracts. Major contracts concerned the Verbund (the grid and the major generators), with fifteen further contracts between the Verbund and regional utilities. It was agreed in advance that the western Verbund was to take over its eastern counterpart of three combines (gas, coal and nuclear) and the grid company.

The overall objective was to privatize the GDR electricity supply with majority western participation. The energy sector was sold by the Treuhand in June 1994. Veag, the eastern electricity company (see below) run by a consortium of three western utilities and five regional ones, was sold for DM8 billion, with DM2 billion paid directly to the new owners. The Treuhand shouldered about two-thirds of Veag's debts. This withdrawal of money means that Veag has to borrow to modernize. In spite of declining demand (still 0.6 per cent in 1993) it had a surplus balance sheet of DM8 billion in 1993. Compared with 1989, electricity sales have dropped by 40 per cent.

These electricity contracts were agreed in general terms in August 1990 (before final unification in October) after negotiations between the East German Minister for Environment, Nature Protection, Energy and Reactor Safety, the Treuhand (still a GDR body) and West German utilities. The contracts were severely criticized from the very start and worried the last GDR government. However, when the West German president of the Association of Communal Utilities (VKU), Manfred Rommel, recommended acceptance, the Volkskammer (East German parliament) ratified it in September 1990. The SPD immediately complained that the 'deal' involved the passing of a state-owned monopoly into the hands of a private one. Part of the strategy of the big utilities was to weaken an old opponent, the municipal utilities sector, by preventing its re-emergence in the new states. This strategy has largely failed, but true to the German regulatory culture, a complex and not entirely clear compromise was agreed in July 1993 as a precondition for privatization.

These electricity contracts allowed for the rapid adjustment of East German prices to those in the West and legalized the management of the GDR electricity system by western utilities, with Veag acting as caretakers for the Treuhand. Part of the legal complications which bedevilled these contracts was the previously mentioned Communal Property Act of the last GDR government. This had changed 27 energy combines to capital-owning companies, which were then taken over by the Treuhand for the purpose of privatization. In a coalition agreement of April 1990, the GDR government had promised to set up a decentralized heat and energy supply system, promising the communes the return of small power stations which had been nationalized after the war. This was formalized in June 1990 in a law about the privatization and reorganization of state-owned property, based on a combined Green/SPD initiative.

In February 1990 the former GDR energy combines joined to form a trade association to represent the interests of regional energy suppliers. Voices calling for the resurrection of communal power supplies were becoming ever louder as the financial difficulties of local government increased. Contradictory promises had clearly been made and conflicting obligations accepted which the legal system would eventually have to sort out. In the meantime, the large western energy supply companies and owners of the high-voltage grid (joined in the powerful Verbund) were, initially at least, able to implement their own ideas in the prevailing power vacuum.

By mid-1991, three big western utilities – RWE Energie (Essen), PreussenElektra (Hannover) and Bayernwerk (München) – had set up Veag (Vereinte Energiewerke AG) and taken over the management of the high-voltage grid. They were operating most power stations for the Treuhand and hoped to gain a majority shareholding in all electricity generation and distribution. By late 1991, however, the promised investment had hardly begun and the East German media reported that communes were demanding their rights and property. In principle, communal participation was not ruled out, but the intention was to reduce the status of communes to that of minority shareholders with no management responsibility and limited income.

The industry itself presented the electricity contracts as agreements for the modernization of the energy economy in the GDR through which leading energy supply utilities had accepted economic responsibility. The big utilities were in a hurry to stake out new markets and hoped to have the whole business completed before the end of 1991. According to their original proposal to the Treuhand, once the grid was 'fused', the 'big three' were to become 75 per cent shareholders of Veag. In return, they promised an immediate investment of DM1.9 billion out of a total of DM60 billion they claimed was needed for the modernization of the entire electricity sector. Eastern power stations would become subject to the full application of German and EC environmental legislation, with only some rescheduling permitted: for example, one extra year to comply with the 1988 EC Large Combustion Plant Directive and the West German TA (Luft) standards, which together comprehensively and very stringently regulate the emission of a large number of pollutants, including those responsible for 'acid rain', sulphur dioxide, dust and nitrogen oxides.[32]

The fuel mix retained brown coal for base load, hard coal for middle load and gas for peak demand. By 1991, investment estimates for power stations and the grid over the next decade had risen to DM70 billion. Flue gas desulphurization (FGD) units were to be retrofitted to two power stations, with existing brown coal plants being refurbished rather than closed down. New levies on gypsum wastes produced by desulphurization and the carbon tax were, however, worrying the utilities and added to their reluctance to actually invest. Neither has been imposed although the latter is still desired by the German government and environmental groups.

A constitutional challenge

The impoverished communes and the large Verbund generators (RWE, Preussen-Elektra and Bayernwerk) were competing for shares in the regional companies, for which the Treuhand had hoped to reserve at least a 49 per cent shareholding for the regions. An attempt to buy these out through financial compensation in November 1990 failed. In August 1991, 123 (later to become 167) regional utilities and towns hoping to have their own *Stadtwerke* took their case to the Federal Constitutional Court, asking for an injunction to stop the Treuhand from implementing the contracts on the basis of existing arrangements for both electricity and gas. The communes in particular were hoping to be able to run integrated supply systems for energy and water as part of their commitment to CHP and district heating. This constituted a major challenge to the large electricity suppliers, which had buttressed their interests by determining the new structure both legally and economically. The communes base their claim on their constitutional right to self-administration, which they consider, most probably correctly, to be violated by the electricity contracts and the unification treaty. By mid-1994, 30 *Stadtwerke* had been licensed and another 115 applications submitted.

The communes were not without allies; backed by their *länder* governments and with the full support of the Western Association of Communal Utilities, environmentalists and the SPD, they managed to achieve the compromise mentioned above, which allows many municipalities to operate their own power stations. Residual questions of waste liability, job security and prices remain to be resolved. The first indication of how such a compromise might work could be observed in Chemnitz, where the city had agreed to own 50 per cent, RWE 40 per cent and Stadtwerk Düsseldorf 10 per cent – a compromise which collapsed, however, as the court hearing was approaching and the city decided that it wanted 100 per cent after all.

None of the 15 regional utilities have so far accomplished their 1991 investment plans, involving an investment log-jam of DM798 million. Negotiations take time and cost money 'up front', but appear to create socially fairer and implementable solutions in the end. They are thus likely to be cheaper in the longer run. By mid-1994, the long saga of the *Energiestreit* was approaching its resolution. This should at last allow investment to flow into 'real' jobs.

DISCUSSION AND CONCLUSIONS

The GDR had been living off its declining capital stocks for at least a decade, during which time pollution was undermining the value of fixed assets. Increasing dependence on domestic brown coal as the basic raw material for industry and energy production was the primary cause of this. Energy remained 'dirty' though cheap and the resultant air pollution crossed frontiers fast and measurably. It made the GDR (with the UK) one of the worst transfrontier polluters at a time when West Germany was rapidly cleaning up in response to *Waldsterben* (forest death) and other, less environmental motives.

Air quality in Germany has improved significantly though the forests everywhere remain in poor health. The reasons are less well understood than they once seemed.[33] Despite this, environmental pressures for emission reductions will continue and, combined with new environmental problems, will constitute a dynamic driving German environmental technology policy. East Germany will remain an experimental area, but the experiment will slow down because of financial and social constraints.

Closer analysis reveals that the image of the East as an ecological disaster area, whilst useful within pre-unification politics, was an exaggeration. Environmental damage stemmed from the inability of the socialist system to extract sufficient wealth from a society to which it had promised western living standards to invest in technical progress. In the end, it no longer managed even minimal maintenance regimes.

Energy politics in the united Germany now involves a search for both solutions to old problems (coal subsidies, nuclear power, competition) and for ways to reach new goals, such as energy efficiency, European integration, and access to gas and oil supplies from Russia. In this search, environmental regulations continue to play a major role. The energy/carbon tax is therefore best seen as much more than a purely environmental instrument. There is as yet insufficient evidence for a full 'paradigm shift' toward an ecologically benign energy system, but policy is moving in the right direction. While a programme for significantly improving energy efficiency is in preparation,[34] the collapse of 'old' industries has been the major route towards reduced emissions.

Only time will tell the extent to which these developments are politically sustainable, whether they will benefit society and culture as well as nature, especially in the East. One conclusion with wider implications can be ventured, however. Without massive transfers of public money and traumatic societal changes the 'economic miracle' expected to follow from the combination of democracy and the market has proven extremely difficult and patchy, even under highly favourable conditions. The German state may manage another miracle, but only if 'Europe' does not undermine these efforts by asking for too much too quickly. The costs of German unification are clearly costs for the whole of Europe and raise questions about the limits of the free market and the nature of the 'real' failures of communism.

The limits of the market

West Germany has always recognized the existence of limits to the market by avoiding narrow concerns over cost effectiveness and low energy prices (as recommended by neo-classical economic theory) and considering wider parameters required for an orderly public policy. For energy these are: energy security, meaning that the state decides the 'fuel mix'; equity, through a price systems that is not primarily competitive; and the promotion of new technology, especially by regulation of industrial processes.

The long-term benefits accruing to society were recouped through indirect payments. Whenever these primary objectives are promoted by environmental regulation, an effective, pro-active environmental policy can be negotiated. Public policy convergence dominates and the pursuit of environmental friendliness becomes relatively unproblematic. When such convergence does not take place, priorities will have to be established through bargaining and over time.

In the five new *länder*, energy policy could not immediately follow market principles, dominated as it was by the already existing energy situation and its problems. Whilst environmental considerations and modernization invited urgent change in the context of European objectives, these often clashed with the West German 'mission' in the East. The evolving German bargain for energy and environment stressed the technical and financial capacity of western utilities to solve energy-related environmental problems, combined with the regulatory powers of the state to force private investment.

In the united Germany, energy-related environmental issues now have to be decided in a common context, that of European integration. The implementation of a common European energy market (i.e. a common energy policy defined on market principles but regulated in Brussels) will involve continued conflicts, with the Germans likely to remain opponents to liberalization, free trade and open procurement. In this it will have the support of environmentalists and the communal utilities, and therefore the *länder*, whose local autonomy would be lost if market-driven policies prevail. Areas of resistance include third-party access to transmission systems (gas and electricity) and ending the subsidy of domestic hard coal.

Partly to protect itself against the implications for domestic prices of rapid technological change and environmental improvement, and partly to promote markets for 'green' technology, Germany is also pressing hard for the further harmonization of environmental standards, thus laying itself open to charges of inconsistency. The promotion of the European Energy Charter (a deal with eastern Europe involving investment and advice in return for the export of coal, oil and especially gas) offers new opportunities for fuel importers but threatens political bargains struck between German authorities and the electricity sector. Keeping such bargains may well be a condition for achieving the transition in East Germany.

Free-market doctrines interfere with long-term investment. Companies are not easily sold when burdened with enormous liabilities. Whilst liabilities depress the sale price of ventures they can also be a disincentive to further investment because of the perceived hidden costs. One way to devalue East German state assets was to generalize and exaggerate environmental failings, which while undoubtedly considerable, were surely not extraordinary if viewed from a historical global perspective. Beckoning markets for replacement technology encouraged the negative assessments of the East German industrial base. As one observer puts it rather subtly, 'who is in the greater hurry to clean up central and eastern Europe – eastern or western Europe?' (Russell, 1991).

Privatization in East Germany therefore led to a phenomenon which was also observable to a much weaker degree in the UK during the 1980s: the devaluation of nationally owned assets prior to privatization because of their environmental failings. The British government, however, worked hard to deny the environmental weaknesses of its nationalized industries. In Germany, political considerations prevented official efforts to protect the value of nationalized property. The West German state's aim of demonstrating the political inferiority of the socialist system

– thus legitimizing its legal and political take-over – converged for a while with the economic self-interest of West German producers and investors who wanted to buy cheap or sell new products fast. Only political intervention, or collusion with industry, can oppose such trends.

West German utilities clearly possessed considerable bargaining powers in their negotiations with the Treuhand. These powers reflect the nature of West German electric utilities – their high profitability, high cash flows and very high reserves.[35] This in turn made them a most attractive instrument of public policy; that is, for investment and the delivery of the much vaunted environmental clean-up. The German Deregulation Commission recently commented wryly that:

> If current rules and dominant practice are not changed, in future every new environ-mental requirement which forces utilities to invest will be a stroke of luck for the utilities. Electricity customers will pay for the new measures in a very short time and the utilities will have a high cash flow, which they can make the best of, before they hopefully have to gradually pay the sums back ... the German electricity industry will ... loyally fulfil environmental requirements and without unseemly opposition.[36]

Neither the enormous political advantages of such an arrangement, nor the political importance of the desire of the former GDR energy combines and communes to imitate their wealthy brothers, should be underestimated. They saw their interest represented by the existing trade associations (*Verbände*) rather than in proposals from either green theorists or those who wanted a common energy market based on more competition. Private sector investment displaces the need for taxation to finance public expenditure. Market and state are working with rather than against each other and energy-related conflicts of interest can be resolved gradually and at the local level. In this process, the role of environmental regulation has been decis-ive in defining frameworks of action promoting non-zero-sum outcomes. Such local lobby pluralism should not be cynically dismissed as a continuation of dominance by vested interests. The *Verbände* provide a wide range of peripheral services, which dedicated energy providers do not.

Higher electricity prices, the state argues in turn, encourage energy saving on the demand side, which promotes energy-efficient technology in the export-oriented appliance industry. Germany has therefore become a major supporter of an EU carbon/energy tax. Environment-friendly restructuring may be encouraged as indus-tries with high electricity needs are replaced by 'high-tech' ones. All this has yet to be tested by future developments; the energy politics in progress in East Germany do not yet provide significant evidence that a fundamental restructuring of the energy sector along ecological lines is under way. The next decade will therefore be an extremely challenging one, with the future of both German coal and nuclear power remaining at the centre of energy politics and with the municipalities, as the owners of utilities, increasingly important actors.

The limits of political autonomy

The collapse of the GDR demonstrates the severe limits of the socialist policy of autarky, presumably imposed by the USSR in its pursuit of political autonomy, as well as the failure of the East German political elite to understand their fundamental problems and make necessary adjustments early enough.

Apart from the politics of the Cold War, the second oil crisis of 1978 and its aftermath was the second major factor in the deterioration of the energy infrastructure in the GDR. For a small country poor in natural resources, heavily industrialized, uncompetitive at world market prices but tied to the USSR as an exporter of manufactured goods and importer of oil and gas, the 1980s became a struggle for economic survival. The political system was particularly ill-prepared for this struggle and lacked the flexibility to adjust.

In the early 1980s the USSR reduced its oil exports and thereby forced the GDR to become even more dependent on brown coal. The plan was to increase mining by 330 million tonnes annually, with a mooted further doubling in the future. This doubling, a West German figure, is rejected by IfE – the maximum annual increase ever considered was 450 million tonnes per annum. Brown coal had to be mined for survival without attention to environmental impact. Valuable domestically produced fuels made from brown coal (briquettes and coal powder for pulverized bed combustion) were exported in growing amounts to the West to earn hard currency. Political stability could be bought for a little longer.

Another strategy considered in response to the oil crisis was the rapid and significant expansion of nuclear power and further restrictions on the importation of gas and oil. Nuclear expansion was under way when unification put a stop to it, to the deep regret of many East German engineers. Air quality did not, therefore, improve markedly during the 1980s, in contrast to the situation in West Germany. As comparisons with the West became starker they also became a political liability. As the current situation demonstrates only too well, given certain political parameters which the GDR could not change by itself, it had very little freedom of action left by the mid-1980s. The FRG today is in a similar, if far less dire situation, with respect to policies emerging from Brussels. The loss of sovereignty comes in many forms and requires that we re-examine many underlying assumptions about society, ideology and economy, as well as human–nature interactions.

NOTES

All German texts have been translated by the author.

1. Air pollution problems did not worsen in the East; the output of SO_2 remained somewhat over 5 million tonnes until unification, though there had been some decline. For detailed emission data see Mez *et al.* (1991).
2. Mez *et al.* (1991: 176) give the following 1985 NO_x deposition as tonnes per square km (1985) for the GDR, UK and the old FRG respectively as: 7.4, 8.7 and 11.8. Total NO_x emissions in the GDR were estimated as about half those of the Federal Republic, but these values remain uncertain.
3. The term did not make it into environmental parlance, largely I believe, because it was replaced by two Anglo-Saxon terms with which its overlaps – sustainable development and clean technology.
4. The term is *nachhaltige Entwicklung.*

5. The words of an energy planner after having received and rejected advice from the Eco-Institute in Freiburg on how to transform the energy supply system of Dresden.

6. The decision-making process appears similar to that adopted by the Thatcher administration and its successors in the UK.

7. This picture emerged during discussion with energy planners at Leipzig. A longing for simpler procedures and 'less politics' was observed in 1993, but East Germans were learning fast as fundamental institutional change was reshaping the decision-making process. Benefits, however, seemed to be accruing to the West.

8. Personal observation and discussion with engineers at the Technical University of Dresden. In the last years of the GDR students had invariably reported back to their teachers that they could not use what they had been taught but were engaged in permanent repair jobs.

9. The small farmers' party and the FDP.

10. For example, H.-J. Grunow at the Martin Luther University in Halle-Wittenberg.

11. Interviews have confirmed general press reports – the ruling elite had repeatedly been warned by its planners/economists of the implications of this policy but refused to act for fear of political repercussions.

12. An earlier article considers the CO_2 problems in some detail and uses it to challenge the futurology of people like Hermann Kahn. The socialist answer was, in essence, recycling (Boehemer-Christiansen *et al.*, 1993).

13. *Berliner Zeitung* 15 November 1984: 9. Because multinationals are moving their old technology to the third world, it was argued that the West had to say that the ecological crisis could only be prevented by an end to economic growth.

14. *Die Zeit* (12 September 1991: 23) suggested a deficit then of DM21 billion and estimates the number of companies run by the Treuhand as 10,000. Burdened by a debt liability reported as about DM100 billion, in mid-1991 it had sold rather less than half of its companies for DM12 billion. Its first director was assassinated.

15. Only 20 per cent of the population have telephones in the East compared with 93 in the West; for cars, fridges and washing machines the ratios are 51:68; 60:70; 37:86, respectively (*DIW Report Wochenbericht* 24/91: 326).

16. Such a tax has been discussed by the EU since 1990 as a contribution to solving the alleged greenhouse problem. No agreement has been reached, since it would of course serve many other purposes as well. The UK is a major opponent.

17. Natural gas produces less CO_2 per unit of electricity, virtually no acid emissions and can also be burnt more efficiently than coal or oil in combined cycle plants. Its use in power stations had been discouraged, but its wide availability (although requiring pipeline systems) and cheapness make it the fuel of the 1990s. It will run out long before coal, however, and its supplies are very localized.

18. In May 1992, regional government, Ruhrgas, Greenpeace and the World Wide Find for Nature formed a working group to oppose bringing gas across the shallow North Sea.

19. Twenty-four such reactors were in operation, or about to come on line, in 1990 (*Power In Europe* 1 March 1990: 22). Providing nuclear services has indeed become a major German export, especially for Siemens.

20. These reactors were built during the 1980s and were sufficiently similar in design to get regulatory approval together, rather than on a case-by-case basis. This was to speed up licensing procedures and frustrate protestors, who had caused long delays and costs to the industry.

21. VDEW, *Stromthemen* June 1991: 1. He was restating part of the German energy 'deal': government decides the energy mix, and government means party consensus.

22. Federal environment minister Töpfer reported from a speech about 'environmental crises' areas in Saxony and Thuringia (*Freie Presse*, Zwickau, 2 June 1991).

23. *European Energy Report* No. 345, 23 August 1991: 4 and *Power in Europe* No. 112, 21 November 1991. So far only the hard coal industry has managed to recycle its ash and gypsum wastes. The levy came into force in 1994 in the West and 1996 in the East, and combined with a CO_2 levy would, according to the industry, almost double the cost of German brown coal.

24. For example, W. Herz, Verdrängte Wahrheit, *Die Zeit* No. 36, 30 August 1991. Estimates in 1991 suggest a transfer of public money of DM9000 per capita of East German population; that is, DM2000 per capita West (*Die Zeit* No. 32, 2 August 1991: 1). Chancellor Kohl admitted to serious errors having been made in 1992.

25. One argument is that had Chancellor Kohl not acted as he did when he did, the Russians would not have released the GDR.

26. The *ECE Energy Series* No. 7, cited in Russell (1991: 30), claims that this raising of standards would cost DM220 billion for electricity and heat supply alone, excluding the cost of neutralizing damage already suffered. Total costs for the modernization of the East mentioned by economics minister Möllemann are 5 per cent of GNP; the Saxony Prime Minister, Professor Biedekopf, estimated the need for capital investment as DM1200–1500 billion.

27. When visiting Meissen in 1992 by car, just reaching the town centre took almost an hour. A hole had appeared in the only bridge across the River Elbe. In 1993, most roads were building sites (in order to become eligible for a subsidy) and parklands had been turned into car parks.

28. This was put to the British delegation mentioned in the Acknowledgements by the environment minister of Saxony, a CDU member, and deeply resented by the many professional women with whom I was able to talk.

29. The main victims of this neglect were probably in Poland, with the GDR receiving some of its 'transboundary' emissions from the West.

30. *Stromthemen* September 1990: 7. The definition of district heating was broader in the East than the West, including, for example, large central heating units.

31. *Freie Presse*, Zwickau, 2 July 1991. Wismut once employed half a million people. The number of victims of radiation damage, Töpfer argued, was larger than the 7000 suggested by Wismut.

32. While European legislation applies only to new plants, the Germans (in response to the alleged dying of the forests in the early 1980s) applied these standards to existing plants as well, thereby closing many small coal-fired stations down and improving the competitiveness of nuclear power, as well as its image as a saviour of the German *Wald*. The surviving 160 large combustion plants had to comply by July 1996 and another 6735 plants faced closure or compliance with the tough air pollution norms of the TA (Luft).

33. It is now known that acid rain alone has not been the main culprit, the new proposed villain being the extra nutrients trees receive from ammonia and nitrates.

34. Both the Leipzig Institute für Energetiks and the energy engineering departments of the Technical University of Dresden are participating in the IKARUS programme of assessing the potential for efficiency improvements and CO_2 reduction for the Federal Ministry for Research and Technology.

35. For a damning economic review of the absence of competition and hence high electricity prices in Germany, see the report of the Bonn Deregulation Commission, reviewed in *Power in Europe* No. 101, 20 June 1991: 9.

36. *Power in Europe* No. 101, 20 June 1991: 9.

REFERENCES

Boehmer-Christiansen, S., Merten, D., Meissner, J. and Ufer, D. (1993) Ecological restructuring or environment friendly deindustrialisation? The fate of the East German energy sector and society since 1990. *Energy Policy* 21(4), 355–373.

Mez, L., Jänicke, M. and Pöschk, J. (1991) *Die Eneergiesituation in der vormaligen DDR*. Edition sigma, Berlin.

Russell, J. (1991) Energy and environment conflicts in East/Central Europe: the case of power generation. Royal Institute of International Affairs, London.

ACKNOWLEDGEMENTS

This chapter draws on a study tour of East German energy institutes during the summer of 1991 funded by the British Council and the Anglo-German Foundation for the Study of Industrial Society, less than a year after unification. Further information, observation and experience were gained during a ten-day visit to Germany in October 1994 as a member of a group of environmental 'experts' invited by the Goethe Institute. East and West German places and institutions were visited, including local government in Freiburg, national policy-makers and environmental lobbies in Bonn, and regional government and brown-coal mining areas in and around Leipzig. The 1991 visit included a collaborative effort between the author and energy experts from the Institute for Energetics (IfE) in Leipzig and the Technical University of Dresden and benefited from the assistance of Dr Lutz Mez of the Research Institute for Energy and Environment at the Free University of Berlin, as well as contacts with many people in Saxony, who have kept the author informed about developments in the region where she grew up. Ian Welsh is thanked because without his gentle persistence I would not have found the time to update and reorganize an earlier publication to suit this book. I am grateful for all this assistance but remain responsible for the interpretation of events and for any errors of fact.

CHAPTER 4

ENVIRONMENTAL SOCIOLOGY IN POLAND AND THE ECOLOGICAL CONSCIOUSNESS OF POLISH PEOPLE

Jacek Wódz and Kazimiera Wódz*

INTRODUCTION

The notion of environmental sociology has not, thus far, found a clear equivalent in Polish sociology. This does not mean, however, that environmental problems (primarily those of the environment of residence, or human habitat) have not been addressed by Polish sociologists. On the contrary, Polish sociology has great traditions in environmental studies going back to before the Second World War, including work by such authors as Znaniecki (1938) and studies that have been seminal in the development of urban sociological research in Poland (e.g. Rychliński, 1935). In addition, scholars such as Ossowski – who crossed the borderline of sociology and town planning – devoted much attention to the mutual relationships between these fields (see especially Ossowski, 1945). Thus from the outset of the post-war period, urban sociology in Poland included a strong environmental trend, often linked critically to the output of the Chicago School. However, research carried out within this framework did not extend much beyond analyses of socio-spatial structures of Polish towns or the spatial behaviour of their inhabitants (e.g. see Kaltenberg-Kwiatkowska, 1982).

Many years then passed before Polish sociologists became interested in ecological problems in the current understanding of the phrase. This re-awakening of interest was probably related to a number of phenomena dating back to the 1970s. These included the fall from grace of the concept of 'socialist industrialization', the emergence of small and diffuse ecological movements, and, finally, the growth of interest in research on social problems (including urban social problems) connected with the symptoms of economic, social and political crisis, which were already visible in the latter half of the 1970s. These factors culminated in the workers' strikes and the formation of Solidarity (Solidarność) in the summer of 1980 (see Kabala, 1993a: 119 on the environmental significance of the independent Polish trade union movement). To differing degrees, environmental issues were inextricably linked with activities of a clearly political character – a fact which did not escape the interest of either the ecological movements or sociologists more widely.

---

* With additional material by Andrew Tickle.

Typically, this political character accompanies many contemporary ecological movements, not only in Poland.

It is clearly difficult to present a full overview of the complex problems of environmental sociology in Poland, but the rest of the chapter attempts to deal with some of the most important elements of the development of sociological reflections on the environmental problem and how this is shaping the ecological consciousness of Polish people. In addition, an attempt is made to consider the role of the environmental movement in these processes.

SOCIALIST INDUSTRIALIZATION AND THE ENVIRONMENT

After the Second World War, particularly after the formation of the Polish People's Republic in 1949, Poland (as in other central and eastern European countries) found itself closely aligned politically with the Soviet Union. This meant the acceptance of the specific line of economic development which, in relation to an environmental sociology perspective, can be termed 'socialist industrialization'. This is not the place to characterize in detail this phenomenon,[1] which is generally known to most observers today from its early roots in 'Soviet industrialization' (see, for example, Kotkin, 1995). It should be stressed, however, that this type of industrialization meant not only the intensive building up of heavy industrial capacity and the development of allied power and energy sources (in Poland based mainly on coal) but also a specific type of change in social and geographical structures. In structural terms, this 'involved draining the traditional farm labor force for industrial employment, bringing women into the work force, and forcing heavy direct investment in industrial capacity at the expense of both consumption and social and economic infrastructure' (Kabala, 1993a: 118).

Socialist industrialization was realized in economic conditions directly antithetical to a free-market economy. Thus the Polish state accepted the model of the centrally planned economy in which prices and costs were decided arbitrarily by central planners according to socialized requirements rather than being shaped by market relations and the law of value (Smith, 1994). In this type of economy the costs of the possible degradation of the natural environment were included (*de facto*) in general, arbitrarily decided costs of industrial investment as part of the total cost of realizing the social change envisaged as leading to a future 'socialist industrial society'.

Economic investment from the end of the 1940s until the latter part of the 1970s was mainly focused in the heavy industrial sector (as part of the 'extensive strategy' of industrialization), which was most damaging to the environment. At the same time almost no modernization (intensification) took place in the existing (pre-war) heavy and energy-producing industries. The social aim of the investment was to employ large numbers of what became mainly the young working class, who, according to the Party's ideological assumptions, were to be the political base of the new communist power (in Poland these were mainly people of peasant origin). Little attention was paid to the fact that this resulted in the destruction and depopulation of sometimes even fertile country areas – possibly because this was the direct corollary of the assumed political aim: the realization of a new social structure in which a decisive role was to be played by the so-called 'manufacturing industry working class'. It was for such workers that new towns were built around the large new complexes of heavy industry, such as Nowa Huta near Kraków, as well as new districts, such as the district of Dąbrowa Górnicza near the great metallurgical works of Huta Katowice in Upper Silesia.

The realization of this type of industrialization also had implications for the system of social values. The totalitarian state (using the Soviet-based educational system) wanted to bring up 'the new man of socialism' or *'Homo sovieticus'*, characterized by a social personality adapted to or born of 'socialist industrialization'; that is, the creation and reproduction of a wider proletarian class, mostly from a peasant base. In Poland this appears to have had very little effect in instilling class consciousness; instead, workers tended to accept political passivity in return for improving standards of living – a tacit bargain implicitly encouraged by the state (see Matejko, 1974: 111–115 and Tickle and Vavroušek, in this volume, for its Czechoslovak variant). In many socialist countries the Party also sought to undermine the role of the family and family values in favour of more collective forms of organization (Kotkin, 1995: 159). This was attempted by a variety of means, which were largely unsuccessful (Crampton, 1994: 254), the Polish family remaining a bastion of traditional values and a bulwark against political socialization. However, in some other states in central Europe the provision of social facilities (see below) by dominant local enterprises appeared to be a reasonably successful form of patronage – thereby ensuring the reproduction of the worker collective (Smith, 1994: 408–409).

It is obvious, therefore, that the socialist industrialization project was overwhelmingly political in character. This is perhaps best evidenced in some of the locational choices for investment in heavy industry, which were often unrelated to the efficient sourcing of either labour or materials. Thus steel mills such as the Warszawa Mill were located in the capital and the Lenin Steelworks at Nowa Huta near Kraków, the 'intellectual capital' of Poland. In the latter case this was done 'to counterbalance the local well-entrenched intelligentsia' (Werner, 1992: 296) in addition to the policy of establishing such plants 'in regions of the worst peasant overpopulation' (Ascherson, 1981: 48). This overt politicization of economic strategy is worth stressing as it appeared to prompt a clearly political aspect to some of the initial ecological movements organized in the 1970s. Furthermore, in specific reference to the forced industrialization of the Kraków region and its populace, the antagonized local intelligentisa then went on to form the Polish Ecological Club (Polski Klub Ekologiczny or PKE), one of the foremost environmental groups of the 1980s.

However, the perception of rapid industrialization and its attendant effects was clearly contingent on social position. Those employed in the new industrial professions had the possibility of obtaining flats earlier than other citizens; they also had access to numerous social services (e.g. vacations organized by the larger factories, holiday camps for children, etc.). Such workers had little or no reason to think about the ecological costs of the overall industrial investment. In their system of social values their situation – still in the 1970s – was usually seen as definite social promotion. Thus paying attention to the necessity of slowing down the speed of development of this type of industrial investment (often aggressive towards the natural environment) was seen as threatening their chances of improving their individual situation.

Therefore one can say in concluding this section that, whilst totalitarian authority managed to conceal data on the negative influence of industrial pollution on public health (up to about 1980, when this ban was largely lifted; see Kabala, 1993b: 53), and until the consequences of environmental degradation were directly felt by the population,[2] the majority of Polish society was reluctant to pay attention to the relation between the state of the environment and individual living conditions. This may also have been due to the relative novelty of the issue in a recently industrialized region (where smokestack industries were also potent ideological symbols of progress and the production ethic) and the acceptance of the oft-quoted Party dictum that pollution was the price society had to pay for such progress.

Ecological consciousness of society

One should also briefly note that little attention has been paid by Polish sociological researchers to the issue of the ecological consciousness of the population. There are potentially many reasons for this phenomenon; foremost among them would surely be the fascination of Polish sociology in the 1950s and 1960s with examining macro-scale change, with few researchers asking questions as to how large-scale industrialization and the associated changes in social structure could influence the attitude of society towards the natural environment.

It must also be admitted self-critically that even if the great majority of Polish sociologists of that period did not wholeheartedly accept the political and social changes occurring, they at least appreciated many positive changes resulting from the modernization of Polish society. Neither was there in those years any considerable critical trend in Polish sociology favouring reflections concerning the state of the environment and the degradation associated with socialist industrialization. In turn, when the first organized movements for the protection of environment emerged in the 1970s, they were understood as categories of political contestation (since they were always 'against' the current policy of the authorities, no matter what premises such policies originated from) rather than in the context of their influence in shaping the ecological consciousness of society.

More serious analyses of the reasons for, and consequences of, the degradation of the natural environment in Poland occurred at the end of 1980. Of particular importance in this field were critical analyses of the state of Poland's spatial economy originating from the borders of economics, social geography and sociology (Anon., 1982a, 1982b; Kukliński *et al.*, 1983). The 1980s also brought a number of works of a diagnostic–postulate character (e.g. Wierzbicki, 1983; Kozłowski, 1986, Ginsbert-Genert, n.d.). It was in this period that the macrostructural trend took shape in Polish urban sociology (e.g. Kisztal and Miszia, 1982; Jałowiecki, 1988; K. Wódz,

1990), deriving its main inspirations from the radical critical theory of Castells (1977) and Marxist political and economic geography. Although some may regard this dynamically developing orientation of Polish urban sociology as marginal, its greatest achievements lay in revealing an alternative paradigm of urbanization processes in the post-war period. Here the definition of such processes was connected with the realization of the effects of intensive industrialization and the incoherence or even conflict between investment programmes in the field of the development of industry, housing, technical and social infrastructure. These latter tensions crystallized between the ideologically justified requirements of production and the necessity of protecting nature and human health from environmental degradation.

Recent critical evaluations of the state of Polish space undertaken by sociologists and social geographers have been directed primarily towards the main actors in the social production of space in the Polish People's Republic – the state and its planning agendas, the Party and economic bureaucracy in general. Thus the state apparatus (i.e. the Party), acting on the basis of the doctrinally justified (*ex ante*) model of the extensive development of heavy industry, had at its disposal the nation's natural resources. The completely free and wasteful way in which these resources were 'managed' led finally to the state of ecological catastrophe apparent by the 1980s (see studies such as Kukliński, 1983 and Jałowiecki, 1988). In the majority of cases such studies were attempts at objective analyses of situations with particular characteristics but lacked, however, any sociological research on ecological consciousness. These latter dimensions were analysed, primarily, at a regional level. This resulted from two important features characteristic of the development of interest in the sociology of the environment in Poland. The first, and most important, factor is the clear division of the country into agricultural regions, regions of old industry and new industrial regions. Due to this, the very nature of societal reference to the natural environment is heterogeneous throughout Poland. The second factor was the mainly regional – rather than national – scope of engagement of environmental and social movements (dating from the end of the 1970s) in making public opinion sensitive to the problems of the sociology of the environment. This mainly occurred through the work of the regional chapters of Solidarity in 1980 and the increasing influence of its 'organizational offspring', the PKE (also organized into a nationwide network of club chapters; see Kabala, 1993a: 123).

Regional case study: Upper Silesia[3]

> Upper Silesia in southern Poland is a very intensively industrialized region constituting the major centre of the coalmining industry and the most important region for metallurgy and metal industries in the country (dating from the latter part of the nineteenth century). The region is limited in area, but industry was developed there for economic reasons (proximity to the coal mines). The metals industry is still adjacent to the coal mines, and the great majority of these works are very old and still utilizing outdated technologies. The consequent pollution of the natural environment (on an enormous scale) is due both to the concentration of industrial works and the use of old technology. ▷

Upper Silesia is also the most heavily populated of all Polish industrial agglomerations. There is a continuous network of towns located so close together that urban boundaries run down the middle of streets, with no inter-urban zones, no suburbs, and no open spaces. The poor living conditions of the population are largely a result of a very low standard of housing. Much of the population resides in old districts and worker settlements that were built at the end of the nineteenth century and which have not been repaired for many years. Only a few towns have newer central districts and newer housing estates.

Characteristic living conditions

The Upper Silesian agglomeration of towns and industries includes the highest population concentration in Poland, with over 10 per cent of the nation living in an area that constitutes only 2.1 per cent of Poland's land area. In such cramped conditions, the outdated heavy industry has particularly harsh effects on both living and working conditions. The coal mines have a predominant influence on the quality of life in the region: they have dangerous concentrations of methane gas and the threat of explosion is always present. More generally, there is continuing danger of serious accidents at work; working conditions in the iron foundries compare with those found elsewhere at the end of the nineteenth century. Unsurprisingly, demographic data clearly show that the structure of employment in Upper Silesia is distinctly different from that in the rest of Poland. There is a disproportionately high concentration of employment in heavy industry and very little in agriculture or service industries.

A particular feature of the region which influences the length and quality of life is the daily commuting pattern of workers, which, in a number of socialist countries, has been linked to under-urbanization (Fuchs and Demko, 1977). An average inhabitant spends at least two hours daily commuting to work using a very poorly organized intercity transport system. Very often workers have to get up at 5.00 a.m. to arrive at work by 8.00 a.m. First they have to take a tram or a bus to connect with an overcrowded train, and then a further bus or train to the place of work (occasionally special works buses are available for miners or ironworkers). This travel often takes place in poor environmental conditions (winter smogs etc.). Such long journeys leave workers tired even before they begin work. Health specialists report this as causing a number of serious accidents in the workplace.

To give further flavour to the daily microcosm of life that influences living conditions, two additional features of the communities of Upper Silesia must be noted. The first is typical of worker communities elsewhere in Europe: the custom of cultivating small pieces of land, either in one's own garden or in the so-called workers' allotments or workers' gardens. Contamination of soil and air by heavy industry is a fact that is ignored by such workers as all kinds of vegetables and fruit are traditionally grown here and consumed by the family. Attempts to explain the contamination of the natural environment and the allied dangers of such practices fall on deaf ears.

The second feature is the lack of opportunity to visit traditional and cultural locations for rest and to take holidays outside the region. As a result, the average inhabitant inhales all possible harmful substances and does not leave the region even for short periods of relief. The habit of going away was popularized for a time in the 1970s by the larger industrial works (mines and ironworks), but later, due to financial difficulties, these holidays were abandoned and the custom did not spread. ▷

Environmental degradation

The influence of the degradation of the natural environment on mortality in the Upper Silesian region has never been investigated systematically, and hence data at our disposal are largely incomplete. However, they do allow some insight into the scope of environmental degradation. For example, Sroczyński (1989) suggests that over 3 million people in the region are affected by pollution from heavy industry and outdated processes. The concentration of harmful substances in the air, such as dust, benzo[*a*]pyrene (for which the World Health Organisation sets no safe limit: WHO, 1987), phenols and various heavy metal compounds, exceeds the permissible norms for good health several times. According to Sroczyński (1989), at least twenty-four of the most toxic substances exceed set norms, often by a factor of ten. The impact of such pollution is of course greater, given the population concentration in the region.

The major sources of environmental contamination include outdated industry, the municipal power plants, smoke from domestic coal-fired stoves (either individually or in communally heated blocks of flats), transport (particularly important because of the density of the infrastructure), low-quality petrol, outdated engine technology and poor maintenance, lack of vehicle emission controls and cattle-breeding farms that do not process or purify their chemical sewage. Thus many elements of pollution are introduced into the environment, including dust, gases, sewage and bacterial and viral contaminants.

Sroczyński (1989) further identifies the annual average levels of excessive contamination for several toxic materials. The permissible norm for dust pollution, mainly from smoke, is exceeded annually in the Upper Silesian region by four times. Such regional averages do not show the much higher levels that occur in localized areas and in winter, when domestic premises are heated with coal. However, more serious than dust pollution is contamination by metal compounds, particularly heavy metals known to affect human health adversely. For example, lead compounds exceed permissible emission standards by about fifty-five times, zinc compounds by about three times, and cadmium by a factor of two. In terms of gaseous pollution, sulphur dioxide (SO_2) exceeds legal norms by four times and carbon monoxide (CO) by as much as thirty times. Such levels are related to the common use of high-sulphur coal as the basic source of energy. Finally, certain other compounds that are particularly harmful to health appear in the Upper Silesian environment in quantities clearly exceeding all permissible norms, including those set internationally. For example, benzene exceeds the norm by about 100 times[4] and phenol by a factor of twenty.

Such data are examples of the general and specific degradation of the environment caused by excessive exploitation of old industrial works concentrated in Upper Silesia. It is obvious that there are many places with much larger local concentrations of harmful substances than the averages just described. It should also be pointed out that work outside some industrial plants is carried out under conditions of much higher concentrations than those listed.

Mortality and environmental degradation

An informed demographic analysis of the influence of environmental pollution on mortality is problematic in Upper Silesia due to incomplete and often unreliable data. For many years, not all accidents at work were registered and causes of death were only given as the immediate or direct cause, without identifying the primary underlying factors, which may have been related to environmental degradation. $\triangleright$

Table 4.1 Tumour disease rate in Poland and Katowice province per 100,000 people

Year	Katowice Province	Poland
1977	169.4	185.0
1978	185.0	195.8
1979	175.4	183.2
1980	182.6	182.6
1981	166.6	177.4
1982	177.1	193.3

Source: Żmuda *et al.* (1988).

A major further problem in determining mortality rates for the region is the manner of recording mortality data. Many people who work in Upper Silesia do not permanently reside there. Administratively and statistically, such people are treated as living outside the region and only temporarily working and living in so-called lodging houses. It is known from previous sociological research that these 'outsiders' tend to work in the most difficult environmental conditions and have the greatest health risk. Thus the degree of negative influence of environmental degradation on their health and mortality is difficult to determine from demographic research. One of the older ironworks exemplifies the extent of this problem; as many as 65 per cent of the production workers are inhabitants of lodging houses and are therefore officially inhabitants of other regions.

The frequent lack of statistical data or their extremely low reliability is best shown using an example. Table 4.1 illustrates the tumour disease rate in the whole of Poland and in Katowice province. However, additional – yet contrasting – data on this problem are available: Mantorska (1989: 59) points out that in the Upper Silesian area death rates are higher than the country's average, with 11.6 per cent of males and 10.3 per cent of females dying in Upper Silesian towns annually (1985 data).

The main cause of death cited in such cases was diseases of the circulatory system. From 1970 to 1985 the number of deaths caused by this group of diseases grew from about 3 per 1000 inhabitants to more than 5 per 1000. In the Upper Silesian towns, deaths due to circulatory system diseases in 1985 were 5.4 per 1000 for males and 5.5 per 1000 for females. In rural areas, women had even higher rates (5.5 per 1000) compared with men (4.9 per 1000) (Mantorska, 1989: 59). The second cause of death after circulatory system illnesses was malignant tumours. From 1979 to 1985 the number of deaths caused by tumorous illnesses grew from 1.4 to 1.8 per 1000 inhabitants. In 1985, in both urban and rural areas of Upper Silesia the rate of deaths among men due to tumorous illnesses was higher than that for women (2.4 versus 1.9 per 1000, respectively, in towns; 2.1 versus 1.6 per 1000 in country areas). It is also worth mentioning that in the period reported, of all deaths in the Upper Silesian region about 70 per cent were due to circulatory system illnesses or tumorous diseases.

The third most important cause of death was respiratory system diseases. This category also had a significant increase between 1970 and 1985 (Mantorska, 1989: 59). Sroczyński, on the basis of his research, suggests that excessive mortality in Upper Silesia is largely influenced by high infant mortality rates (53 deaths per 1000 per year) – an average higher than for Poland as a whole (Sroczyński, 1989: 49). Based on his extensive studies of environmental contamination and human health, ▷

Sroczyński has highlighted a direct relationship between excessive infant mortality and the mothers' living conditions, with multifactorial causation including disturbances of genetic coding, foetal damage through maternal inhalation of toxic substances, and the everyday conditions of the mother's life (commuting to work, hard physical labour, too little sleep, etc.).

A further factor influencing mortality, especially among men in Upper Silesia, is the large number of accidents at work. We do not have precise data at our disposal, because most accidents are not made public for various reasons. Even the causes of fatal accidents are hidden by highlighting other reasons. Accidents are important factors in mortality, both directly from fatalities and indirectly as a result of the worsening of an individual's physical condition and even disability. Data on another suspected factor – environmental contamination of the food chain (including drinking water) – and excess mortality are largely absent but there seems to be little doubt about the anecdotal evidence on the connection between deaths from tumorous ill-nesses and the widespread toxic contamination of air, soil and water. Other regional influences, such as the highly urbanized life-style and the stressful commuting and working conditions suffered by most, can also be assumed to give rise to negative influences on human health.

Case study overview

It is not easy to draw firm conclusions from these limited data. Demographic analysis, even if it is enriched with biological and chemical data as well as sociological informa-tion, is only possible here to a limited extent. There is therefore a strong argument for acquiring improved demographic data in any future work. If lack of data in demo-graphic research is a common phenomenon, then in the case of mortality research in Upper Silesia this lack of data is of a specific character. In a totalitarian country, as Poland was for forty years,[5] all enterprises (mines, ironworks, etc.) are owned by the state, and it is likely that information relating to any harmful activities of these enterprises has been concealed or falsified. Thus, the problem is not just simply the lack of data, it is also that access to data has been impeded and information falsified in the interest of the state.

Hence, it has only recently become possible to gain access to data concerning environmental pollution. Thus data concerning public health are still incomplete and mortality data are not yet reliable, although attempts have been made at partial ana-lyses (e.g. Sroczyński, 1989). However, state interests have not prevented sociological research on particular conditions or particular towns which has attempted to describe the influence of environmental degradation on the quality of life.

This last observation also throws up the urgent need for better methodology for such complex research; the data highlighted in this case study are provided primarily as a starting point for discussion and methodological development for further studies of the Upper Silesian region (and other parts of Poland) rather than facts in themselves.

THE SOCIOLOGY OF REGIONAL DEGRADATION

Throughout the 1980s, in addition to the work described in the case study, Upper Silesia was also the subject of systematic sociological research (based to a large extent on the methodological traditions of the Chicago School) considering both the problems of environmental degradation and environmental conditions of life, and also social problems resulting from the organization of social life in the conditions of a degraded environment (e.g. Czekaj and Wódz, 1991; Wódz, 1991). These long-term studies were principally conceived within the discipline of urban sociology and although the problems of ecological consciousness occupy a very important place in them, it would be difficult to consider them as research in the particular field of environmental sociology.

Political case study: Kraków and the PKE

The only other region in Poland with such a high degree of environmental degradation as Upper Silesia is that of Kraków and its surrounding area (Kraków province). Kraków is the third largest city in Poland (750,000 inhabitants) and, together with Upper Silesia, produces 30 and 50 per cent of total Polish solid (dust) and gaseous emissions, respectively (Carter, 1993: 128) The historic town is surrounded by several old industrial works but the main factor influencing regional degradation is the Nowa Huta ('New Mill') factory complex built in the 1950s – an enormous metallurgical works (including the Lenin Steelworks) created in the main by large-scale investment under the 'extensive strategy' phase of 'socialist industrialization' (mimicking the original Soviet strategy pursued between the 1930s and 1950s). By the end of the 1970s, Nowa Huta – together with other nearby industrial complexes and domestic sources – had been identified as a major environmental threat (Atlas, 1979: 19).

As a consequence, the Polish Ecological Club (Polski Klub Ekologiczny or PKE) formed spontaneously in Kraków in 1980, its emergence probably also helped by the new social and political openess associated with the rise of the Solidarity trade union movement. The PKE was originally founded as a local organization being, on the one hand, a social movement for the improvement of ecological conditions and, on the other, a specific consortium of scientists of different disciplines (from natural to social sciences) intent on examining and discussing environmental degradation and thereby shaping the ecological consciousness of society. With the increasing availability of environmental data, the PKE published research revealing serious environmental degradation, principally from local industrial sources.

One of these plants was the aluminium smelter at Skawina, 14 km from Kraków, whose emissions of fluoride had been linked to human health and cattle poisoning problems in the region (Kabala, 1993a). Given the favourable political climate at the time (1980), this prompted an informal coalition of environmentalists, scientists, Solidarity and the local press, which demanded the closure of the plant forthwith. Almost immediately, part of the plant was closed – reducing emissions by 30 per cent – and continued pressure (from a group now including PKE as a formal entity plus the Kraków city authorities) forced its complete and permanent closure in January 1981. As Kabala (1993a) has noted, the significance of this episode, both in terms of the opportunity to campaign freely against state-directed industry and the national importance of the plant (which produced 50 per cent of Poland's aluminium), cannot be underestimated.

In other parts of the country during this period, local Solidarity groups worked on specific environmental campaigns. Nationally such activities were reflected in ▷

the central inclusion of environmental reforms in Solidarity's famous 1981 demands (Kabala, 1993b), although it has been suggested that at this level (as opposed to locally) the Solidarity leadership's adoption of environmental concerns was simply a cynical political tool (Glinski, 1993). However, when martial law was imposed at the end of 1981, the PKE was tolerated by the state (whilst Solidarity was suppressed) and the movement quickly became regional in its scope; within a year it had seventeen regional chapters throughout the country (Carter, 1993: 124) plus a national board (based in Kraków). By the mid-1980s, environmental issues were firmly back on the public agenda after a series of officially sponsored high-level reports had appeared (e.g. Kassenberg and Rolewicz, 1985; Andrzejewski *et al.*, 1987)[6] and PKE was often pre-eminent in espousing and influencing new policy directions, both at local and national levels (Kabala, 1993a: 124).

The government was also now becoming pro-active on this issue by creating a new environmental ministry, albeit with little influence relative to the heavy industry lobby and its governmental sponsors. The government also sought to influence the development of the environmental groups by creating the Social Movement for Ecology (Ekologiczny Ruch Społeczny or ERS) to act as an umbrella organization for the extant movement. However, such quests for self-legitimation were constantly undermined by non-official discourse in the alternative press, PKE reports and *samizdat* material – all of which, for the majority of people, were more trusted sources than government information.

The power and legitimacy of the environmental opposition was finally formally recognized with the formation of the 'Round Table Ecology sub-team' as part of the government–opposition round table talks of early 1989, which heralded the collapse of the communist regime. Here the Solidarity representatives were largely drawn from environmental groups, particularly from the PKE. The resulting protocol now forms the implicit agenda of environmental policy issues for the 1990s in Poland, although the importance assigned to such issues, both politically and publicly, has now declined drastically in the face of other societal issues. However, the work of groups such as the PKE continues both nationally and in local groups such as Kraków to document environmental problems of the region (e.g. Gumińska and Delorme, 1990a, 1990b), thus continuing pressure on the new generation of democratic policy-makers at all levels of government.

We have pointed above to two examples of regional studies. However, it was only in the 1980s that the wider interests of mainstream Polish sociology focused on the problems of the ecological consciousness of Polish society and ecological education (see Gliński, 1988; PAX, 1988). Regional work also continued: on the basis of the research experience in Upper Silesia there was also an interdisciplinary attempt to collect methodological reflections on examining the ecological conscious-ness of Polish society (J. Wódz, 1990).

Summing up this part of our reflections it must be stressed that sociological research on the environment is still of a diffuse character, with studies developed mainly in those regions in which environmental degradation is particularly visible. Indeed, examples of situations in particular regions also serve to underpin empiric-ally wider methodological and theoretical reflections. However, such reflection con-cerning the general problems of environmental sociology is still a marginal trend in

Polish sociology. This is a result of both Polish society being in a period of very fast transformation during which many serious social problems have occurred and the specific politicization of the problem of environmental protection not always being concomitant with the pursuit of pure sociological research in the field of the ecological consciousness of society.

ACTIVITIES OF THE ENVIRONMENTAL MOVEMENT

We have already mentioned that throughout much of the post-war period the ideology of socialist industrialization was a dominant influence in Poland. Campaigns during the 1980s against some of its negative consequences (primarily against environmental degradation) therefore had a double-edged character. They were, of course, always campaigns for the improvement of the environment but they also represented a specific form of political challenge to the existing state system. Thus one cannot understand the situation of Polish environmental sociology without taking into account this second political element. Such political campaigns were practised by virtually all the environmental movements, which, in the 1980s, sought (by various forms of action) to improve the state of society's ecological consciousness. Full analysis of these movements is not undertaken here (but see Hicks, 1996), partly due to the complexity of these diffusely characterized groups, which were differentiated in terms of both their political programmes and territorial and social scope. It must be admitted, however, that all such groups and their activities fulfilled, and still fulfil, an important function in shaping Polish ecological consciousness (how ever low that may generally be).

However, many of these groups primarily emphasized certain political choices open to society, with issues concerning the value of environmental protection and preferred ways of improving the degraded natural environment being almost secondary considerations. It may be speculated that this political emphasis has been one factor in the relatively low effectiveness of the contemporary social influence of these movements, not only in the sphere of social or political activities, but also in the sphere of raising the ecological consciousness of the population. Thus if we allude to the observable efficiency of ecological movements in Poland in the 1990s, we refer only to small local communities or individual actions or campaigns against a specific factory's environmental impact. But this then raises the question of whether we are examining the effectiveness of ecological movements or the innate ability or desire of local communities to organize against damaging developments. And how much have such campaigns influenced state policy compared with outside influences? It is difficult to answer this question unequivocally, although examples such as the closure of the Skawina aluminium plant near Kraków in 1981 (see case study 2) and the cancellation of the Żarnowiec nuclear power plant project clearly rank as major policy changes engendered by lobby pressure from environmentalists acting in a wider sphere than simple so-called 'NIMBY'-type ('Not In My Back Yard') issues.

Since we stress the political character of these movements so clearly, it is necessary to point out that the political differentiation between the groups can be large, ranging from Catholic movements (e.g. the Gdansk-based Franciscan Environmental Movement, Franciszkański Ruch Ekologiczny) to groups of an entirely secular (lay) character and youth groups often inspired by counter-cultural traditions (Gliński, 1993). In addition, from the purely political point of view, there exist movements referring both to the tradition considered as extremely right wing (e.g. Movement of Healthy Poland) and to the leftist values related to the reform communist period of 1968. Further examples include the strong 'Freedom and Peace' movement, with its programme combining environmental protection with active pacifist ideas (e.g. refusing military service). This movement is notable because it has retained an active and ongoing campaign base and also has quite a long tradition going back to the middle of 1985 (see Zieliński, 1988). Furthermore, its actions are known all over the country due to their spectacular 'direct action' character (e.g. blocking the roads to the dam being built at Czorsztyn in the Pieniny Mountains). Yet despite the political bias to the environmental movements' activities, it is significant that in the parliamentary elections in autumn 1991 as many as four parties describing themselves as ecological took part without any concrete success (i.e. none won seats in the Sejm – the lower seat of the Polish parliament).

CURRENT ISSUES AND THE FUTURE

It is worth paying attention to one further aspect of Polish ecological movements: their relation to other central and eastern European states and the region as a whole. The profile of the environmental groups has often been raised through publicizing problems actively kept secret for whole decades under the communist regime. In specific instances this has involved pointing to industrial activities of neighbouring countries which have cross-border effects on the Polish environment. Now, having obtained freedom of speech and independence from the Soviet bloc, such activities have gained a certain popularity as Polish society appreciates any efforts aimed at the protection of national goods. Thus nationalistically oriented campaigns have indirectly contributed to raising ecological consciousness.

Two major examples stand out. First of all, there is the border with the former Czechoslovakia (now the Czech Republic): here the Polish ecological movements have protested against the building of a coking plant at Stonawa, in the Moravian–Silesian region, close to the Polish–Silesian border. It will emit significant pollution loads likely to degrade the natural environment on the Polish side (Kapala, 1990). Secondly, there is the area of the Karkonosze (Giant) Mountains (part of the Sudety range) on the south-western border of Poland, the Czech Republic and the former GDR. The concentration of industrial pollution deposited on the Polish side, but which is partly sourced from both the neighbouring states, has given rise to serious degradation of the natural environment. This particular example has often been depicted by Polish television as a national ecological disaster (almost total destruction of the mountain forests). In both cases Polish ecological movements contributed to the social construction of the problem of ecological protection of border regions, whilst at the same time sensitizing society at large to ecological problems. Following on from such transboundary issues, there have also been attempts to establish agreements between Polish ecological movements and their Czech, Slovak and former East German counterparts.[7]

Yet in contradiction to such nationalistic overtones being used in individual campaigns, an important overall element of many of the environmental groups' activities is the increasing attempt to put across the common belief that ecological threats do not have state borders – a non-partisan 'internationalization' of the problem. This is also linked to the notion of the necessity of defining common policies for the protection of the natural environment by the countries of the old Soviet bloc (a demand of scientists often quoted in the press). In all these countries of eastern Europe after the Second World War a similar model of 'socialist industrialization' was realized (although with certain differences due to the politics and economies of particular countries: e.g. see Hamilton, 1971), and yet in many of them there is today a high degree of pollution of the natural environment but a relatively low ecological consciousness of society. A future challenge for environmental sociology is to explain this relationship.

NOTES

1. Instead, for example, see Hamilton (1971) for its general application in eastern Europe and Werner (1992) for the Polish experience.
2. Opinions differ as to the beginnings of environmental concern in Poland. Szacki *et al.* (1993: 12) suggest that environmental degradation was becoming an increasingly visible problem in the 1970s, provoking 'a growing public resistance'. Other sources (Kabala, 1993a, 1993b) also identify the early 1970s but instead describe concern as being limited to the scientific community rather than occurring more broadly across society.
3. Much of this section is drawn from Wódz (1992) and is reproduced here with the kind permission of the publishers.
4. World Health Organisation air pollution guidelines state additionally that 'no safe level for airborne benzene can be recommended, as benzene is carcinogenic to humans and there is no known safe threshold level' (WHO, 1987: 54).
5. Some sources such as Mason (1993: 37) suggest that Poland cannot be classified as a totalitarian state, given that 'in both religion and agriculture, there were large sectors of the population and important aspects of social life, that were largely outside the control of the communist authorities'.
6. Such reports were often compiled or written by experts who were involved in closely overlapping epistemic communities of scientists (Polish Academy of Sciences), policy advisers and activist groups (often the PKE). Examples include Professor Andrzej Kassenberg, a well-known environmental scientist and long-time PKE activist (see also Kabala, 1993a: 130). This situation has clear analogies to the relationships occurring between state bodies, scientists and environmental and dissident groups in Czechoslovakia between 1983 and 1989 (see Tickle and Vavroušek, this volume).
7. For example, the NGO Strategy Seminar on Transboundary Air Pollution within Czechoslovakia, Germany and Poland held in Katowice in October 1990 resulted in the first

trilateral agreement between Polish, Czech and East German green groups on the priority actions needed for the environment in the heavily polluted 'Black Triangle' border region comprising North Bohemia (Czech Republic), Upper Silesia and south-eastern Germany. Groups signing the declaration included the PKE, the Czech Union of Nature Conservationists (ČSOP), Brontosaurus, Children of the Earth, Ecoforum Teplice, the Ecological Society and Duha (Czechoslovakia), Green League, Arche, Ümweltbund Ökologie-Leipzig (NIKA/ČSOP, 1990).

REFERENCES

Andrzejeski, R., Kozłowski, S. and Kassenberg, A. (1987) *Ekologiczne podstawy rozwoju społecznego-gospodarczego kraju [Ecological Elements of the Socio-economic Development of the Country]*. National Planning Commission, Warsaw.

Anon. (1982a) Problemy polskiej przestrzeni [The problems of Polish space]. *Biuletyn Komitetu Zagospodarowania Przestrzennego Kraja PAN* issue 118.

Anon. (1982b) Strategia uprzemysłowienia a proces urbanizacji [Strategy of industrialization and the process of urbanization]. *Biuletyn Komitetu Zagospodarowania Przestrzennego Kraju PAN* issue 119.

Ascherson, N. (1981) *The Polish August: The Self-limiting Revolution.* Allen Lane, London.

Atlas (1979) *Atlas Miej. Woj. Krakowskiego.* Kraków.

Carter, F.W. (1993) Poland. In *Environmental Problems in Eastern Europe* (eds F.W. Carter and D. Turnock). Routledge, London.

Castells, M. (1977) *The Urban Question: A Marxist Approach* (trans. A. Sheridan). MIT Press, Cambridge, MA.

Crampton, R.J. (1994) *Eastern Europe in the Twentieth Century*, Routledge, London.

Czekaj, K. and Wódz, J. (1991) *Miasto – ekologia społeczna, patologia społeczna [Town – social ecology, social pathology].* Katowice.

Fuchs, R. and Demko, G. (1977) Commuting and urbanization in the socialist countries of Europe. *Bulletin of the Association of Comparative Economic Studies* 19, 21–38.

Ginsbert-Genert, A., ed. (n.d.) *Ekonomiczne i socjologiczne problemy ochrony środowiska [Economic and Sociological Problems of the Protection of Environment].*

Gliński, P. (1988) Świadomość ekologiczna społeczeństwa polskiego – dotychczasowe wyniki badań [Ecological consciousness of the Polish society – current results of research]. *Kultura i Społeczenstwo* 32(3).

Gliński, P. (1993) Co-operation between environmental NGOs and the government in Poland. In *New Horizons* (eds P. Hardi, A. Juras and M. Toth Nagy). Regional Environmental Center for Central and Eastern Europe/Institut für Europäische Umweltpolitik, Budapest, 145–157.

Gumińska, M. and Delorme, A., eds (1990a) *Klęska ekologiczna Krakowa [Ecological disaster of Kraków].* Kraków.

Gumińska, M. and Delorme, A. (1990b) *Wadliwe uprzemysłowienie Krakowa w świadomości jego mieszkańcow [Faulty Industrialization of Kraków in the Consciousness of its Inhabitants].* Kraków.

Hamilton, S.E.I. (1971) The location of industry in east-central and south-east Europe. In *Eastern Europe: Essays in Geographical Problems* (ed. G.W. Hoffman). Methuen, London, 173–221.

Hicks, B. (1996) *Environmental Politics in Poland: A Social Movement Between Regime and Opposition*, Columbia University Press, New York.

Jałowiecki, B. (1988) *Społeczne wytwarzanie przestrzeni [Social Creation of Space]*. Warsaw.

Kabala, S.J. (1993a) The history of environmental protection in Poland and the growth of awareness and activism. In *Environmental Action in Eastern Europe: Response to Crisis* (ed. B. Jancar-Webster) M.E. Sharpe, Armonk, NY, 114–133.

Kabala, S.J. (1993b) Environmental affairs and the emergence of pluralism in Poland. In *Environment and Democratic Transition* (eds A. Vari and P. Tamas). Kluwer, Dordrecht, 49–66.

Kaltenberg-Kwiatkowska, E. (1982) Koncepcje ekologii społecznej w socjologii polskiej [Concepts of social ecology in Polish sociology]. In *Przestrzeń i społeczeństwo. Z badań ekologii społecznej [Space and Society. From Research on Social Ecology]* (ed. Z. Pióro). Warsaw, 133–159.

Kapala, J. (1990) Prognoza wpływu projektowanej koksowni w Stonawie na jakość powietrza w Polsce [Forecasting the influence of the projected coking plant at Stonowa on air quality in Poland]. *Ochrona Powietrza* 4.

Kassenberg, A. and Rolewicz, C. (1985) *Prezestrzénna diagnoza ochrony środowiska w Polsce [The Spatial Diagnosis of Environmental Protection in Poland]*. Polish Academy of Sciences, Warsaw.

Kisztal, P.A. and Miszia, B. (1982) Rola procesów spontanicznych i kontrolowanych w przebiegu socjalistycznej urbanizacji [The role of spontaneous and controlled processes in the course of socialist urbanisation]. *Studia Socjologiczne* 3–4, 115–134.

Kotkin, S. (1995) *Magnetic Mountain: Stalinism as a Civilization*. University of California Press, Berkeley, CA.

Kozłowski, S. (1986) Poszukiwanie koncepcji ochrony i gospodarowania zasobami przyrody [Looking for the concept of protection and managing natural resources]. *Studia KPZK PAN* 91, 9–74.

Kukliński, A., ed. (1983) Gospodarka przestrzenna Polski. Diagnoza – rekonstrukcja – prognoza [Spatial economy in Poland. Diagnosis – reconstruction – prognosis]. *Biuletyn Komitetu Zegospodarowania Przestrzennego Kraju PAN* No. 125.

Kukliński, A., Jałowiecki, B., Kołodziejski, J., Kozłowski, S. (1983) Diagnoza stanu gospodarki przestrzennej Polski [Diagnosis of the state of Poland's spatial economy]. *Biuletyn Komitetu Zegospodarowania Przestrzennego Kraju PAN* No. 123.

Mantorska, T. (1989) The demographic consequences of natural environmental pollution. In *Social Problems of a Highly Industrialised Region* (ed. L. Frackieicz). Silesian Scientific Institute, Katowice, 40–67.

Mason, D.S. (1993) Poland. In *Developments in East European Politics* (eds S. White, J. Batt and P.G. Lewis). Macmillan/The Open University, Basingstoke.

Matejko, A. (1974) *Social Change and Stratification in Eastern Europe*. Praeger, New York.

NIKA/ČSOP (1990) Common solutions for Black Triangle. Press release, mimeo, 22 October, Prague.

Ossowski, S. (1945) Urbanistyka i socjologia [Town-planner and sociology]. *Problemy* 1.

PAX, ed. (1988) *Edukacja ekologiczna społeczeństwa [Ecological Education of the Society]*. Warsaw, PAX.

Rychliński, S. (1935) Socjologia miasta [Urban sociology]. *Przegląd Socjologiczny* 3.

Smith, A. (1994) Uneven development and the restructuring of the armaments industry in Slovakia. *Transactions of the Institute of British Geographers*, NS 19, 404–424.

Sroczynski, J. (1989) The influence of environmental pollution of the Upper Silesian industrial basin on the population's health condition. In *Barriers of Functioning of Upper Silesia* (conference proceedings). Mimeo, Katowice.

Szacki, J., Głowacka, I., Liro, A. and Szulczewska, B. (1993) Political and social changes in Poland: an environmental perspective. In *Environmental Action in Eastern Europe: Response to Crisis* (ed. B. Jancar-Webster). M.E. Sharpe, Armonk, NY. 11–27.

Werner, A. (1992) Marxism and pollution – some east European experiences before the revolution. In *Pollution Knows No Frontiers* (ed. K. Schleicher). Paragon House, New York, 291–303.

Wierzbicki, Z.T. (1983) Ekologia człowieka a socjoekologia społeczna [Ecology of man and social socio-ecology]. In *Teorie socjologii miasta a problemy społeczne miast polskich [Theories of Urban Sociology and Social Problems of Polish Towns]*. Wrocław, 61–74.

Wódz, J., ed. (1990) *Problemy świadomości ekologicznej [Problems of Ecological Consciousness]*. Katowice.

Wódz, J. (1992) Effects of the degradation of the biophysical environment on mortality in Upper Silesia, Poland. *Society and Natural Resources* 5, 307–312.

Wódz, K., ed. (1990), *Problemy metodologiczne badań procesów planowych i żywiołowych w mieście [Methodological Problems of Examining Planned and Spontaneous Processes in Town]*. Katowice.

Wódz, K., ed. (1991), *Przestrzeń wielkiego miasta w perspektywie badań nad planowaniem i żywiołowością [Space of a Large Town in the Perspective of Research on Planning and Spontaneity]*. Katowice.

World Health Organisation (1987) *Air Quality Guidelines for Europe*, European Series No. 23. WHO, Regional Office for Europe, Copenhagen.

Zieliński, M. (1988) *Ruchy neopacyfistyczne w Polsce w latach 1983–1986 [Neopacifist Movements in Poland in 1983–1986]*. Warsaw.

Żmuda, S., Surmacz, A. and Zadrożna, J. (1988) Environmental threat to health of the Katowice agglomeration inhabitants. In *Conditions of Life and Existence of the Inhabitants of Upper Silesian Agglomeration* (ed. L. Frąckiewicz). Silesian Scientific Institute, Katowice, 173–198.

Znaniecki, F. (1938) Socjologiczne podstawy ekologii ludzkiej [Sociological bases of human ecology] *Ruch Prawniczy, Ekonomiczny i Socjologiczny* 1.

CHAPTER 5

ENVIRONMENTAL POLITICS IN THE FORMER CZECHOSLOVAKIA[1]

Andrew Tickle and Josef Vavroušek[2]

The roots of our deep ecological crisis lie in the political history of the past 42 years. The mutual relations among our people were equally deformed and distorted as were those between Man and Nature. (Moldan *et al.*, 1990: 9)

INTRODUCTION

Czechoslovakia, in common with the majority of Soviet bloc satellite states in central and eastern Europe, experienced a relatively rapid transition from over forty years of totalitarian rule to a fledgling democracy, beginning with the 'velvet revolution' of 17–27 November 1989. The day-to-day events of that initial transition period have been quickly captured and documented in both personal (Garton Ash, 1990; Urban, 1990) and meticulous historical accounts (Otáhal and Sládek, 1990). It has taken slightly longer, however, for more detailed analyses to be undertaken, identifying key causative factors underlying the nature and timing of the regime's downfall in Czechoslovakia (e.g. Wheaton and Kavan, 1992; Kabele, 1993; Holy, 1996).

Such accounts, in common with broader analyses of the end of communism in central and eastern Europe (e.g. Glenny, 1990; Schöpflin, 1993; Hobsbawm, 1994), describe a series of intertwining and cumulative economic, political and social factors that combined to question the legitimacy of the party-state, leading to its final swift fall from power. In the Czechoslovak situation, three main threats to the government have been identified: the increase in public criticism, economic difficulties, and events external to the country (Wheaton and Kavan, 1992: 24ff.) The latter were dominated by Gorbachev's reforms in the Soviet Union (*perestroika*) and the changes being wrought in neighbouring countries, notably Poland, Hungary and East Germany.

In common with other countries such as Hungary and Bulgaria (see Fisher, 1993; Persányi, 1993; Baumgartl, 1993; Mitsuda and Pashev, 1995; Enyedi and Szirmai, this volume), it has also been suggested that the gross environmental mismanagement of the former socialist regime, plus the activities of critical environmental groups and other dissidents, were significant contributory factors in the transformation of the Czechoslovak political system – both as catalysts for change and, in the case of environmental activists, as prominent players in the establishment of new democratic structures – at least in the early transition phases (Tickle, 1990; French, 1991; Slocock, 1991; Andrews, 1993; Carter, 1993; Fisher, 1993; Murphy, 1993). Such assertions have held wide sway (anecdotally) with key actors in the transition process and in certain fields of study (notably, and obviously, environmental policy: see e.g. Jancar-Webster, 1993 or Vari and Tamas, 1993).

However, few of these claims have been based on critical analysis or first-hand experience. As such, the pluralist concept of 'green revolutions' should be treated with some caution until it can be better tested against competing theories, particularly those of a structuralist, political–economic nature. Obviously, trying to ascertain the relative influence of the environment and environmental activists is of central importance in this chapter, given the overall scope of this research – the role of environmental issues in pre- and post-transition politics in Czechoslovakia. However, it must be noted that, even with the benefit of hindsight, the complexities of the transition process essentially dictate that any finer resolution of the dominant factors of revolutionary causation will still remain – to a large extent – empirically untestable and thus subjective and partial.

But before examining the validity of the 'green revolution' thesis, it is necessary to put the subject into context by also examining the history of Czechoslovak environmental policy and regulation prior to the events of 1989 and the success or otherwise of this framework in protecting the main components of the country's environment. This also calls for a brief introduction to the relatively short political and legislative history of Czechoslovakia.

Political history

Czechoslovakia was created as a state in 1918, out of the ashes of the Austro-Hungarian empire. By 1920 it included Bohemia, Moravia and parts of Silesia (these three areas forming the Czech lands) plus Slovakia (formerly Upper Hungary) and Ruthenia (later recovered by the Soviet Union in 1945). In the interwar period (Masaryk's First Republic, 1918–38) a liberal social democracy existed, before creeping Nazi occupation began in 1938 with Hitler's annexation of the Sudetenland (sanctioned by Britain and France as part of the Munich 'appeasement' package). After liberation by the Soviet Red Army in 1945, the last free elections took place in May 1946 with the Communist Party (Komunistická strana Československa, KSČ) winning a plurality (38 per cent) of the total vote,[3] although a coalition with the Social Democratic Party was required to give the KSČ a working majority in the national assembly (Bankowicz, 1994: 148). However after the Soviet-inspired coup of February 1948, the KSČ gained complete control – acting through the 'multi-party' National Front (Národní fronta) – and thereafter Czechoslovakia's short-lived democratic tradition was suppressed until the next free elections in June 1990.

Throughout this whole period (1948–89), despite a few hiccups (notably the radical reform programme of the 1968 'Prague Spring'), the KSČ concentrated and centralized its powers, strengthening its totalitarian grip on the country. This was particularly evident in the 'normalization' period of the 1970s,[4] when the population's acquiescence was gained by the state's acceptance of private non-compliance with the regime's ideology provided the public behaved *as if* they were compliant. This has been described as the 'as-if' game and led, *inter alia*, to a mental and physical[5] 'inner emigration' and 'a monumental mental corruption that left few untouched' (Wheaton and Kavan, 1992: 9–10). In addition, the 'pill' of normalization (primarily involving a tripartite package of savage party and institutional purges, hegemonic control of public discourse and mild economic reforms: Wheaton and Kavan, 1992: 9–10) was sweetened by providing a relatively high standard of living (bought with the latter, short-term reforms). As Kabele puts it:

> Nearly all citizens passively accepted anarchy masquerading as a powerful communist country, the state bureaucracy, and the security forces. In return for their loyalty, they were provided with a series of socialist contrivances based on the principle of officially organized and unofficially tolerated redistribution processes. . . . Society paid for these genuinely comfortable social certainties with the constant pressure of lawlessness and a forced abandonment of its ideals. Communism as an end in itself was quietly forgotten in socialist Czechoslovakia sometime around the early '70s. (Kabele, 1993: 767).

Unfortunately, part of the cost of providing this unwritten social contract was the unsustainable exploitation of Czechoslovakia's natural resources. As it was simply put by Moldan (1990) at the outset of this chapter, this unhappy political history (post-1948, but particularly 1969–89) forms much of the basis for the country's severe environmental problems.

The legislature

Until 1968, the country had a single parliamentary body (i.e. a unicameral legislature), the National Assembly. After the 'leading role' of the KSČ was enshrined in Article 4 of the constitution enacted in May 1948, the Assembly had few significant powers and these only became gradually apparent in the period after the new constitution of 1960, climaxing in the Prague Spring in 1968 (Norton, 1990). This brief period (in 1968) of true parliamentary activity was snuffed out with the Soviet invasion that followed the attempted reforms. However, with federalization (one of the sole remaining reforms enacted from the radical 1968 programme) a bicameral legislature was created, incorporating the House of the People and the House of the Nations. The legislature, together with the unicameral republican parliaments (the Czech and Slovak National Councils), remained in this guise until the dissolution of federal structures at the end of 1992.

As this chapter goes on to describe later, once the single-party system had been irreparably broken, new systems of environmental protection could be introduced alongside fundamental economic reforms, albeit with varying degrees of success.

This is still an ongoing process, although the impetus for environmental reform has been slowed since the secession of Slovakia from the former federal state on 1 January 1993. This date forms a convenient endpoint for this current analysis, although some comments are offered on the likely success of future environmental strategies and policies in both the Czech Republic and Slovakia – a future strongly related to the ability of environmental groups (either as social movements, environmental NGOs or political parties) to compete in the new style of politics.

ENVIRONMENTAL PROTECTION UNDER THE COMMUNIST SYSTEM

We can be sure that even communists personally prefer clean air or water to that which is polluted, healthy trees to the cemeteries of dying forest ecosystems, or healthy children compared to children beginning their lives with genetic defects, pulmonary diseases, allergies or even cancer. But in essence, the whole nature of the communist totalitarian regime – based on narrow-minded Marxist–Leninist dogmas[6] – led inevitably, *inter alia*, to severe environmental degradation.

This latter statement reinforces the perception of other commentators that eastern European citizens (in this case, in the Soviet Union and East Germany) probably view 'both environmental deterioration and poor consumer goods supply . . . as symptomatic of the pervasive inefficiency and skewed priorities in the economic sphere. Environmental deterioration is simply an additional burden, a reflection of the unresponsiveness of the political economic system to popular demands and needs'(DeBardeleben, 1985: 38).

DeBardeleben's analysis also suggests that although the practice of Marxism–Leninism as a guiding doctrine generally did have adverse effects on the environment, the social problems that environmental deterioration presented challenged extant interpretations of Marxism–Leninism and, on occasion, caused doctrinal re-evaluation. However, to pursue that analysis further, it seems unlikely that any such re-evaluation significantly altered the overall impact of the party-state on the environment, at least in Czechoslovakia. This may, to some extent, reflect the more obdurate nature of the KSČ (especially in the later years of normalization) compared, for example, with the relatively freer policy debate in the Soviet Union (DeBardeleben, 1985: 56ff.).

Thus we continue to adjudge the central reason for environmental degradation to be directly connected with the 'leading role' of the Communist Party, even if in Czechoslovakia the KSČ was not the only officially recognized party. In fact, in Czechoslovakia there had been five 'official' parties making up the Národní fronta,[7] compared with Romania, Bulgaria and the former Soviet Union, where the 'true' one-party system existed. But the roles of the other parties were very small, if any: all the main decisions were generally made by the Central Committee of the Communist Party of individual countries, usually directly influenced by Moscow.

The consequences were clear: even if in theory there was 'the division of powers' – legislative, executive and judicial – in practice all these powers were concentrated in the hands of the same people, the KSČ. The system had no effective system of checks and balances. The same group of people had been setting the legislation – including a number of environmental protection laws, directly managing factories serenely violating these laws, and directly controlling environmental protection institutions as well as the 'independent' judicial system. Thus it could be said simply that – given its history – the communist system could not operate without producing violations of human rights, an inefficient economy and ecological catastrophes.

This stands in stark contrast to the near mantra-like assertion of Marxism–Leninism that whilst 'improper natural resource exploitation is a result of the capitalist mode of production . . . a socialist economy necessarily pursues the wisest possible use of natural resources' (Pryde, 1972: 136). Rephrased in a more modern idiom, this suggests that private ownership puts its primacy in profits rather than meeting environmental quality targets whilst public ownership of the means of production allows for a more enlightened view to be taken, with social equity and social justice, including environmental safeguards, guiding decision-making. So where had *socialismus* gone wrong?

Problems at the macro level

From the outset it should be stated that the largest problem affecting the efficacy of environmental protection, in either the East or West, is that political priorities largely rest on the twin pillars of economic growth and military security, with social welfare (health, education, etc.) close behind.

It is plain that Soviet-type economies were too heavily tied to non-economic criteria (mostly ideological) and thus were unable to deal properly with the needs of either consumers or producers. Indeed the post-war economy of the eastern European region – especially in relation to resources – has been characterized as 'a kind of slash-and-burn policy' (Schöpflin, 1993: 227), whereby the system was kept alive by a series of resource 'injections' (in fact, mostly depletions) ranging from pre-war capital accumulation, depletion of natural resources (both renewable, e.g. soil and landscape, and non-renewable, e.g. mineral resources), failures to invest in infrastructure, and finally attempts to borrow from the West in the 1970s. Against this background of economic decay, it is clear that resources available for environmental protection were likely to be heavily circumscribed.

Furthermore, the system of the centrally planned (or command) economy did not – and actually could not (as the system was arranged) – take into account specific factors, crucially important for 'environmentally friendly' production and consumption. Natural resources were – in relation to Marxist analysis – economically worthless (as labour was seen as the only true source of surplus value) and thus unpriceable. The centrally dictated prices of all goods include only labour costs, not the scarcity of resources or the external costs of their conversion to goods such as wastes or pollution of air and water. Here convergence is again shown with the West, as both systems (centrally planned or market economies) have found it problematic to cost environmental externalities (Füllenbach, 1981: 105).

The structure of central and eastern European economies was also excessively oriented towards production processes that consumed prodigious amounts of energy and raw materials, with enormous outputs of all kinds of wastes.[8] This was strongly linked to satisfying the dictated – and usually distorted – production norms of the 'internal market' of the Soviet bloc, as controlled by the Council for Mutual Economic Assistance (Comecon or CMEA). Czechoslovakia, with 15 million inhabitants, had been producing, for example, more than 15 million tonnes of steel and nearly 2.5 million tonnes of cement per year (in 1988), and consuming more than 120 million tonnes of coal, most of it of very poor quality. A very similar situation often obtained in other central and eastern European countries, where 'socialist industrialization' based on politically motivated industrial location and the use of largely outdated technology also prevailed (see Wódz and Wódz, this volume).

After the occupation of Czechoslovakia by Soviet and other Warsaw Pact troops in 1968, it was becoming quite clear that the huge, and still growing, social, economic and environmental problems typical of most central and eastern European countries could not be solved within the framework of the socialist system, as some of the reform communists had believed at the beginning of the 1960s. As a number of experts were beginning to suggest clandestinely (e.g. Vavroušek, 1990: 10[9]), the only solution appeared to be a complex transformation of the political, economic and social systems of central and eastern European countries, with a strong environmental orientation.

In the cases of East Germany and the Soviet Union it has also been described how socialist commentators have sought to explain the deficiencies in their own systems in relation to the premises of the 'relations-of-production' and the 'forces-of-production' (DeBardeleben, 1985: 45ff.). The former premise describes the unique character of socialism in offering long-term solutions to environmental problems (see Pryde, 1972) but also emphasizes the key input of 'scientific' advice. In the case of Czechoslovakia, such advice – emanating from the various academic and policy institutes supporting individual government departments – was routinely disregarded in the 1970s and 1980s (see Kabele, 1993: 767) as the regime became increasingly isolated and unable to do more than offer 'sticking-plaster' reforms to what were, by then, major arterial wounds in the economy. In addition, as we later go on to describe in greater detail, this blatant disregard often led to the unintended and eventually counter-productive (in terms of regime legitimacy) politicization of the experts concerned, together with some of the social problems they addressed.

The second internally discussed macro-scale problem that DeBardeleben identifies are the 'forces-of-production', centring on the ambiguous nature of the scientific and technological revolution. This theme, whose roots go back essentially to the Enlightenment, also highlights an area of study within the sociology of science common to both East and West. Furthermore, the ambivalent utopian–dystopian aspects of science have been the subject of environmentalists' debate from the movement's earliest days, giving rise to deep divisions between deep ecologists and 'lighter green' thinkers. The Soviet penchant for 'science conquering nature', as evidenced by many Stalinist 'gigantomania' projects[10] did not always lead to an inherently dystopian construction of the science–nature dialectic in Czechoslovakia.

Instead the narrowness of the science base or its poor translation into policy was questioned instead, especially by ecologists and environmental scientists, who tended to advocate more holistic and interdisciplinary approaches.

Policy explanations

It has suggested that practical ('micro-level') failings or 'mistakes' of state social-ism within the arena of environmental protection can be attributed to three broad causes: policy deficiencies; inadequate scientific–technical knowledge; and 'improper attitudes' (i.e. poor management, ranging from policy-making elites to the populace as a whole) (DeBardeleben, 1985: 56). Clearly, these explanations are not exclusive to the socialist states of central and eastern Europe. Whilst science input to policy and personal and professional attitudes to environmental management are clearly important factors, they are not discussed here. Instead, the following analysis focuses briefly on the area of environmental policy and its administration (for more extensive summaries of Czechoslovak policy in the environmental sphere see Füllenbach, 1981; Hrbacek *et al.*, 1989; Moldan, 1990; Adamová, 1993; Andrews, 1993).

Although a number of laws relating to conservation were enacted in Bohemia and Slovakia in the nineteenth and early twentieth century, environmental legisla-tion as we know it today did not appear until the State Nature Conservancy Acts of 1955/1956 (Čeřovský, 1988: 25). In the following decades, legislation was essen-tially piecemeal, aimed at individual components of the environment (human health, soils, air, water and forests). Attempts had been made to integrate these laws into more over-arching legislation (i.e. some form of broad environmental protection act), starting in 1970;[11] this work was to continue until 1987 but never resulted in a new law, despite the provision of approved expert drafts (Madar, 1988). Currently, specific reasons for this legislative failure are not apparent.

A further problem was that within the legislature itself (i.e. the federal and republic parliaments) there were no specific environmental committees; this partly explains why the environmental legislation was generally obsolete. But even in the areas where the legislation was comparatively satisfactory, widespread and severe violation of laws had been officially tolerated. For example, the Water Act promul-gated reasonably high standards, but there were c. 2400 officially recognized 'exemp-tions' from this law. Most of these exemptions (one included the whole of Prague) were related to uncontrolled municipal sewage discharge (i.e. without wastewater treatment). Such an approach to law not only resulted in a degraded environment but also undermined the regime's environmental legitimacy and the whole concept of the 'rule of law'. This was despite the fact that (nominally) 'national committees' had wide-ranging powers to enforce swingeing fines on, or closure of, enterprises exceeding environmental standards (Hrbacek *et al.*, 1989: 148).

The use of economic 'inducements' to encourage environmental compliance is clearly analogous to the economic 'instruments' currently being promoted (with vary-ing success) in the market economies of western Europe (notably Sweden) and the USA. Indeed, the introduction of such economic levers in both capitalist and social-ist economies is tacit recognition of the difficulties of protecting the environment through either free markets or centrally planned directives alone. In the case of this enterprising Czechoslovak regulatory scheme several weaknesses were revealed. First, the likely charges and fines were built into the enterprise's budget, thus discounting pollution costs in advance; furthermore, the fines did not fully reflect the cost of the pollution and were never revised to take this, or other inflationary pressure, into account. For example, levels of fines for air pollution were set in 1967 (Andrews, 1993). Money collected from emission charges and fines was set aside for special environmental protection funds, clearly analogous to the market economy concept of hypothecated taxation. However, it has been suggested that a large proportion of the revenue raised was not spent on environmental projects (Andrews, 1993).

In addition to the lack of parliamentary oversight, and in common with most central and eastern European countries (see also Enyedi and Szirmai, this volume), there was a persistent lack of ministries or governmental institutions directly responsible for environmental protection. In Czechoslovakia, responsibility for the protection of different parts of the environment had been spread among a dozen or so federal or republic ministries,[12] lacking sufficient co-ordination. For all these institutions the protection of the environment was a secondary, subsidiary role: for example, the Ministry of Agriculture and Food was directly responsible for the amount of agricultural production, and the protection of soils and rural landscape. However, whereas the realization of the first role had been carefully controlled by the party ('fulfilment of plans'), the second role had been systematically underestimated As a result, soils in both republics have deteriorated through erosion, misuse of chemicals and poor management (Moldan, 1990; Carter, 1993).

The ministerial 'branch system' for the environment (Adamová, 1993: 51) was reinforced by the 'narrow departmentalism' noted as a basic feature of the totalitarian system (Moldan, 1990: 17). Indeed, this can be seen to work in two ways, with *neither* inducing positive features in relation to environmental protection. First, and primarily, environmental systems and problems usually cross political as well as physical boundaries. With departmentalism, under which the individual ministry's (and minister's) fiefdom were absolute, cross-sectoral responsibility or initiatives were virtually unknown. Secondly, the division of environmental responsibility over so many government departments and agencies meant that the endemic habit of *obezlička* ('passing the buck') also numbered environmental protection among its victims, despite the nominal existence of the official system of collective responsibility (Moldan, 1990).

Deficiencies in the administration of environmental legislation had clearly been noted by the former government, as evidenced by their attempts to create a more integrated approach (see also note 11). In 1971 an Environment Council of the Czech government was created to foster a more comprehensive approach, but this quickly degenerated into a 'talking shop' with little real power (Moldan, 1990: 21). A further, last-ditch attempt (in the face of increasing environmental problems) involved appending an overall environmental remit to the feared Ministry of the Interior, which became the Ministry of the Interior and the Environment in 1988 (Moldan, 1990; Adamová, 1993).[13]

International policy

In common with the other Soviet satellite states, Czechoslovakia participated in international policy in two spheres of influence. The first sphere was that of the CMEA states, where countries were linked by the multilateral co-operative Programme No. 1 (Socio-economic, organizational and legal and pedagogical aspects of environmental protection: see Madar, 1988: 79). This programme (begun in 1972) confined itself in the main to a largely academic review of environmental protection in the 'really existing' socialist states,[14] rather than addressing cross-border environmental problems. However, by 1988, increasing environmental problems on the Czechoslovak, Polish and East German borders (mostly related to forests killed by acidic air pollution) forced the first high-level (deputy prime ministers) trilateral meeting (on any subject) between the three countries.[15]

Although isolated bilateral agreements on water management had been signed between Czechoslovakia and West Germany (1970 – in fact with the Bavarian state) and Czechoslovakia and Austria (1967), international environmental co-operation with western states began principally with the *détente* process of the 1960s and 1970s.[16] Through the Helsinki Process (Conference on Security and Co-operation in Europe or CSCE) and its final accord (in 1975), a channel of East–West environmental diplomacy was opened up – occurring subsequently through the United Nations Economic Commission for Europe (UN ECE).[17]

The most significant outcome of the multilateral negotiations that followed was the creation of the UN ECE Convention on Long-range Transboundary Air Pollution (Levy, 1993: 81), adopted by 34 states, including the entire eastern bloc (bar Albania), in November 1989. The Convention and the protocols that followed aimed mainly at controlling and reducing air pollution contributing to acid rain and related problems. In 1985 Czechoslovakia signed the Helsinki Protocol of the Convention (commonly known as the '30 per cent club'), thereby pledging to reduce its emissions of sulphur dioxide by 30 per cent (from 1980 levels) by 1993. Although at the time of signature various plans were in hand that could help meet this target,[18] contemporary observers have suggested that the commitment was little more than a cynical attempt to legitimize the government's environmental record with the West.[19]

ENVIRONMENTAL DEGRADATION UNDER THE COMMUNIST REGIME

Although information on the state of the environment was often considered 'top secret' by the state and therefore strongly suppressed,[20] control began to be relaxed towards the end of the 1980s, linked to increasing *glasnost* in the Soviet Union and wider government commitments made internationally (see note 19). This allowed for the first comprehensive summary of Czechoslovakia's environment to be compiled and published, albeit on the margins of legality (Vavroušek and Moldan, 1988).[21] Since that date (and often using much of the same basic data), a number of authoritative reports have provided overviews of the state of Czechoslovakia's environment (e.g. Moldan, 1990; Federal Committee for the Environment, 1992; World Bank, 1992; Carter, 1993; Carter and Turnock, 1996). Whilst it is not proposed to review such detailed data here, it is, however, important to note how environmental problems became progressively acute and began to be perceived as social and political issues.

Although local damage from air pollutants had been noted in central and eastern Europe in the late nineteenth century (Stoklasa, 1923), it was not until after the Second World War that environmental damage began to be noted on a wider scale.[22] By the 1960s, the issue could be said to have been politically recognized, as the scale of the problem was such that environmental legislation was enacted to try and protect various media (air, soil, water). By the 1970s environmental problems had become acute and led to eight affected areas in the Czech Republic being designated officially as 'emergency areas'.[23] Clearly, under such circumstances, it is inconceivable that the seriousness of environmental problems had not passed into wider public consciousness.

Certainly, one did not need to be any kind of expert to realize that something was wrong with the living environment in Czechoslovakia. Some 4 million people (about a quarter of the population) lived in the most heavily contaminated areas. During the winter, when continuous smog conditions could prevail for weeks, children were forbidden to indulge in strenuous activity, playground time was curtailed and people retreated into their houses with their doors and windows firmly closed. Even having the window open just a fraction during the night would result in a throbbing headache the next day. People described industry – and thereby the government – as 'waging chemical war against their own people' (Charter 77, 1987).[24]

Such widespread public perceptions of the environment constituted a major challenge to regime legitimacy, requiring either active management of quiescence by the authorities ('palliative strategy'), or the deployment of direct measures to solve the underlying problem (Kabele, 1993: 769). The preponderance of managed acquiescence under 'problem-free' socialism meant that the environment (which could be asserted to have been one the few officially acknowledged social problems, along with housing problems, the divorce rate and women's unemployment: Kabele, 1993) became propelled forward into the claim-making arena by the politically active opposition and environmental groups, as described below.

THE ROLE OF ENVIRONMENTAL ACTIVITIES IN THE DOWNFALL OF THE COMMUNIST REGIME

In common with many green groups across Europe and North America, the Czech and Slovak environmental movements trace their roots mainly via a 'preservationist stream' (Eckersley, 1992: 39) to the romanticism of the eighteenth and nineteenth centuries (Kundrata, 1992). By the turn of the nineteenth century, a number of virgin forest reserves had been established in the Šumava mountains in South Bohemia (then part of Austro-Hungary) by the aristocracy. Furthermore, at the community level, numerous 'decorative' clubs had been formed, mainly concerned with landscape preservation. At the height of their popularity (before the First World War), membership of these clubs (numbering 378, plus their over-arching Union) is thought to have totalled c. 50,000 – mostly comprising the middle class and intellectuals (Kundrata, 1992). The early twentieth century also saw the general emergence of ecology as a scientific discipline, which in many countries, such as Britain (Sheail, 1976), increasingly served as a professional base and rationale for the nature conservation movement. Czechoslovakia was no exception to this trend and soon after the end of the Second World War, ecology was a flourishing discipline within many universities. This led to the existence of a large cadre of well-informed, environmentally conscious scientists and experts, whose central role in eastern European environmental protest has been noted (Waller, 1989: 308–309; see also below).

Thus by the time the KSČ assumed power, early forms of environmentalism were already well-established as an extra-state activity – born of the Austro-Hungarian Empire and then nurtured in the nascent civil society of the First Republic. With the adoption of scientific socialism, ecology as an academic discipline *per se* was not threatened but clearly its practical incorporation into state activities would have profound consequences. The first and least surprising of these was the forced dissolution of the decorative clubs in 1951. However, by 1958 Tis (Yew) – the first true nature conservation group – was formed, organized along similar lines to current voluntary ecological organizations (Kundrata, 1992). But this group and its successor organizations (see below) cannot be described truly as environmental 'non-governmental organisations' (NGOs) in the modern sense, as they were still tied, albeit often loosely, to the state *apparat*. As Waller has suggested 'it has been in the nature of the [Soviet-type political] system not to suppress such movements, but to channel and encadre them, if possible by setting up an officially sponsored movement' (Waller, 1989: 305).

Pre-1989 environmental movements

The movements, already characterized as largely preservationist in origin, can be divided into two basic categories: those organizations linked to the state (members totalling some 50,000), and independent, that is, illegal or dissident groups (participation countable in hundreds, at the most). Although the activities of some of the groups and their members overlapped, state-sponsored organizations largely addressed practical nature conservation tasks, whilst the independent groups tended to concentrate on more politically focused environmental activism. Refining this crude analysis, Vladimír Ondruš, a noted Slovak environmentalist, offered a four-fold 'streaming' of the ecological movement encompassing:

- 'traditional nature conservationists;
- nature conservation as an attempt at authentic life;
- commercialization of nature conservation;
- politicization of nature conservation' (cited in Kundrata, 1992).

To this Kundrata adds a fifth group comprising state conservation functionaries or *apparatchiks*.

The traditional nature conservationists were those largely working within the state conservation movements, descended from Tis, which by 1969 had split, spawning the Slovak Union of Nature Conservationists (Slovenský zväz ochrancov prírody, SZOP; later adding the term 'landscape' to become Slovenský zväz ochrancov prírody a krajiny, SZOPK), whilst leaving the original organization in Bohemia and Moravia. Tis was later abolished in 1979 (partially for political reasons: Kundrata, 1992), paving the way for the Czech Union of Nature Conservationists (Česky svaz ochráncu prírody, ČSOP) formed the same year.

Two other state-linked organizations existed, both aimed at youth environmental education (generally through conservation). These were the Czech Brontosaurus and the Slovak Strom života (Tree of Life) movements, linked to the Socialist Union of Youth (Socialisticky svaz mládeže, SSM – part of the government in the guise of the Národní fronta). Set up in the wake of the 1972 UN Stockholm environment conference, Brontosaurus' and Tree of Life's activities mostly involved summer work camps, although, like certain sections of SZOPK and ČSOP, they later became more politically focused (see below). Nevertheless, it has been suggested that involvement in the summer camp programmes (dating back to 1963) could often be transformative – adding core intrinsic values that maintained long-term political commitment; many of the leading activists of the late 1980s and 1990s had attended such camps in their youth (Kundrata, 1992).

The second stream of conservation activity described by Ondruš can be seen partly as a response to the post-normalization culture of social apathy and alienation (Kundrata, 1992). Although such movements have elsewhere been characterized as 'indicating back-to-earth sentiments' or 'rural romanticism' (DeBardeleben, 1985: 37–39), these appeared to be concerned mostly with humanist values and the preservation of cultural diversity. This fits well with DeBardeleben's further remarks that 'environmental deterioration may evoke disillusionment with urban, industrial, anthropocentric values' (1985: 37–39). Clearly, such anti-industrial sentiments invoke a clear challenge to the project of modernity, as envisaged by Marxist–Leninist scientific socialism. Indeed, Kundrata (1992) defines the attitudes of such conservationists as 'coherent with post-modern streams of global thinking'. Groups such as this, which included the Bratislava town branch (*mestský výbor*, MV) of SZOPK, also concerned themselves with human welfare in the domestic and urban environment – an activity that brought them into direct conflict with the regime.

The third commercial 'stream' identified by Ondruš relates almost entirely to environmental consultancy activities that sprang up with the post-revolution introduction of the market economy. Although this has created clear tensions with the more traditional, altruistic conservationists (Kundrata, 1992), this grouping is not discussed further here. Instead we wish to focus more intently on the fourth, politicizing stream of conservationists, who were most directly involved in the environmental challenge to regime legitimacy in the decade prior to the velvet revolution. However, a great deal of overlap existed between the various streams of environmental activity, particularly as the subject of the environment became increasingly politicized throughout the 1980s and the power of the state to control criticism waned in the immediate years before the revolution.

The environmental challenge to the regime

In the 1980s severe and continuing environmental deterioration – with few indications of improvement – was so evident in all central and eastern European countries that the environmental consciousness of people awoke, especially in the most polluted regions of coalmining, metallurgy and power plants, such as in northern Bohemia, Silesia in Poland, southern East Germany or the Donetsk regions of the former Soviet Union, and large urban areas, including Prague.

From this point of view, it is not surprising that the political connotations of environmental problems were not lost on the human rights dissident group Charter 77 either, although other sources have indicated that Charter's addition of peace and ecology activities to its core cause of human rights may have stemmed from pressure from the peace movement in western Europe in the early 1980s (Waller, 1989: 311). In fact, soon after their eponymous inception in 1977, Charter had already been active in drawing attention to environmental abuse – issuing a document questioning safety in nuclear power stations in 1978 (see Prečan, 1990: 393). Although the number of Charter signatories who were also active environmentalists could literally be counted on the fingers of one hand, Charter maintained a relatively steady output of ecological statements over the thirteen years of its opposition period.[25] The crossover Chartists/environmentalists really represented the 'tip of the iceberg' underneath which was a complex web of links between Charter, ecological groups and individual activists, whose work fed into one another's activities as and when required. Within this nexus, Waller (1989: 316) has supported the notion of a central 'aggregating role' for Charter; however, in terms of pure environmental dissidence in the latter half of the 1980s, this is questionable given the higher profile of other groups (e.g. SZOPK MV Bratislava) on key issues.

All over central and eastern Europe in the same time period, new environmentally oriented NGOs emerged and grew up rapidly. They organized themselves to fight against huge projects endangering the environment (e.g. the Gabčíkovo–Nagymaros water dams system on the Danube: see Enyedi and Szirmai, this volume). The Danube dams scheme and other regional 'investment' projects (see note 10) were also instrumental in the gradual politicization of the more traditional conservation groups such as SZOPK, ČSOP and Brontosaurus. Early battles to save the mead (unique floodplain) forests of the Danube and southern Moravia, or to prevent an international motor-racing circuit being built in the forest surrounding Brno, were unfortunately lost (Kundrata, 1992), although the public support that the activists gained during these campaigns gave some indication of the increasing currency of environmental issues within a wider constituency. By the late 1980s, however, a number of small but significant victories had been won.[26] One particular campaign method, organized by the Brontosaurus movement, was that of open public meetings on 'hot topics' described thus by Boužková (1989: 9):

It is our new way of fighting unsuitable projects and it is rather efficient. You get to know who is connected with the project and what the background is. Mostly it is the first truthful information after gossip about the issue. It allows journalists to write about it – it is much easier for them to come there than to run from one person to another asking them questions. And surprisingly all the invited ministries and enterprises send their representatives there.

The central involvement of professional ecologists in such debates underlines the prominence given by the environmental groups to scientific rationality, and more broadly supports the noted increase in expert opinion expressed in environmental dialogue in pre-1989 eastern Europe (Waller, 1989: 308). The pre-eminent group in Czechoslovakia in this respect was the Ecological Section of the Biological Society of the Czechoslovak Academy of Sciences (Ekologická sekce Československé biologické společnosti při, ČSAV), which from its founding in 1979 aimed to collect and analyse information describing the deterioration of the natural and human environment, factors influencing the quality of the environment, and the social, economic and political impacts of these changes. All this information had been hidden by the communist regime as 'secret' or even 'top secret'.

Akin to the 'arms-length' relationship between Brontosaurus and the centralized Socialist Union of Youth, the Ecological Section was generally able to manipulate its relationship with the monolithic Academy of Sciences in its own favour. In its final guise, the group consisted of a network of over 400 scientists, mostly working in various scientific institutes of the Academy, giving good access to national and international research data. This unprecedented 'database' of information led to the compilation of the first (preliminary) report on the state of the Czechoslovak environment in 1983 (see Csepel, 1985). Originally commissioned by the government, a copy was quickly leaked to Charter 77, which then forwarded its own accompanying analysis to the government (Prečan, 1990: 244–246) and to the western press,[27] underlining the embarrassing fact that the environmental dissidents had a deeper understanding of the scale of environmental problems than the ruling Communist Party. Although extant copies of the text were seized and destroyed (see also note 21) and contributing authors harassed, the Ecological Section survived relatively unscathed. Indeed, the involvement of so many scientists from state institutions in the Ecological Section made it difficult for the government to close off such channels of communication (Wheaton and Kavan, 1992: 29). Furthermore, the repetition of such material in the official journals of the nature conservation organizations (e.g. *Nika*, the journal of the Prague town branch of ČSOP) also proved uncomfortable for the regime.

Four years later another group of experts, this time from the Bratislava branch (MV) of SZOPK, released a long and damning report, *Bratislava nahlas* (Bratislava aloud), describing the state of the city's human and physical environment (see Stansky, 1988). Although by this time (late 1987) criticism from independent and officially recognized ecological groups had increased in both tone and volume, the detailed nature of the SZOPK critique caused a swift crackdown, with the editor of the report being summoned on criminal charges and other authors being threatened. The public sphere was also now more open in terms of the state's response: the report was dignified by an attack on it from the Slovak Communist Party daily *Pravda*, which described it as an attempt by 'opposition groups to destabilize efforts towards an economic and political revitalization of the dynamic development of our socialist society'.[28]

Whilst describing *Bratislava nahlas* as a subversive 'hijack [of] Czechoslovak *perestroika*'[29] was a typical over-reaction, *Pravda* was quite correct in identifying the report as useful ammunition for 'anti-Communist and anti-Czechoslovak centres [abroad]' (Stansky, 1988: 26) and in suggesting that 'ecological problems and those of the environment have also their political aspects. Anti-Communist propaganda is now attempting to use ecological arguments in its struggle against socialism' (Stansky, 1988: 26). Indeed, in the late 1980s, the ecological movement had often provided a home for those who wished to engage in more overt political activity, but who felt it wisest – for the time being – to cloak it with a green mantle.

In the same year as *Bratislava nahlas* was published (1987), nearly 300 citizens in the Chomutov district sent a petition protesting against poor local environmental conditions to the Czech Prime Minister.[30] Thus, because of perceived weakening (or openness) in the government and the growing seriousness of the environmental threat, ecological opposition was taking on a more open, mass-based character. By 1988, the political opposition in general was emboldened to leave behind narrow protest appeals (largely circulating in limited opposition circles as *samizdat*) as the main form of activity, in favour of large-scale petitions and open demonstrations. Although the particular petitions and demonstrations that caused the greatest challenge to the regime generally related to calls for religious and political freedoms (see Wheaton and Kavan, 1992: 24–30), environmental issues became a later target for public anger.

Thus in the final days before the 'velvet revolution' began, a large two-day demonstration in Teplice focused on environmental problems (11 and 13 November 1989: see Tickle, 1990: 18) and a smaller march in Prague on 15 November, protesting about the likely damage to the city's Stromovka Park by new road plans, was dispersed by riot police.[31] Such activities were clearly prefigured by the emergence of many new independent environmental groups (mostly Prague-based) in the preceding year or so. These included the Independent Ecological Group and its successor, the Ecological Society (both closely connected to Charter 77, with the latter being run in conjunction with the unique *samizdat* ecological journal, *Ekologicky Bulletin*[32]); the Prague Mothers (Pražské Matky) – a women's group focusing mainly on health and children's issues); Children of the Earth (Děti Země) – styled partially on the western green group, Friends of the Earth; and Hnutí Duha (Rainbow movement) – a Brno-based student group favouring more direct action, taking some of its inspiration from the international activist organization Greenpeace.

The pattern of such demonstrations, and the typically crude repressive response of the state to them, foreshadowed the student march in central Prague on 17 November 1989, which culminated in the so-called *masakr* (massacre) or beatings. It was clearly this act (now thought to have been caused by *provocateurs* – possibly linked to the KGB) which precipitated the public outrage (expressed in strikes and city-centred mass demonstrations) that led to the final collapse of the regime.

Environment actors in the political transition

Although some sources have pointed to the decisive part played by other social groupings in the revolution (setting aside the over-arching category of 'dissidents'), such as students (Wheaton and Kavan, 1992), actors and artists (Urban, 1990; Holy, 1996), it is also clear that environmentalists played a significant role in the growth, organization and politics of the new 'official' opposition.

In Prague and the Czech Republic, opposition centred on the swiftly formed Civic Forum (Obcanské Fórum, OF), which acted as an umbrella group for dissident groups and other civil initiatives, including environmentalists. Indeed, one of the eighteen founding members (Josef Vavroušek) was the co-chair of the Ecological Section, whose previous activities had led to extensive cross-fertilization of ideas between the political opposition and environmental thinkers.[33] Vavroušek quickly assumed a prominent role within Civic Forum, chairing the 'Programme commission' responsible for strategic policy development (Otáhal and Sládek, 1990: 490). It is not surprising, therefore, that in Civic Forum's first clear elucidation of its overall demands ('*Co chceme*' – What we want: see Wheaton and Kavan, 1992: 206) environmental protection and values featured among the seven major topics covered.[34]

The prominence of the environment on the opposition agenda did not stem solely from elite, idealistic values or green entryism but closely mirrored public opinion. Surveys taken just prior to the publication of OF's programme showed the environment to be one of the major social problems identified by the public (see, for example, Wheaton and Kavan, 1992: 220). Neither was Civic Forum alone in its astuteness in responding to environmental concern as, by the time of the first elections (June, 1990), most other political groupings had promised ecological initiatives as part of their manifestos (Jehlicka and Kostelecky, 1995: 214).

In Slovakia, the role of environmental actors was more significant. Here almost no dissident groups existed (with the exception of Roman Catholics working in deep illegality),[35] and thus leading personalities within SZOPK (especially the Bratislava town branch: see Kundrata, 1992) became the backbone of the new democratic force, Public Against Violence (VPN – Verejnosť proti násiliu). In addition, the long-established countrywide network of SZOPK branches also helped speed the spread of VPN outside Bratislava (in the Czech lands this process had largely occurred through theatre and student networks). Again, the prominence of key environmentalists within VPN led to 'absolute guarantees of the right to a healthy environment' being one of the twelve central demands of the combined opposition in Slovakia (Citizens' Initiatives, VPN and the Co-ordinating Committee of the Slovak Universities: see Wheaton and Kavan, 1992: 215).

Thus although a large proportion of the most well-known Czech and Slovak environmental activists quickly became involved in the political opposition, many other grass-roots activists – either individually or in local organizations[36] – quickly seized the opportunity to protest, publishing commentaries on the events of 17 November linked with demands for political change and new ecological initiatives. Although groups such as OF and VPN had led the way in voicing open criticism of the regime, the dangers associated with such lesser criticisms should not be under-estimated. Even at this stage of the 'revolution', it was far from clear that the regime would not cling on to power and then later purge those that had dared to challenge it so openly.

Other environmental opportunists also surfaced. The Austrian office of Greenpeace was quick, among the general confusion, to enter the political fray, setting up its anti-nuclear stall from an enormous campaign bus on Wenceslas Square. Here, among the nightly crowds, they distributed anti-nuclear literature, together with stickers bearing an image of the half-completed Temelín nuclear power plant, the words 'Stop ČSSRnobyl!' and the Greenpeace logo. The novelty of such western icons combined with anti-state overtones clearly appealed to the youth of Prague, who liberally plastered the stickers all over the capital, probably regardless of their own views on the Czechoslovak nuclear power programme. In contrast, earlier that year on Wenceslas Square a number of Austrian Greenpeace activists had been arrested and summarily deported for hanging a banner with a similar message down the front of the National Museum.

Unsurprisingly, ecological concerns quickly became formalized with the founding of a Green Party in Prague on 21 November. This was the first political party founded after the velvet revolution (Jehlicka and Kostelecky, 1995). Unfortunately, it soon transpired that this was further opportunism – this time being practised by activists of dubious origin, including the StB (secret police). Outside Prague other green parties sprang up without such problems, although – with the exception of Slovakia – the party failed to attract the most well-known environmentalists to their ranks, most activists preferring to work within the OF/VPN coalition or maintain a supra-political role (Jehlicka and Kostelecky, 1995). This absence of legitimating figures, together with the accusations of communist links, fatally wounded the Green Party's electoral aspirations, except in Slovakia, where a number of former leading SZOPK activists later became parliamentary deputies.

After the final collapse of the old regime and the installation of the interim government 'of national reconciliation' on 10 December, the question of the environment still maintained a key place in political dialogue, featuring prominently in both Havel's presidential New Year address and Czechoslovak Prime Minister Marian Čalfa's major 'state of the nation' speech to the joint federal assemblies on 27 February 1990.[37] However, as Wheaton and Kavan (1992: 129) have noted, major social problems such as ecology, health, housing and education were heavily underscored in such dialogue to prepare the nation for future hardships, in a manner clearly akin to Churchill's famous 'blood, sweat and tears' rhetoric.[38]

However, as the new democratic structures were established in the first half of 1990 (culminating in June with the first free elections), mass interest and political concern over environmental issues began to wane – evidenced partly in opinion polls by a steady decline in the Green Party's popularity (Jehlicka and Kostelecky, 1995: 213). The phenomenon, which has been explained in some quarters as 'the environment can wait for democracy' (Jehlicka and Kostelecky, 1995: 213), may also have been due to the creation of new government environment agencies, thus creating the perception that the problem was being dealt with (and by the 'right' people). Indeed, the staffing of these ministries – virtually entirely from the ranks of the pre-1989 environmental movement – also meant that a significant vacuum was created in extra-state environmental activity.

This vacuum persisted despite the fact that many new groups had sprung up in the wake of the events of November and December. Although a number of these new formations were initiated by former members of the pre-1989 groups, the profusion of the new groups and the alacrity with which they arose suggests a powerful latent desire to organize around environmental initiatives – long suppressed by the regime. Many of the new groups tended to focus on either local, 'NIMBY'-style topics or narrow sectional interests, such as recycling, energy conservation and efficiency (Böhm *et al.*, 1990), and as such did not generally gain widespread recognition or influence – at least at a national level. However, as the pre-1989 environmentalists were soon to be in charge of the country's environmental policy, the need for strong NGO opposition could be said to have been reduced for the time being.

ENVIRONMENTAL PROTECTION IN THE NEW DEMOCRACY: ACHIEVEMENTS AND FAILURES

The first step, necessary politically and environmentally, was to destroy the one-party system and the centrally planned economy. This basic reform was attempted in all the former socialist states of central and eastern Europe with very different results, but never with complete success. Even in Czechoslovakia, after the quiet and elegant 'velvet revolution', the former (or 'new') communists still influenced developments, especially in the economic field. Only the former *nomenklatura* – and the mafia members – had either the resources or sufficient management experience. But despite this, their main political power was broken. The transition period, from January to June 1990, was also fundamental for re-establishing the proper separation of legal, executive and judicial powers, as well as a multi-party parliamentary system and the foundations of a market economy.

National policy

In Czechoslovakia, institutional framework building had begun several weeks after the 'velvet revolution': the Czech Ministry of the Environment was created on 1 January 1990, the Slovak Commission of Environment on 1 April (with ministry status) and the Federal Committee for the Environment on 28 June of the same year (with federal ministry equivalence). The members of the Ecological Section, Bedřich Moldan, Vladimír Ondruš and Josef Vavroušek, had been respectively appointed as the first ministers (not without some apprehension – see Vavroušek, 1993: 88). Because of the federal character of Czechoslovakia, the Federal Committee for the Environment had been established as a collective body (a unique status in the federal government) consisting of all three ministers of the environment plus the deputy ministers of economy, foreign affairs, social affairs, foreign trade and public health, but with its own staff (about 170 people). This was an attempt to solve the environmental problems in their broader economic, social and economic contexts, and also to overcome the threat of Slovak secession. In its first year, the strategy was largely successful but after the decision of the Slovak environmental minister Ivan Tirpák (successor to Ondruš) to support the secession of Slovakia, the work of the Federal Committee became complicated by many obstructions.

Despite these problems, the new policy-makers had established a framework of new environmental legislation, compatible with (and largely modelled on) the legislation of the European Union (EU) and other developed countries.[39] The major pieces of new legislation included a waste management law (the first in the history of the country), a new air pollution act with stringent emission controls as well as air quality standards, a framework environmental law (which also included environmental impact assessment procedures), a regional planning law, and new nature and landscape protection laws. Many of these laws included transitional periods (typically between five and seven years) for adaptation to the new standards.[40]

All three governments (federal and two republics) also adopted a long-term State Environmental Policy (April 1990) and later the State Environmental Programme (May 1991), which comprised a 'wish list' of about 220 specific short-term projects covering all major environmental areas. The passage of this environmental legislation was not achieved without difficulty, however. First, all the parliaments (Czech, Slovak and federal) were under enormous pressure to create a new democratic system overnight, with major pieces of legislation (e.g. the new constitution) requiring considerable time for discussion and debate. Secondly, not all political groupings were convinced of the need for a binding web of stringent environmental laws, despite the necessity of harmonization with the EU. Although the environment did indeed have to 'wait for democracy', others felt that it could also 'wait for prosperity' (Jehlicka and Kostelecky, 1995: 230). Such feelings were perhaps best summed up by the so-called 'cake theory' of the forceful federal finance minister (later Czech prime minister), Václav Klaus. Here the economy is the 'cake' to be 'baked' first, followed by the 'icing' with the environment. Clearly, most environmentalists – drawing on concepts of sustainable development – directly rejected such views and the relationship between the respective federal ministries quickly deteriorated to a stand-off of mutual incomprehension (see also Slocock, 1996: 508ff). Thus in areas of legislation where the boundaries of economy and ecology crossed (e.g. ecological taxes, environmental liability within the privatization programme), battles for innovative policy-making were often lost to the economists.

After the second national elections of 1992, when the free-market economists of Klaus's Civic Democratic Party (Obcanská demokratická strana, ODS) were preferred over the more humanist, social-justice-oriented remnants of OF (prominent environmentalists joining the Civic Movement, Obcanské hnuti, OH), this process of economic ascendancy became largely complete. This is perhaps best illustrated by the formulation of the article of the new 1992 Czech Republic constitution dealing with the environment. This speaks only of efficient economic exploitation of natural resources and protecting 'Nature's wealth' (*sic*) (International Institute for Democracy, 1995). Although the evolution of this article's formulation may be partly traced back to the original (1990) OF electoral programme,[41] the phrasing could equally have passed for the rhetoric of the previous regime.

In Slovakia, environmental influence within the government (represented by VPN and the Greens) also declined, this time to the burgeoning nationalism of the Movement for a Democratic Slovakia (Poboda, 1998). At the second elections in Slovakia, the Slovak part of the Green Party lost its mandate, although its Czech wing, through its participation in the Liberal Social Union, had three deputies elected (Jehlicka and Kostelecky, 1995). As the same authors commented, the 'brave hopes of 1989' had 'fallen into near oblivion' (p. 208). At least, however, in Slovakia the environmentalists had won themselves a more fitting epitaph in the new state constitution – a well-balanced and comprehensive statement of personal and state responsibilities towards the environment (International Institute for Democracy, 1995).

International developments

Perhaps taking their lead from the general post-revolution notion of the country's 'return to Europe' and Havel's global presidential diplomacy, the new green ministries also became very active in international environmental affairs. Partly this represented a continued participation in UN environmental conventions on acid rain, ozone depletion and global warming – albeit with far more honest and realistic intentions. In addition, the new government sought to establish a new type of pan-European environmental dialogue, based on a return to more humanist and ecocentric values (Vavroušek, 1993: 98).

Thus in June 1991 Czechoslovakia organized the first pan-European conference of environmental ministers (with the additional participation of ministers from the USA, Japan and Canada) at Dobříš Castle, near Prague. Opened by Václav Havel, who strongly endorsed the ethical and philosophical basis of the meeting, the conference focused on three main objectives:

- to prepare and establish a European Environmental Protection and Restoration System, co-ordinating – on a voluntary basis – the efforts of individual European countries and organizations in the field; the first steps in this direction would be the regular conferences of European environmental ministers (the second was held in Lucerne, Switzerland, in 1993 and the third in Sofia, Bulgaria, in 1995) and the European Environmental Agency, which was to be established as soon as possible;
- to develop, implement and periodically revise the Environmental Programme for Europe, as the common framework for environment-oriented activities. This included specific programmes for the protection of the main European river basins (Rhine, Elbe, Oder) and the preparation (by the EU) of the first State of the European Environment Report (Stanners and Bourdeau, 1995);
- to seek human values and environmental ethics for sustainable development (or living) as the basis for such ways of life which can re-establish the harmony between humankind and nature.

In the main, the first two objectives were well reflected in the resolutions of the final conference document (see Vavroušek, 1993: 109–112) and have largely come to fruition since. However, it would be fair to say that a number of those initiatives were in train before Dobříš, such as the European Environment Agency. But as Vavroušek (1993: 102) later noted: 'very little progress has been made in the public discussion of human values and environmental ethics since Dobříš'. This largely reflects the dominance of 'realist' dialogue in international environmental diplomacy over the possibly naive (but worthy) aspirations of environmentalists who had helped bring down the communist regime. As Vavroušek put it: 'we had learned during the Velvet Revolution that nothing is impossible, and so the first truly pan-European meeting was taking place in newly liberated central Europe. Was there a place more appropriate to talk about basic human values?' (1993: 99).

And concomitant with the international *realpolitik* rejection of a moral basis for environmental dialogue (later underlined globally at the UN Earth Summit in Rio in June 1992), the social justice aspirations of the Prague-based intelligentsia who ran the revolution and the 'honeymoon' government of 1990–2 were swept away by the free-market ideologies of the new right.

Looking forward

So what has happened to the environment since the fall of the communist regime? The most obvious indicator has been that levels of major pollutants (particulates, sulphur dioxide and nitrogen oxides) have been reduced by 42–68 per cent during 1990–95 (Český ekologický ústav, 1996), partly because of new measures that have been taken for the protection of the environment, but mostly due to a decline in industrial production and GNP in general. But new threats have emerged. In some ways, perhaps the most worrying (from the point of view of environmental politics) is the fall of environmental issues from second position in the public's consciousness of serious social problems at the end of 1989 and beginning of 1990 to a situation in the mid-1990s where economic and social issues generally predominate. The citizens of Czechoslovakia and its successor states have also been the recipients of new opportunities, but also new social problems (crime, unemployment, etc.). There is also strong pressure to locate dirty industries and waste dumps on the territory of former Czechoslovakia and other central and eastern European countries, in attempts to become as rich as soon as possible without any environmental considerations (Greenpeace, 1991; Kruszewska, 1993), though this has now been tempered by OECD membership and the desire for EU membership (and hence harmonization with EU legislation). Much of the two countries' ageing industrial plant is still running, and therefore polluting, including a number of Russian-designed nuclear reactors that are unlikely ever to meet western safety standards. But perhaps the biggest political failure of the new-born democracy in Czechoslovakia was the fact that it was unable to avoid the loss of the formal federal state, despite the clear indications that referendums on the topic were likely to support continued union. Whilst the environmental ramifications of this separation are largely unclear at present, it must, however, be noted that the secession occurred peacefully (the 'velvet divorce') compared with the former Yugoslavia, with its human and ecological destruction.

The central and eastern European countries have found themselves at a crossroads: either to introduce the 'pure' market economy based principally on monetarist theories or some kind of socially and environmentally oriented market economy combined with systematic and dedicated efforts to find and implement sustainable living patterns. The choice has been made clear, at least for the Czech Republic, after the general elections of 1992 and 1996. The ruling coalition dominated by the Civil Democratic Party (ODS) chose a path of no experiments, instead simply introducing and maintaining a 'traditional' market economy based on the rights of the individual (translated by most into selfishness and hedonism) with low – if any – environmental consciousness. But environmentalists are maintaining the hope that the public may in time realize (or be persuaded of) the short-sighted nature of such policies and, together with western European countries, seek other, more sustainable ways of development. The likelihood of environmental NGOs being in a position to sway public opinion and policy-making towards such a goal is discussed below.

CONCLUSIONS

This chapter has attempted to outline an outwardly simple scheme of events, running from the communist *coup d'état* in 1948 to the 'velvet revolution' of 1989, throughout which environmental politics played an ostensibly minor, yet significant role. Following this green thread of Czechoslovak communist history necessitates the acceptance of several key assumptions. It is widely accepted that the political economy of the communist regime, acting through the doctrine of Marxism–Leninism, led to gross environmental mismanagement. By the early 1970s, nearly a quarter of the country's population lived in heavily polluted areas, principally in the largest cities (Prague and Bratislava) and regions adjacent to heavily industrialized areas (e.g. North Bohemia and the Silesian region of Moravia). By this time, in common with most European countries, Czechoslovakia possessed a large and professionalized conservation and ecology movement, largely concerned with the preservation of the 'natural' environment (landscape, fauna and flora, etc). Clearly, the cumulative economic development since the Second World War presented wide-ranging threats to that environment, thereby politicizing the conservation movement – or at least, a significant proportion of more forceful activists, operating at the movement's margins (in terms of the central *apparat*).

But it was not only landscape and biodiversity that were on the receiving end of communism's environmental policy failures: humans and the fabric of society itself were also affected. This not only made the environment a human rights issue (the right to fresh air, clean water, etc.), inviting the intervention of political opposition groups such as Charter 77, but also gave a direct political saliency to the problem. In addition, the increasing importance of green issues in Europe as a whole, as a social problem spanning both 'East' and 'West', meant that the environment had an added and wider geopolitical legitimacy as a discussion topic. As has been shown for other state socialist countries, the environment then became a site for significant and contested discourses, both among and between the Party (and all its organs), scientific experts and environmentalists (from state organizations to dissident groups).

It does in fact seem slightly ironic that the initial legitimization of the environment as an issue in the socialist states came about partly through Soviet attempts to find common ground within the CSCE conferences of the 1970s (and thus dissipate western criticism on human rights). The same CSCE process also spawned the Charter 77 movement, which, in the following dozen years or so, was the most active critic of the Czechoslovak regime and its human rights record, including environmental abuses. Indeed, it has been suggested that the activities of dissident groups in eastern Europe, such as Charter, have helped in the emergence of a recognizable environmental movement (Waller, 1989).

However, the opposite has also been argued for Czechoslovakia: that environmentalists, organizing diffusely on the margins of legality, in fact made political 'space' for the emergence of more clear-cut oppositional groups (students, actors, intelligentsia) that formed the backbone of the revolution (Kundrata, 1992). This suggests that, through their opposition to the regime in the pre-revolutionary period, environmentalists can be directly implicated in the maintenance of a civil society which otherwise largely hibernated throughout the communist years. In doing so, the best-known activists often gained 'unprecedented social credit' (Kundrata, 1992), perhaps suggesting why they came to occupy important organizing roles (either by initiative or nomination) in the transition period.

The basic argument made above – environmental protest as a vehicle for transition – has also been advanced elsewhere for other countries (Baumgartl, 1993) and suggests strongly that, despite the political suppression of civil society by Soviet-type political systems, a limited form of pluralism was able to catalyse a 'bottom-up' political movement which – with massive popular support – brought down a totalitarian regime. However, even looking through the most rose-tinted of spectacles, it is clear that protest movements associated with the poor state of the environment did not bring about a revolution on their own. The 'truth' as to whether the dissidents created space for the environmentalists or vice versa can remain a moot point; however, continuing the pluralistic argument, it is plain that the dissident movement (largely Charter 77) constituted a more direct political challenge to the regime. As a result of their occupation of the moral highground, Charter's leading activists (together with other able academics and experts, including environmentalists) inherited the mantle of political authority as the regime rapidly lost its last vestiges of legitimacy.

This brings us to structuralist arguments for change (i.e. was the regime 'pushed' by pluralist elements, or did it simply 'fall', weighed down by inexorable macro-scale political and economic forces?). Unsurprisingly, many authorities favour such structural factors in general explanations of 'the end of socialism' (e.g. Hobsbawm, 1994: 461ff.; Hirst, 1997), with the main problems being identified as economic decay – or more precisely, 'the exhaustion of the development potential of the state socialist mode of production' (Bryant and Mokrzycki, 1994: 2) – and the inability of the socialist states to reform politically. In addition, the unwillingness of Gorbachev to intervene in the Soviet satellite states was perhaps the most important predisposing factor in allowing the transformations to occur when they did. More specifically for Czechoslovakia, although such political and economic factors have been cited as major catalysts of the events of 1989, the role of public opposition has also been emphasized, including ecological protest (Schöpflin, 1993; Wheaton and Kavan, 1992).

It is clear that the environment occupied a special position in public dialogue, being one of the few social problems around which some form of contested discourse took place between various elements of society (notably experts and the environmental groups) and the state. The state could not avoid this: the magnitude of the problem was plain to see and the state had legitimized the topic through its own ideologically derived stance, both nationally and internationally. Furthermore, the state had also sanctioned the growth of a widespread environmental movement which, although not politicized in a wholesale manner, became a fertile ground for increasingly combative campaigning.

The character of environmental protest was not homogeneous, either in terms of its subject matter (though most often it focused on the threats to landscape from technocratic projects) or its philosophy. Part of the protest *did* relate to challenging the underlying assumptions and methods of centralized socialist planning, but it also exposed the economic and technological failures of the state, thus widening the critique significantly. In this sense, it becomes difficult to isolate a distinct environmental locus within anti-state dialogue as the width of the protest agenda permeated so many areas of policy responsibility. For this reason, the construction of a counter-factual test of the environment's significance (i.e. if the environment had not been a problem, how much later or sooner would the regime have fallen?) becomes an almost impossible task.

Nevertheless, it is concluded here that the environment can be seen as playing a significant role in both pluralist and structuralist interpretations of the regime's fall in Czechoslovakia. However, only time will tell whether the changes that took place in the country represent an early example of how environmental issues may challenge current notions of governability, or a small deviation along the road to the type of environmental politics currently predominating in western-style market economies.[42]

Other authors have referred to the prominent role of intellectuals (or the 'intelligentsia') in the revolutions[43] and their often temporary grasp of the reins of power as they were swept aside by neo-liberal economists (Bauman, 1995). The speedy elevation of environmental experts from the former protest groups into ministerial posts in Czechoslovakia and their equally swift decline illustrates this phenomenon well. The increasing exclusion of intellectuals from government between 1990 and 1992 served as a foretaste of the gradual narrowing of the overall governmental agenda to a centripetal core dominated by the supremacy of parliament, allied with an increasing disregard of public opinion or pressure.

Thus the future of environmental politics and policy will be strongly related to the ability of environmental groups (either as a social movement or political party, or both) to compete in the new style of politics. Thus far the activities of the Green Party do not provide much cause for optimism (Jehlicka and Kostelecky, 1995). In addition, although the re-creation of civil society has been a much vaunted goal in

Czechoslovakia (as in most other former communist states), the current political climate operates strongly against the expression of countervailing views by interest groups, especially those of a grass-roots, pluralist nature (which would often include environmental groups) (Wheaton and Kavan, 1992: 184). A vivid example of this intolerance was the listing in January 1995 of Greenpeace, Hnutí Duha and Animal SOS (an anarchist animal rights group) as subversive organizations to be monitored by state intelligence. As Wheaton and Kavan (1992: 184) perceptively observe, 'a mind-set of an adversarial character has been generated tending to regard opposing interests of whatever kind as illegitimate'. The similarities between the authoritarian response of the post-communist Czech government to Duha and Greenpeace and the former regime's treatment of environmental groups in general are not difficult to discern. Obviously, such an example does not bode well for the future of environmental politics in the Czech and Slovak Republics. Nonetheless, with the re-establishment of democratic processes in these two countries (despite current unease among some observers), it must be axiomatic to state that the conditions in which environmental issues may be raised within the sphere of civil society have been drastically improved. The continuing challenge for environmental politics now seems to lie mainly with persuading government and public alike of the continued legitimacy of the environment as a core issue for post-communist society.

NOTES

1. The material in this chapter largely covers events prior to the secession of Slovakia on 1 January 1993. Therefore the name Czechoslovakia and the term 'former Czechoslovakia' are used in preference to the more recently adopted Czech and Slovak Federal Republic (ČSFR). This, it is felt, is more consistent with the longer usage of the former name.
2. Sadly Josef Vavroušek (together with his daughter Petra) was killed in an avalanche in the Roháče mountains in Slovakia on 18 March 1995. The chapter was finalized after his death with the kind permission of his widow, Eva Vavroušková, and the advice of some of his former friends and colleagues. However, the views finally expressed in this chapter do not necessarily reflect the views of those who commented on previous drafts. Any errors are the responsibility of the remaining author (AT).
3. This desire for change through some form of utopian socialism appeared to be a significant feature in post-war Europe, ranging from popular support for communism in countries such as Czechoslovakia and Hungary (see e.g. Kopacsi, 1989; Glenny, 1990; Moldan, 1990: 15) to the surprise Labour landslide in Britain in 1945.
4. i.e. the imposition of Soviet-style 'norms' or standards of political control.
5. Characterized most commonly by the weekend and summer occupation of *chata*, small 'cottages' (some little more than glorified garden sheds) usually located within easy commuting distance of major towns and cities (see also Wheaton and Kavan, 1993: 9). Many families had access to such cottages; for those living in large, inhuman 'concrete city' housing estates, the *chata* provided a much-needed physical and mental safety-valve.

6. Together with others, such as DeBardeleben (1985), we seek to differentiate between Marxism–Leninism (as a continually evolving ideology or doctrine of the Soviet bloc) and Marxist social science theory. Clearly the two share wide epistemological roots but it is accepted here than the guiding principles of the socialist (i.e. Marxist–Leninist) state had long diverged from those of communism, as originally posited in Marx's writings. This view would obviously be denied by party ideologists, who would describe changed doctrinal interpretations as being synonymous with Lenin's interpretation of Marx (DeBardeleben, 1985: 7).

7. These comprised the Communist Party of Czechoslovakia (KSČ), the Czechoslovak Socialist Party, the Czechoslovak People's Party, the Slovak Revival Party and the Slovak Freedom Party. The latter four parties of the Národní fronta comprised the left-wing factions of pre-1948 political groupings (see Bankowicz, 1994: 151 for further details).

8. See Jänicke, M., 'Structural change and environmental impact', *Environmental Monitoring & Assessment* 12, 1989, 99–118 for an interesting East–West comparison of industrial intensities in various sectors.

9. This book was first available in *samizdat* form in June 1989 under the variant titles of *Životní prostředí a sebeřízení společnosti* (The Environment and the Self-management of Society) or *Péče o Životní prostředí v procesu sebeřízení společnosti* (Care of the Environment Within the Processes of Societal Self-managment). A copy of the book had been carried illicitly to London by one of the authors (AT) in September 1989 and was being prepared for publication when the collapse of the regime made it unnecessary.

10. This is not to suggest that projects of this kind are not also associated with western countries. Indeed, western multilateral development banks (e.g. the World Bank) have been commonly cited as encompassing a similar planning vision, especially in relation to projects executed in developing counties. Examples of neo-Stalinist gigantomania in Czechoslovakia include the Gabčíkovo–Nagymaros dams scheme on the Danube between Bratislava and Budapest, which generated enormous controversy on environmental grounds [see also 'Gabčíkovo–Nagymaros project: Hungarian misgivings', *East European Reporter* 1(1), 1985, 9–10; 'Unfinished past: the Gabčíkovo–Nagymaros project: 1953 and now', *East European Reporter* 1(3), 1985, 25–27; Enyedi and Szirmai, this volume; Persányi, 1993; Galambos, 1993], the Danube–Oder–Elbe canal scheme [Mrazek, P., 'Ekologie krajiny: k průplavu Dunaj–Oder–Labe', *Ekologicky Bulletin* 18, Říjen 1989, 16; SZOPK (1989) *Danube–Oder–Elbe Canal*. Mimeo, Bratislava] and the Nové Mlyny dam project [Kundrata, M., 'Francouzi pod Pálavou', *Veronica* rocník III, 4/1989, 22–23; Nečas, Z. *et al.*, 'Diskuse. Vypustíme Nové Mlyny', *Veronica* ročník IV, 2/1990, 25–31].

11. This began with a government decree (Resolution No. 80, April 1970) based on the document 'Conception of Environmental Protection in Czechoslovakia' drawn up by the then Federal Committee for Technical and Economic Development. The decree set in motion a series of working groups (working mostly under the Institute of Law, Czechoslovak Academy of Sciences) to draw up an integrated environmental law. These reported to the Presidium of the Academy of Sciences in 1980 with further studies being completed in 1987 (Madar, 1988).

12. These included at the federal level: the State Commission for Scientific and Technical Developments and Investments (this succeeded the Federal Committee for Technical and Economic Development, see note 11), the Federal Ministry of Agriculture and Food, the Federal Ministry of Mining, Heavy Industry and Electronics, the Czechoslovak Commission for Nuclear Energy, the State Planning Commission and the Ministry of Finance; on the level of the republics: the Ministry of Water Management and Forest

Industry, the Ministry of Agriculture and Food, the Ministry of Culture, the Ministry of Health, the Central Authority of Mining, the Ministry of Building and Construction, and latterly the Ministry of the Interior and Environment (Adamová, 1993).

13. The Ministry of the Interior was also responsible for the activities of the secret police or StB (Státní tajná bezpečnost). Whether this had any explicit link to the monitoring of ecologically related dissident activity is unknown.

14. See *Sotsializm i okhrana okruzhayushchey sredy* [Socialism and Environmental Protection] (Yuridicheskaya literatura, Moscow, 1979) and its German edition *Sozialismus und Umweltschutz* (Staatsverlag der DDR, Berlin, 1982) (Madar, 1988).

15. The meeting took place 1–3 March 1988 in Jelenia Góra, Poland, and agreed a number of joint initiatives and plans, none of which appeared to have been implemented. For further details of Czech and Polish environmentalists' response to the meeting see 'Independent Ecological Seminar at Gliwice', *East European Reporter* 3(2), 1988, 48.

16. Although Czechoslovakia – in common with most eastern European states – had boycotted the 1972 UN (Stockholm) Conference on the Human Environment because of disagreements over UN recognition for East Germany.

17. For a much fuller discussion of the CSCE negotiations and the role of the UN ECE, see Füllenbach (1985). Further details on the UN ECE's environmental initiatives can be found in Chossudovsky, E.M., *East–West Diplomacy for Environment in the United Nations*, (UNITAR, New York, 1989) (cited in Levy, 1993).

18. As part of the 1986–1990 Five Year Plan, a sum of £7 billion was allegedly set aside for environmental improvements, which would have included air pollution control projects (see 'Czechs plan cleaner air by 2000', *New Scientist*, 7 August 1986). By 1988 the main strategy to meet the 1993 target appeared to be building new nuclear power plants and some desulphurization measures. In relation to the latter, an attempt had been made to use Soviet desulphurization technology at the Tušimice power plant in North Bohemia, but the equipment never functioned properly. Additionally, in 1987 agreements were being made with West Germany over the installation of pollution control equipment, again in North Bohemia: see *East European Reporter* 2(4), 1987, 15. Official documents (although never promulgated at the time) in 1989 suggested, however, that the planned pollution control programme would not realize the 30 per cut, even by 1995 (Moldan, 1990: 62). This also would have been exacerbated by delays in the construction of new nuclear plants.

19. From interviews with Czechoslovak and other western government officials (who wished to remain anonymous) involved in the negotiations leading up to the Protocol. It may also be added, however, that involvement in UN ECE affairs also brought with it the commitment to provide various environmental data for the compilation of European overview reports, including emission totals for a wide variety of pollutants [e.g. United Nations, *Airborne Sulphur Pollution*, Air Pollution Studies No. 1 (UN, New York, 1984)] and politically sensitive figures on forest decline [UN ECE/UNEP, *Forest Damage and Air Pollution*. Report of the 1986 forest damage survey in Europe, UN ECE/FAO, 1987). This reporting requirement also had the secondary effect of loosening internal suppression of data and encouraging the slow development of professional information systems which could be accessed more widely (Moldan, 1990: 29).

20. Indeed a number of cases exist of citizens who were prosecuted and jailed for disseminating critical environmental information (usually under Article 98 of the Penal Code: 'subversion of the Republic'): e.g. Aleš Machaček, sentenced to three and a half years in 1977 [see 'Interview with Czech civil rights activist – Aleš Machaček', *East European Reporter* 1(2), 1986, 43–45]; two students, Pavel Křivka and Pavel Škoda,

jailed for between twenty months and three years in 1985 [see Ward, A., 'Young nature enthusiast on trial', *East European Reporter* 1(4), 1986, 38–39; Moldan, 1990: 32–33]. All were first offences. More commonly (and more latterly), authors of critical articles were subjected to varying combinations of harassment by the secret police, loss of professional privileges and status, censorship and restrictions on foreign travel (including within the eastern bloc).

21. A previous summary document from the same source (the Ecological Section of the Czechoslovak Biological Society within the Academy of Sciences) had been confiscated and destroyed after a copy had been leaked to Charter 77 and thence to the western press in December 1983. This document and others formed the basis of ongoing discussions between dissidents and concerned scientists and experts in the following years. See Charter 77 (1987) and also the 1987 *samizdat* report, *Bratislava nahlas* (Bratislava aloud) summarized in 'Pollution: the tale of Bratislava', *East European Reporter* 3(3), 1988, 26–30.

22. For example, by 1955 some 1200 hectares of forest in the Krušné hory (Ore mountains or Erzgebirge) were noted to be damaged by industrial emission, presumed to emate from the smokestack industries of North Bohemia, Saxony (GDR) and Upper Silesia (Poland).

23. These were Karlovy Vary-Sokolovo; Plzeň; Ústí nad Labem-Chomutov; Prague; Mělník-Kralupy; Hradec Kralové-Pardubice; Brno; Ostrava-Karvinná. The naming of these areas by government decree dated from as early as 1974.

24. This information is reproduced from Tickle, A., 'Ice cracks but the water is still polluted', *New Ground* 25 (Summer 1990), 10–11.

25. A crude content analysis of the main Charter bibliography (Prečan, 1990) shows that from 1978 onwards Charter usually issued up to two documents or statements per year relating to environmental problems (excepting three years: 1980, 1982 and 1984). This totalled fifteen formal documents over thirteen years from a total output of 565 documents (c. 3 per cent). The most oft-addressed issues were: the Gabčíkovö–Nagymaros dams controversy (3 documents); the ecological situation in Czechoslovakia (3); nuclear safety, including the Chernobyl accident (3) and air pollution problems (3). Interestingly, the year 1989 saw an unprecedented four statements, perhaps indicative of the increasing saliency of the environmental issue and its potential for putting pressure on an already ailing regime.

26. These included stopping the Krívoklátsko hydroelectric power scheme, preventing a new radio tower being built in the internationally recognized Pálava Biosphere Reserve and postponement of a cable-car scheme in the Krkonoše (Giant mountains) (see Kundrata, 1992: 15).

27. See for example 'Alarm over acid rain damage in Bohemia', *The Times* 5 October 1984.

28. See Piskorová, D., 'Nothing new under the sun', *Pravda* (Bratislava) 3 February 1988.

29. Limited reform attempts were being made by the party from 1987 onwards, associated with the new leader, Miloš Jakeš, and pressure from Moscow.

30. *East European Reporter* 2(4), 1987, 15; also described and analysed by Waller (1989).

31. 'Environmental protest in Prague', *Daily Telegraph* 16 November 1989; see also Urban (1990: 116).

32. For example in an open letter in 1989, Charter 77 spokespersons and the editor of *Ekologicky Bulletin*, Ivan Dejmal (also an original Charter signatory), combined with well-known Austrian anti-nuclear activists to petition Austrian and Czechoslovak leaders on a variety of energy-linked environmental issues [Hradilek *et al.* (1989) 'Petition', mimeo, Vienna/Prague]. This also parallels increasing international links being made by the environmental movement in the late 1980s. For example, in June 1989, the

Brontosaurus and Tree of Life groups, in conjunction with the international 'Greenway' network, European Youth Forest Action (a network of youth groups concerned with acid rain damage to forests) and the Dutch Milieukontakt Oosteuropa group, organized an international environmental youth meeting (the Bohemian Forest Ecological and Peace Meeting) attended by many foreign environmentalists. Unusually attended by the first (and last) communist Czech environment minister, it culminated in a forceful statement (signed on behalf of about 300 participants) sent to eastern European governments (see Tickle, 1989).

33. For example, on 6 September 1989, with a group of like-minded scientists, Vavroušek helped found the Circle of Independent Intelligentsia (Kruhu nezávislé inteligence, KNI). This group aimed at the 'rehabilitation of those European values which could help in bringing Czechoslovakia onto the path of democratic development' (Gabal *et al.*, 1989) by re-establishing the social responsibility of those engaged in scientific and cultural activities.

34. The other areas identified for political change were the law, the political system, foreign policy, the economy, social justice and culture.

35. Charter 77 had never been popular in Slovakia, possibly because of the group's disregard of Slovak national pride and ambitions. One source suggests that out of a thousand Charter signatories in 1977, only four were Slovaks (Ulč 1992: 28). The same author also states that the 'velvet revolution' was predominantly a 'Czech affair', a contention challenged both here and elsewhere, e.g. Urban (1990: 129–30).

36. For example, various local branches of ČSOP, the Green Club in Litoměřice, the newly formed environmental NGO umbrella group Zelený kruh (Green Circle), the Prague Mothers, students at Charles University (Prague) and youth groups in Teplice. Statements of these groups were collated in Petrlík, J. (ed.) (1990) *Ekoton.* Mimeo, ČSOP/Děti Země, Prague.

37. See *East European Reporter* 4(1), 1989, 56–58 and 4(2), 1989, 8–10, respectively.

38. A formal comparison with Churchill's famous speech was later made in OF's election programme: see *East European Reporter* 4(2), 1989, 20.

39. This was also part of a wider strategy to ensure the country could move towards membership of the EU as quickly as possible. Association status was soon granted (alongside Hungary and Poland) and an application for full membership was made in January 1996.

40. For more comprehensive summaries of the new legislation see Andrews (1993: 27–34) or Adamová (1993: 44–50).

41. See *East European Reporter* 4(2), 1989, 21.

42. This relates to the twin concepts of 'environmental politics as rupture' and 'environmental politics as continuity' developed by Welsh (1995). These arguments are developed further in relation to eastern Europe in the Conclusions.

43. See, for example, Isaiah Berlin in New Europe!, *Granta* 30, 148–150.

REFERENCES

Adamová, E. (1993) Environmental management in Czecho-Slovakia. In *Environmental Action in Eastern Europe: Response to Crisis* (ed. B. Jancar-Webster). M.E. Sharpe, Armonk, NY.

Andrews, R.N.L. (1993) Environmental policy in the Czech and Slovak Republic. In *Environment and Democratic Transition: Policy and Politics in Central and Eastern Europe* (eds A. Vari and P. Tamas). Kluwer, Dordrecht.

Bankowicz, M. (1994) Czechoslovakia: from Masaryk to Havel. In *The New Democracies in Eastern Europe: Party Systems and Cleavages* (eds S. Berglund and J.Å. Dellenbrant). Edward Elgar, Aldershot.

Bauman, Z. (1995) After the patronage state: a model in search of class interests. In *The New Great Transformation? Change and Continuity in East–Central Europe* (eds C.G.A. Bryant and E. Mokrrzycki). Routledge, London.

Baumgartl, B. (1993) Environmental protest as a vehicle for transition: the case of Ekoglasnost in Bulgaria. In *Environment and Democratic Transition: Policy and Politics in Central and Eastern Europe* (eds A. Vari and P. Tamas). Kluwer, Dordrecht.

Böhm, V., Eichler, J., Fibír, T. and Vatral, I. (1990) *Zivotní prostredí v Československu: Zelená Hnutí 1990*. ČSOP, Stará Boleslav.

Boužková, Š. (1989) *Brontosaurus Movement*. SSM, Zdarma.

Bryant, C.G.A. and Mokrzycki, E. (1994) Introduction: theorizing the changes in East–Central Europe. In *The New Great Transformation? Change and Continuity in East–Central Europe* (eds C.G.A. Bryant and E. Mokrzycki). Routledge, London.

Carter, F.W. (1993) Czechoslovakia. In *Environmental Problems in Eastern Europe* (eds F.W. Carter and D. Turnock). Routledge, London.

Carter, F.W. and Turnock, D. (1996) A review of environmental issues in the light of transition. In *Environmental Problems in Eastern Europe*, rev. edn (eds F.W. Carter and D. Turnock). Routledge, London.

Čeřovsky, J. (1988) *Nature Conservation in the Socialist Countries of East Europe*. Ministry of Culture CSR, Prague.

Český ekologický ústav, ed. (1996) *Statistická ročenka životního prostředí české republiky 1996* [Statistical Environmental Yearbook of the Czech Republic 1996]. Ministerstvo životního prostředí české republiky/česky statistický úrad, Prague.

Charter 77 (1987) Aby se dalo dychat [Let the people breathe]. Dokuement 33/87, mimeo, Prague [translated in *East European Reporter* 2(4), 15–20, 1987].

Csepel, A. (1985) Marxism and the ecological crisis. *East European Reporter* 1(2), 41–43.

DeBardeleben, J. (1985) *The Environment and Marxism–Leninism*. Westview, Boulder, CO.

Eckersley, R. (1992) *Environmentalism and Political Theory: Towards an Ecocentric Approach*. UCL Press, London.

Federal Committee for the Environment (1992) *Atlas of the Environment and Health of the Population of the Czech and Slovak Republic*. Geographical Institute of the Czechoslovak Academy of Sciences, Brno and Prague.

Fisher, D. (1993) The emergence of the environmental movement in eastern Europe and its role in the revolutions of 1989. In *Environmental Action in Eastern Europe: Response to Crisis* (ed. B. Jancar-Webster). M.E. Sharpe, Armonk, NY.

French, H. (1991) Green revolutions: environmental reconstruction in eastern Europe and the Soviet Union. *Environmental Policy Review* 5(1), 1–9.

Füllenbach, J. (1981) *European Environmental Policy: East and West*. Butterworth, London.

Gabal, I., Hlavatý, L., Jůna, J., Katětov, M., Kopecký, L., Kratochvíl, P., Pátý, L. and Vavroušek, J. (1989) Komuniké ze zakládající schůze Kruhu nezávislé inteligence [Communication regarding the founding meeting of the Circle of Independent Intelligentsia]. Bulletin KNI No. 1, mimeo, Prague.

Galambos, J. (1993) An international environmental conflict on the Danube. In *Environment and Democratic Transition: Policy and Politics in Central and Eastern Europe* (eds A. Vari and P. Tamas). Kluwer, Dordrecht.

Garton Ash, T. (1990) *We the People*. Granta Books, Cambridge.

Glenny, M. (1990) *The Rebirth of History: Eastern Europe in the Age of Democracy*. Penguin, London.

Greenpeace (1991) *Avoiding Western Mistakes: A Guide to Clean Investment in Eastern and Central Europe*. Greenpeace International, Amsterdam.

Hirst, P. (1997) *From Statism to Pluralism*. UCL Press, London.

Hobsbawm, E. (1994) *Age of Extremes: The Short Twentieth Century*. Michael Joseph, London.

Holy, L. (1996) *The Little Czech and the Great Czech Nation*. Cambridge University Press, Cambridge.

Hrabacek, J., Binek, B. and Mějstřík, V. (1989) Czechoslovakia. In *International Handbook of Pollution Control* (ed. E.J. Kormondy). Greenwood Press, New York.

International Institute for Democracy, ed. (1995) *The Rebirth of Democracy: 12 Constitutions of Central and Eastern Europe*. Council of Europe Press, Strasbourg.

Jancar-Webster, B., ed. (1993) *Environmental Action in Eastern Europe: Responses to Crisis*. M.E. Sharpe, Armonk, NY.

Jehlicka, P. and Kostelecky, T. (1995) Czechoslovakia: Greens in a post-Communist society. In *The Green Challenge: the Development of Green Parties in Europe* (eds D. Richardson and C. Rootes). Routledge, London.

Kabele, J. (1993) The dynamics of social problems and transformation of Czechoslovak society. *Social Research* 60(4), 763–785.

Kopacsi, S. (1989) *In the Name of the Working Class*. Fontana/Collins, London.

Kruszewska, I. (1993) *Open Borders, Broken Promises. Privatization and Foreign Investment: Protecting the Environment Through Contractual Clauses*. Greenpeace International, Amsterdam.

Kundrata, M. (1992) Czechoslovakia. In *Civil Society and the Environment in Central and Eastern Europe* (eds D. Fisher, C. Davis, A. Juras and V. Pavlovic). Ecological Studies Institute, London/Institut für Europäische Umweltpolitik, Bonn/ECO-Centre, Belgrade.

Levy, M.A. (1993) European acid rain: the power of tote-board diplomacy. In *Institutions for the Earth* (eds P.M. Haas, R.O. Keohane and M.A. Levy). The MIT Press, Cambridge, MA.

Madar, Z. (1988) Participation of legal science in the development of environmental research. *Environmental Policy and Law* 18(3), 76–80.

Mitsuda, H. and Pashev, K. (1995) Environmentalism as ends or means? The rise and political crisis of the environmental movement in Bulgaria. *Capitalism, Nature, Socialism* 6(1), 87–111.

Moldan, B., ed. (1990) *Životní prostředí České republiky [Environment of the Czech Republic]*. Academia, Prague.

Murphy, T. (1993) Enterprise, economics and the environment in eastern Europe. *European Environment* 3(2), 10–13.

Norton, P. (1990) A legislature in transition: the Czechoslovak Federal Assembly. *The House Magazine* 19 November, 7.

Otáhal, M. and Sládek, Z. (1990) *Deset pražských dnů (17.–27. listopad 1989). Dokumentace [Ten days in Prague (17–27 November 1989) Documentation]*. Academia, Prague.

Persányi, M. (1993) Red pollution, green evolution, revolution in Hungary. In *Environmental Action in Eastern Europe: Response to Crisis* (ed. B. Jancar-Webster). M.E. Sharpe, Armonk, NY.

Prečan, V. (1990) *Charta 77 1977–1989. Od morální k demokratické revoluci [From a Moral to a Democratic Revolution]*. ČSNL and ARCHA, Scheinfeld-Schwarzenburg and Bratislava.

Pryde, P.R. (1972) *Conservation in the Soviet Union*. Cambridge University Press, Cambridge.

Schöpflin, G. (1993) *Politics in Eastern Europe*. Blackwell, Oxford.

Sheail, J. (1976) *Nature In Trust: The History of Nature Conservation in Britain*. Blackie, Glasgow.

Slocock, B. (1991) *The East European Environment Crisis: Its Extent, Impact and Solutions*. Special Report No. 2109, The Economist Intelligence Unit, London.

Slocock, B. (1996) The paradoxes of environmental policy in eastern Europe: the dynamics of policy-making in the Czech Republic. *Environmental Politics* 5(3), 501–521.

Stanners, D. and Bourdeau, P., eds (1995) *Europe's Environment: The Dobříš Assessment*. European Environment Agency, Copenhagen.

Stansky, P. (1988) Pollution: the tale of Bratislava. *East European Reporter* 3(3), 26–30.

Stoklasa, J. (1923) *Die Beschädigung der Vegetationen durch Rauchgase und Fabriksexhalationen [The Damage to Vegetation from Exhaust Gases and Factory Emissions]*. Urban & Schwarzenberg, Munich.

Tickle, A. (1989) Radical call for ecological reform. *East European Reporter* 3(4), 43–44.

Tickle, A. (1990) The environment before and after the revolution. *East European Reporter* 4(2), 18–20.

Ulč, O. (1992) The bumpy road of Czechoslovakia's velvet revolution. *Problems of Communism* XLI(3), 19–33.

Urban, J. (1990) Czechoslovakia: the power and politics of humiliation. In *Spring in Winter* (ed. G. Prins). Manchester University Press, Manchester.

Vari, A. and Tamas, P. (1993) *Environment and Democratic Transition: Policy and Politics in Central and Eastern Europe*. Kluwer, Dordrecht.

Vavroušek, J. (1990) *Životní prostředí a sebeřízení společnosti [The Environment and the Self-management of Society]*. Academia, Prague.

Vavroušek, J. (1993) Institutions for environmental security. In *Threats Without Enemies: Facing Environmental Security* (ed. G. Prins). Earthscan, London.

Vavroušek, J. and Moldan, B. (1988) *Stav a vyvoj životní prostředí v Československu [State and Development of the Environment in Czechoslovakia]*. Mimeo, Prague.

Waller, M. (1989) The ecology issue in eastern Europe: protest and movements. *Journal of Communist Studies* 5(3), 303–328.

Welsh, I. (1995) *Risk, Reflexivity and the Globalisation of Environmental Politics*. SEPEG Working Paper No. 1, Centre for Social and Economic Research, University of the West of England, Bristol.

World Bank (1992) *Czech and Slovak Federal Republic Joint Environmental Report*. Report No. 9623-CS, Vols I and II, World Bank, Washington, DC.

Wheaton, B. and Kavan, Z. (1992) *The Velvet Revolution: Czechoslovakia, 1988–1991*. Westview, Boulder, CO.

ACKNOWLEDGEMENTS

The remaining author wishes to thank all those who helped him with friendship, hospitality, advice and information during many visits to Czechoslovakia and the Czech and Slovak republics, particularly Petr Zvára and Helenka Zvárová, RNDr Ing Václav Mejstřík CSc, Jindrich Tichý and Majka Tichá, Michal Marek, Jana Lihocká, Simona Boužková, Peter Tatar, Josef Vavroušek and Eva Vavroušková, Ivo Šilhavý, Jan Piňos and Eva Piňosová, Žora Pauliniová, Lubica Trubiniová, Hana Pernicová, Jiří Houška and Lída Houšková. I am also grateful to Petr Jehlicka for his comments on the chapter. This work was supported in part by the British Council and Greenpeace International.

CHAPTER 6

ENVIRONMENTAL MOVEMENTS AND CIVIL SOCIETY IN HUNGARY

György Enyedi and Viktória Szirmai

INTRODUCTION

In this chapter, we intend to give an insight into the environmental consciousness of Hungarian society in the period of transition from the state socialist system to a democratic, market economy system. The chapter has three parts. In the first part, we describe how environmental issues were formulated and handled by the state socialist system; in the second, we explain how environmental movements have developed since the 1970s; and in the third part we attempt to characterize the social actors of the environmental scene during the transition period.

We do not wish to present a detailed overview of the state of the environment in Hungary (see, for example, Enyedi and Hinrichsen, 1990; Brown, 1992; Hinrichsen and Lang, 1993). However, one of the foremost environmental problems in Hungary has been water pollution. Long-term monitoring of water quality has shown a striking deterioration during the last thirty years. Water resources originating within the national boundaries of Hungary comprise only 4 per cent of total surface waters. The Danube is the only river which carries water of significant quality. Its gravel bed serves as a drinking water resource for the most urbanized north-western part of Hungary (including Budapest). The water quality of the Upper Danube depends largely on the upstream countries (Austria and Slovakia). The Budapest agglomeration itself is the source of much pollution since most of the sewage from the two and a half million people reaches the Danube without biological treatment. Groundwater reserves, which are mostly in the Great Plain, are close to the surface and are heavily polluted. Thus many drinking water sources in the country are seriously threatened.

Air pollution affects 11.2 per cent of the country's territory, but the areas affected house 44 per cent of the population. The capital city suffers the most serious pollution, predominantly from gaseous pollutants such as nitrogen oxides (NO_x) caused by traffic. The situation in the traditional industrial regions has improved as a consequence of the massive decline in heavy 'rust-belt' industries.

Protection of the population against pollution is poor. The average citizen is not well-informed, the control of food quality in respect of incorporated hazardous pollutants is not adequate and the dumping of hazardous wastes in this densely populated country is not properly regulated (Persányi and Lányi, 1991). It also seems clear that environmental deterioration contributes to the strikingly high death rate of the Hungarian population. But despite this, neither the citizens nor the authorities accord environmental problems any real importance. In this respect, the collapse of the state socialist system has not yet resulted in a fundamental change in the handling of environmental issues. New actors continue to play the old drama (see Szirmai, 1993).

ENVIRONMENTAL ISSUES IN A SOCIALIST SYSTEM

In traditional (pre-modern) Hungarian thinking the environment was God's donation to mankind to be used for mankind's own purpose (Péter, 1987). The notion that nature was a condition of the operation of society but not in itself a social feature legitimized the exploitation of natural resources. Thus Marxist views on society's domination over nature were, in some respects, closely aligned with earlier traditional interpretations (Enyedi, 1987; Szabó, 1989).

The centralized state socialist authorities had an interest in the total relegation of environmental factors. In the 1950s the political authorities realized their ideological and economic interests through the concentration of resources, both geographically and sectorally. They achieved the aims of forced industrialization by channelling all resources, including natural resources, into industry (see Wódz and Wódz, this volume). The centralized command economy that operated without any market or price mechanisms drew freely on natural resources and paid almost no attention to the social costs that resulted. Such an economic system could more easily conceal the limits of productivity and the problems of efficiency (or lack of it).

A limited assertion of environmental arguments was achieved only in the 1970s and 1980s (Enyedi and Zentai, 1986). The government first set up an official body for environmental protection, the National Environment and Nature Protection Office (OKTH), in 1977. However, the office was not given real power, nor was it built into the centralized decision-making mechanism. It never had the same standing as the bodies directing economic processes, such as the Economic Committee or the State Planning Office. In the field of environmental protection its influence covered only the dumping of toxic waste and air pollution issues. Even in this respect, the office shared its authority with other ministries so that, for instance, decisions on toxic waste or clean air were taken in conjunction with the Ministry of Health or the ministry responsible for the manufacture of the given product. Similarly, landscape protection was controlled by the Ministry of Agriculture and Food; mineral resources by the Ministry of Industry; and water quality protection was the realm of the National Water Authority. Thus the National Environment and Nature Protection Office again did not have sufficient political power to fight for its specific interests against other sectors of government (see Tickle and Vavroušek, this volume). Sometimes, ministries controlling special environmental fields (e.g. land, mineral resources) represented both their own sectoral and environmental interests; they promoted the frequently contradictory aims of increasing production and supporting environmental protection.

Nevertheless, the 1970s were important years for environmental protection. In 1972 Hungary (and the other socialist countries) did not participate in the groundbreaking United Nations Conference on the Human Environment in Stockholm. The official explanation for this was that they were protesting against the exclusion of the GDR (which was not a UN member state at that time) from the conference. However, it also appears that ruling communist parties were reluctant to discuss the growing environmental problems in their countries. In this case, their usual excuse of blaming the capitalist past (along the lines of 'we have not yet succeeded in overcoming the weaknesses of our past') did not work – environmental deterioration was generated during the socialist era (Enyedi and Hinrichsen, 1990). But in Hungary under the Kádár regime (which allowed some measure of public debate and political accommodation: Ostry, 1988), 'experts' had enough influence to push the government towards some form of modern environmental thinking (albeit based on technological solutions). The first step was the 1972 revision of the constitution; thus the concept of environmental protection – through which the basic civil right of protection of human life and health should be realized – was included in law. Following this, the National Council for Environmental Protection was founded in 1974 to serve as a direct advisory body to the government. After three years of preparatory work, the 1976 Act on the Protection of the Human Environment was formulated, which put the already existing environmental regulations into a comprehensive legal framework.

In 1988, the Ministry for Environmental Protection and Water Management was established, elevating environmental management to the level of a ministry. Unsurprisingly, this new status did not give more power to the new ministry – the sectoral division of environmental protection remained as it had been in the 1970s.[1] In addition, as the economic and political crisis grew, there were fewer and fewer financial resources for environmental protection, which led to an increase in the incidence of environmental damage (Enyedi and Hinrichsen, 1990).

The interests of social power relations and the power centres sought to develop a fundamentally formal concept of environmental protection. By developing the state environmental protection administration, the central authorities could partly satisfy the expectations of the technical intellectuals who were interested in the development of environmental protection, while at the same time, they were able to control the social forces behind both the intelligentsia and local power groups.[2]

In socialist countries – including Hungary – environmental protection was declared to be one of the state's tasks (Enyedi et al., 1987). Environmental investment and targets in environmental protection were incorporated into national planning. The 'classical' socialist central planning was of a sectoral nature. Economic planning set production targets first and foremost; economic growth was the panacea for all socio-economic problems (mimicking 'western' capitalist models of growth). Planning of infrastructural development was a separate priority, and a much weaker one, compared with production. It was a general principle that environmental protection received funds from the central budget 'according to the capacity of the economy'. This concept indicated that the financial means for environmental protection were drawn from development resources. As economic resources were also limited in the largely inefficient state economy, environmental interests had restricted importance in the national development plans.

Usually, state enterprises were the largest polluters. State ownership was practised by sectoral ministries which stipulated production tasks and provided enterprises with investment funds, including funds for environmental protection investment. Enterprises (and their managers) were evaluated according to their production performance. Thus, enterprises could not be blamed if environmental investment had fallen behind. When another state agency tried to force enterprises to respect environmental prescriptions their efforts were not generally successful. If the socialist state intended to put into force sanctions against enterprises, it meant essentially that its own 'children' should be punished. But in common with other 'really-existing' socialist countries, lack of independent enforcement meant that environmental misdemeanours generally went unnoticed and unpunished.

However, in Hungary, in total contrast to most of the socialist bloc (excluding Yugoslavia), the system of planning directives ended in 1968 and no sectoral plans were prepared thereafter. These economic reforms did not fundamentally change the dominance of state ownership but market conditions were simulated. Consequently, western environmental protection measures – such as the 'polluter pays' principle – could not work properly. Amidst the decentralization that began in the 1970s, and the quasi-market processes that were introduced by the economic reforms ('goulash' communism), the strong state presence caused environmental regulations to operate dysfunctionally. Large state industrial companies tried to profit from the 'environmental fashion' by getting state resources for environmental investment and then using them for other purposes. This was done with the help of backstage deals, which in several cases were achieved on the basis of an alliance with local power groups in the form of financial aid in local ecological conflicts.

THE ENVIRONMENTAL MOVEMENT

Phase one: initial growth

We can distinguish three phases in the short history of the Hungarian environmental movement. Phase 1 started in the 1970s and lasted until the early 1980s. Environmental issues were formulated mostly by intellectuals and expert circles, who followed the birth of the strong western environmental consciousness in the 1970s. This was concurrent with the incidence of the first local ecological crises, which mobilized local authorities, and the period in which the plan for the construction of the Gabčikovo–Nagymaros dams on the Danube drew its first scientific critics. It could not by any means be classified as a grass-roots movement; nevertheless, environmental criticism grew outside the official hierarchy. In the 1970s and early 1980s, when state socialism was not facing deep crisis, ecological social movements involuntarily strengthened the position of state environmental protection, indirectly bringing a temporary stability to state socialism (through participating in policy discussions).

The environmental protection administration, which had always been downgraded to some extent, was forced to assert its interests by means that lay outside the formal decision-making mechanism. For example, it drew its strength and base from local society in order to achieve greater independence and to acquire power/ legitimation. Some of the local discontent over ecological damage erupted, or was allowed to erupt, because the environmental protection administration wanted to show its importance, and because in this way it could win a bigger share of power and resources from the strong economic and political lobbies around the government. It was with their help that the ecological movements of the 1970s hit the headlines.

Local ecological conflicts arose occasionally during the 1970s and increasingly often in the 1980s. In January 1974, there was panic in Dunaújváros when 3000 cubic metres of crude oil were released into the Danube by the Danube Iron Works. In 1978, there was outcry in Budapest after a series of illnesses were linked to lead pollution in the neighbourhood of the Metallokémia Works at Nagytétény (a southern industrial suburb). In 1980, there were a series of reports to the health authorities in Vác that the wells and water supplies were polluted, which was traced to the illegal storage of toxic waste at the Chinoin Pharmaceutical Plant.

There was little mass protest or an organized civil society behind the first environmental movements dealing with local ecological conflicts. As a result of the political and economic modernization in the late 1960s and the 1970s under the 'soft dictatorship' of the Kádár regime, the quasi-market and the large second economy created the opportunity for developing relative well-being, economic autonomy and individual life strategies (a 'social compact' similar to that aimed for during the post-1971 'normalization' years of the Czechoslovak regime: see Tickle and Vavroušek, this volume). One result was the process of petty embourgeoisement, which appeared to be inimical to creating a broad interest in ecological issues. However, financial prosperity was sufficient to meet only the most important primary needs, and only through hard work at that. Thus this was not sufficient to favour the expression of post-materialist values or any form of demand for environmentally friendly products. The recognition of local and global environmental dangers, and their unfavourable effects on health, was limited to certain groups of the intelligentsia: scientists, doctors, teachers and ecologists.

Local environmental groups usually accepted the compromise offered by the state authorities: open criticism of the political system was restrained, discussions and bargaining were largely private and in return the state gave financial and/or technical support for solving the conflict. In this way, the early environmental movement was implicitly integrated within the state socialist system. Thus, as other authors have pointed out (Ostry, 1988; Hajba, 1991), the regime in Hungary – compared with other eastern European socialist states such as Czechoslovakia, for example – did appear to have a more consensual approach to social movement mobilization, at least in the case of environmental issues.

Phase two: new political mobilizations

The second phase in the development of the Hungarian environmental movement took place in the latter half of the 1980s, characterized by grass-roots activities.

They had two origins. First, opponents of the Danube dams scheme turned to a larger public, established the Danube Circle organization (Duna Kör), and propagated their concerns about a possible major ecological disaster if the originally planned system of dams were constructed. The other source was the growing number of protests by local communities. Activities during this period bore little resemblance to the earlier protest actions, nor did they develop any connections with the interest groups represented by the state environmental protection administration, or local power groups (see Persányi, 1993). The movement explicitly attacked state socialism itself, pointing out the dysfunctioning of the system. In this respect, the Danube Circle was especially active. In addition, a number of underground opposition politicians joined the ecological movement, which gave them more opportunity for (semi-)legal activities than openly political groups would have done. However, the earlier tolerance and complicity of the state was over and thus the mass media were forbidden to publish news about the environmental movement.

Hungarian ecological groups seldom comprised any real anti-capitalist approaches, whereas western alternative movements set aims which went beyond the capitalist system (Lowe and Goyder, 1983). This difference between the eastern and western European ecological movements – which faced different social, economic and political problems – appears to derive from the differing challenge of modernization. Western alternative movements searched for a way out of the crisis facing the established market economies, while the eastern movements saw the 'developed' western model as offering a way out of the crisis in state socialism – at least up to (and often beyond) the threshold of the political transition.

Phase three: the transition period

Currently the role of the ecological social movement in the 1990s is far from defined. The germs of potential tendencies seen thus far would suggest that the stronger ecological groups may achieve a new quality of self-stabilization through their critique of the capitalist system, hinted at by the tendencies that can be felt in local communities. However, other authors have been far from optimistic about any measure of real influence in the newly pluralist political arena – at least in the short term (Persányi, 1993; Hajba, 1994).

On the threshold of the transition there were numerous signs, although they have later been proved illusory, that the separate systems of society and natural environment might move into a closer relationship, and that society could integrate the interests of the environment more fully (this feature also characterized the Czechoslovak transition: see Vavroušek, 1993). The ecological movement that developed at the end of the 1980s not only attacked the state socialist system, but also demanded that ecological aspects should be given a bigger role in effecting the transition. However, governmental and parliamentary influences, which largely determined the position of environmental protection on the overall political agenda, brought about a different scenario.

While ecological problems did feature prominently among the electoral promises of the political parties, ecological questions were pushed into the background as new political structures took shape. In the political system that developed, group organization gave way to party politics. The new parties sucked in the representatives of green issues (giving them a background role), whilst other former ecological activists shed their green mantle to work on other social problems or develop full-time political careers. In the government's programme ecological issues featured as discrete problems to be tackled, but were not positioned within the framework of a formal environmental protection concept or strategy. In line with government interests and those of privatization, state environmental protection withdrew from certain ecologically important policy areas. For the most part, the government dealt with environmental matters only where international – mainly political but sometimes economic – interests were at stake. The paltry budgets for environmental protection indicated that ecology was subordinate to political, organizational and – in the cases of certain groups – economic interests. The reorganization and strengthening of the state environmental protection administration was also held back by the continued delay in bringing a new environment law before parliament. A further problem for the environmental movement has been the difficulty of struggling against a social system that it played an important role in creating. But the majority of environmentalists still expected that environmental regulation would be better served by a market economy (Szirmai, 1991).

The environmental movement has now become fragmented and transformed as a result of the transition. There are a great number of environmental associations – over a hundred such associations are registered in Budapest alone. However, their overall impact is weak, especially those that have tried to enter formal politics; the performance of various green parties was miserable, in both the parliamentary and local elections of 1990 (the Green Party got only 0.37 per cent of the national vote in the parliamentary elections). The ecological groups for the most part place their ideological emphasis on the almost exclusive demands for the satisfaction of ecological interests (Zsolnai, 1992). This one-sided ecological attitude appears to make them incapable of any compromise. Such a rigid attitude has been seen by many as unworkable. Thus looking to the future, the environmental movement needs to start to recognize that it will have to develop a more subtle 'ecological–social' approach, which could produce important alliances of interests.

SOCIAL ACTORS ON THE ENVIRONMENTAL SCENE DURING THE TRANSITION PERIOD

There is currently no strong actor who is able or willing to replace the weakened environmental movement. Political parties have environmental programmes, but these programmes are subordinate to most other issues. Political parties do not expect too much electoral support for their ecological programmes. The government environmental protection administration is influenced far more by the government than national activist groups, and the local authorities are more influenced by the political parties (and the polluting companies) than by any actions of the grass-roots movement. Furthermore, the highest-ranking government agency for the environment has been reorganized again, becoming, in 1990, the Ministry of Environmental Protection and Regional Development.

The political and economic actors with an interest in suppressing environmental protection have given the impression that the downgrading of ecological interests will be a long-term feature of the political agenda, and that this is the product of a social consensus that the solution of the social, economic and political crisis is far more important than the management of ecological crisis. The desire for the well-being of a 'consumer society' is portrayed as stronger than the desire for a clean environment. Such a false dilemma of ecological *or* social crisis management offers the chance to conceal the subordination of ecological interests. In addition, the apparent dilemma presents a favourable ideological opportunity for polluting companies opposed to environmental protection to work out their environmentally damaging strategies. The impact of external (western) financial aid has been seen as helpful in presenting alternative paradigms: many international, and particularly World Bank, loans and projects demand that priority be given to ecological issues. However, the government is not hostile to environmental protection *per se* – it simply feels that its political urgency is not excessive; and on a national scale, there is no strong environmental pressure group to construct a viable counter-claim.

A further initial difficulty was the lack of any clear environmental strategy in relation to companies. State-sector enterprises – although still dominating the economy in numeric terms – were falling apart and generally struggling for survival, and were uncertain about the time and form of their privatization. Such structural obstacles meant they were thus unable to invest in environmental protection or to work out any sort of long-term policy. In contrast, large multinational companies operating in Hungary have generally shown more regard for environmental deterioration, and have been more ready to adhere to current standards prevailing in western Europe. As far as the (generally small) private enterprises were concerned, their attitudes were largely contingent upon the behaviour of local authorities; and, in general, they have to be forced to follow environmental regulations.

However, there are a growing number of environmental conflicts, which show an increased 'green' consciousness in the population – at least in terms of local issues. This stems partly from the fact that the role of local authorities in environmental protection is far greater than before. Among their tasks are the protection of local communities' natural environments and the application of legislation in the issuing of permits and so forth.

However, in the latter regard local authorities are limited in their opportunities for action. Property relations of urban land during the early phase of transition were not entirely clear, nor was the new environmental law. Thus local authorities had to base their activities on a legal background that was out of date. This legal gag and the financial pressure of limited resources have, in some cases, forced local authorities to encourage development in 'green belt' areas and to welcome polluting industries. However, the attitude of local government depended to a great extent on its role within the local power structure and the stratification of local society. Local authorities had the most difficult position in the heavy industrial company towns and were cautious towards monopolistic employers in such areas: unemployment was not seen as a realistic alternative to clean air. Local authorities received more support – or pressure – in larger towns, where civil society was better organized, the middle class more powerful and employment opportunities more diversified

(Haraszti, 1990). Within such areas, young parents could be exceptionally militant if pollution was perceived to threaten their children's health.

The growing number of local protests does not necessarily herald a growth in the environmental movement. Local protests are organized by local interest groups, who are lobbying for different purposes: for a new school, or public transport, or (if they judge it important) for broader aspects of environmental protection. However, the existence of such protests at least makes for the possibility – and, for some, the necessity – for local authorities, ecological social movements and different groups of civil society to enter 'horizontal' deals. Indeed the ecological movement may implicitly be going down this policy avenue: it currently focuses its activities on local issues, supporting citizens' groups and local authorities. And as a result of such tactics, environmental views appear in the bargaining process not merely with greater strength: now they are a part of a complex social phenomenon. Thus the forces that are organizing horizontally ('networking') on ecological issues could, through their demands for a complex approach to managing the environmental, social and economic crisis, offer the opportunity to place the present system on completely new foundations.

NOTES

1. The contradiction between environmental protection and water management was of course best highlighted by the enormous political debate surrounding the Gabčíkovo–Nagymaros hydroelectric dams scheme (see Ostry, 1988 or Galambos, 1993).
2. See Ostry (1988) and Persányi (1993) for more detailed accounts of this co-option of the environmental agenda for self-legitimation purposes.

REFERENCES

Brown, L.R., ed. (1992) *State of the World 1992*. W.W. Norton & Co., New York.

Enyedi, G. (1987) Környezet és társadalom [Environment and society] *Forrás* 19(1), 1–7.

Enyedi, G., Gijswijt, A.J. and Rhode, B., eds (1987) *Environmental Policies in East and West*. Taylor Graham, London.

Enyedi, G. and Hinrichsen, D., eds (1990) *State of the Hungarian Environment*. Hungarian Academy of Sciences, Budapest.

Enyedi, G. and Zentai, V. (1986) *Environmental Policy in Hungary*. Discussion Papers No. 2, Centre for Regional Studies, Pécs.

Galambos, J. (1993) An international environmental conflict on the Danube: the Gabčíkovo–Nagymaros dams. In *Environment and Democratic Transition: Policy and Politics in Central and Eastern Europe* (eds A. Vari and P. Tamas). Kluwer, Dordrecht.

Hajba, E. (1991) *The Green Social Movement in an 'Overweight' Political System*. Budapest Papers on Democratic Transition No. 3, Hungarian Center for Democracy Studies Foundation, Budapest.

Hajba, E. (1994) The rise and fall of the Hungarian Greens. *Journal of Communist Studies and Transition Politics* 3, 180–191.

Haraszti, M. (1990) The beginnings of civil society. In *In Search of Civil Society* (ed. V. Tismaneau). Routledge, New York.

Hinrichsen, D. and Lang, I. (1993) Hungary. In *Environmental Problems in Eastern Europe* (eds F.W. Carter and D. Turnock). Routledge, London.

Lowe, P.D. and Goyder, J. (1983) *Environmental Groups in Politics*. Allen & Unwin, London.

Ostry, D. (1988) The Gabčíkovo–Nagymaros dam system as a case study in conflict of interest in Czechoslovakia and Hungary. *Slovo* 1(2), 11–24.

Persányi, M. (1993) Red pollution, green evolution, revolution in Hungary. Environmentalists and societal transition. In *Environmental Action in Eastern Europe: Response to Crisis* (ed. B. Jancar-Webster). M.E. Sharpe, Armonk, NY.

Persányi, M. and Lányi, G. (1991) Waste import at the turn of the epoch: how problems are tackled in Hungary. In *Cities of Europe: The Public's Role in Shaping the Urban Environment* (eds T. Deelstra and O. Yanitsky). Mezhdunarodnye otnoshenia Publishers, Moscow, 123–129.

Péter, S. (1987) Eszmék és realitások [Ideas and realities]. *Forrás* 19(1), 16–27.

Szabó, M. (1989) *Politikai ökológia [Political Ecology]*. Arts Index, Budapest.

Szirmai, V. (1991) Ökológiai társadalmi mozgalmaink [Our ecological social movements]. *Valóság* 34(10), 34–42.

Szirmai, V. (1993) The structural mechanisms of the organisation of ecological movements in Hungary. In *Environment and Democratic Transition: Policy and Politics in Central and Eastern Europe* (eds A. Vari and P. Tamas). Kluwer, Dordrecht.

Vavroušek, J. (1993) Institutions for environmental security. In *Threats Without Enemies: Facing Environmental Insecurity* (ed. G. Prins). Earthscan, London.

Zsolnai, L. (1992) *Ecological and Social Impacts of the Economic Transition in Hungary*. Humphrey Institute of Public Affairs, University of Minnesota.

CHAPTER 7

ENVIRONMENTAL POLITICS, CIVIL SOCIETY AND POST-COMMUNISM

Andrew Tickle and Ian Welsh

BACKGROUND

The preceding chapters have explored the relationship between the environment and transition in the former Soviet Union (FSU) and a number of central and eastern European countries, revealing both common ground and country specificities. This final chapter draws together some central themes and examines them within a comparative context informed by recent social and political science perspectives on the collapse of communism, the transition to democracy and the market, and the future of post-communism. In general, most social science commentators (e.g. Schöpflin, 1993; Bryant and Mokrzycki, 1994; Holy, 1996; Offe, 1996) have had little to say about the role of the environment as a contingent factor in socio-political change. Our interpretations therefore represent a novel re-working of the 'green revolutions' thesis advanced both within this volume and elsewhere (e.g. Waller and Millard, 1992; Jancar-Webster, 1993; Hajba, 1994; Mitsuda and Pashev, 1995; Sööt, 1995; Dawson, 1996) in the context of more recent critical frameworks.

Despite the political, social and cultural differences between specific country regimes, social mobilization around environmental issues within the socialist bloc was remarkably extensive. This general feature can be related primarily to the imposition of the Soviet political model, with its focus on rapid and extensive industrialization and scientific socialism. Very few countries therefore escaped the environmental degradation that, in the eyes of many western observers, epitomizes eastern Europe and the republics of the FSU. However, between countries, the pattern of environmental mobilization differed markedly in relation to a number of factors. These included the development of academic ecology, the presence or absence of official conservation cadres and synergy with other social movements, including the independent opposition. Such patterns may be related to prior socio-political developments, including the extent of pre-Soviet industrialization and the presence or absence of antecedent democratic and/or civil society structures.

In a number of countries the roots of concern for landscape, nature and the environment ran deep: for example, in the interwar years of the first Czechoslovak Republic (1918–38) landscape conservation groups were popular.[1] Earlier developments in the Austro-Hungarian Empire included the establishment of some of the first nature reserves in Europe. Analyses of Russo-Soviet environmentalism (Weiner, 1988; Gare, 1993) also show a range of early (pre-1917) conservation developments, comparable to those occurring in western Europe and the United States. From 1919 onwards, activities relating to scientific ecology were enthusiastically adopted, largely on utilitarian grounds, by Bolshevik leaders such as Lunacharsky and Lenin, resulting in arguably the world's first systematic and extensive network of protected nature reserves (*zapovedniki*). These developments came abruptly to a halt in 1930 with the rise of Stalin and the priority of industrialization at any cost (Gare, 1993). This evidence suggests that early western streams of environmentalism were far from unique and that the patterns noted here fit well with evolutionary models of nature conservation derived for countries such as the UK (e.g. Lowe, 1983). However, other authors have contended that 'the historical-cultural context of movements in the West and East is sharply different' (Yanitsky, 1993: 122), basing their arguments on the differences in the scale of pluralist civil society between eastern and western societies.

In other eastern European states in the post-1948 period, a more common historical factor in the development of environmental consciousness was the influence of science and scientific ecology. This was akin to the Soviet situation in the 1920s and the UK between 1910 and 1970 (Lowe, 1983). Environmental problems were primarily viewed through the twin lenses of science and technology, both made paramount in communist societies by the ideology of scientific socialism and its role in the rapid drive towards modernity (based on Stalin's aim to 'catch up' and 'overtake' the capitalist countries). By the 1960s and 1970s in countries such as Bulgaria (Baumgartl, 1993), Poland (Kabala, 1993), Czechoslovakia (Tickle and Vavroušek, this volume), East Germany (Holmes, 1992), Hungary (Szirmai, 1993), Slovenia (Klemenc, 1993), Estonia (Sööt, 1995), Latvia (Dreifelds, 1995), Lithuania and the Ukraine (Dawson, 1996), and the Soviet Union in general (Mirovitskaya, this volume), official and non-official groups of scientists and intellectuals had begun to discuss environmental problems openly and make critiques based on their analyses.

Although these developments were in part related to the thaw in Soviet totalitarianism after Kruschev's denouncement of Stalin (see Dreifelds, 1995: 116), in a number of countries environmental critiques developed in the West (e.g. the 1971 Club of Rome report) were also highly influential (Holmes, 1992: 73). In addition, the political profile of the environment was also raised throughout the region by participation in environmental *détente*. This was initiated by the Soviet Union within the Conference on Security and Co-operation in Europe (CSCE or Helsinki) process and then carried forward from 1979 by the United Nations Economic Commission for Europe (UN ECE) with the signing of the (Geneva) Convention on Long-Range Transboundary Air Pollution and subsequent protocols.

Within the countries covered in this volume (the Soviet Union, Poland, Czechoslovakia, Hungary and East Germany) a reasonably common pattern of environmental mobilization has been shown to occur, albeit with varied beginnings. However, setting aside the commonality of causes (Soviet industrialization, the existence and involvement of scientific/nature conservationist cadres, the growing international importance of environmental issues), country-specific differences did occur and these should be analysed further in order to help define the structuring of the environment as an issue in these heterogeneous countries.

ENVIRONMENT AND SOCIETY – VARIATIONS AND THEMES

We have already indicated that environmental issues had served as a central locus for small civic and larger-scale political initiatives within Bolshevik Russia. After Stalin's death, these issues emerged again in a relatively fitful manner across the Soviet Union, mainly related to pollution 'hot spots' or the planned development of inappropriate industrial schemes (often nuclear or hydroelectric power plants). Concurrent with these local mobilizations, many people became members of official conservation groups as a protest against industrial monopolization and state paternalism, though this opposition was in general 'silent' – couching criticism in technological and scientific terms and avoiding outright political issues (Mirovitskaya, this volume). However, a large proportion of those involved in Soviet state conservation groups were members in name only, 'participation' for many being politically unavoidable. Related to this observation is the characterization of Soviet environmental politics of this period as resembling a state corporatist model (Ziegler, 1987). This also reflects the prevailing situation in Poland during the 1970s and Czechoslovakia and Hungary during the early 1980s, where specialist criticism was almost solely confined within regime agendas and policies.

The internalist nature of criticism was fundamentally overturned by Gorbachev's policies of *glasnost* and *perestroika*, which were actively pursued from 1985. The initial attempt to cover up the accident at Chernobyl in April 1986 encouraged popular anti-nuclear movements in Armenia, Lithuania, Ukraine and Russia, which during 1988–90 were remarkably successful in opposing plans for nuclear expansion (Dawson, 1996). Elsewhere myriad community demands for industrial plant closures had significant effects on regional economies and green rhetoric pervaded political demands in republics as varied as Tadjikistan and Georgia (Peterson, 1993), being particularly strong in the Baltic republics (Ziegler, 1992). However, almost all of these movements were united by nationalist aspirations or what has been termed 'eco-nationalism' (Dawson, 1996). This 'particularity' has been suggested as a basis for distinguishing Soviet environmental movements from their more 'universalist' or 'anti-nationalistic'-based counterparts outside the FSU (Goldman, 1992: 2). As Ziegler has noted, reflecting on the post-*glasnost* period, 'nationalism and environmentalism have generated highly emotional forms of mass political participation that are directed against the political establishment . . . [and] both . . . are closely associated with physical territory' (1992: 35). Indeed this linkage between political populism (even national extremism) and the environment also characterized the 'blood and soil' movement of Nazi Germany and its weaker vestiges such as the fascist involvement in the organic agriculture movement in 1930s Britain (Bramwell, 1989).

Nationalism (or anti-Soviet sentiment) has also been invoked as a significant factor in the collapse of communist systems, notably in the Czech Republic. In this situation the late Ladislav Holy, by deconstructing oppositional discourse and symbols, suggested that 'the popular opposition to the communist regime in Czechoslovakia . . . was neither triggered by a sense of material deprivation nor carried out in the name of democracy and the free market . . . [but] was carried out in the name of freedom of individuals and freedom of the nation' (Holy, 1996: 53). However, Holy also recognized the importance of ecological discourse in communist Czechoslovakia, where 'the supporters of the ecological movement considerably outnumbered the dissidents, and during the last years of communist rule . . . ecological protest became the most important form of expression of disagreement with the communist system' (p. 169). However, whilst Holy saw ecological discourse as important, it stood 'primarily as a tangible symbol of the wider ills of the socialist system' (p. 171), reflecting wider anxieties of a society in crisis. He illustrated this by the decline in popular environmental consciousness after 1989.

It has been argued that environmental movements became the symbolic focuses for wider anti-state and anti-Soviet sentiments in a number of other countries, including Bulgaria (Mitsuda and Pashev, 1995) and Hungary (Hajba, 1994; Lomax, 1997; Pickvance, 1997). This general argument applies to many of the countries described in this volume. This in turn raises complex questions about the relationship between the environmental and other movements during this period. Dawson (1996) has described this as *movement surrogacy*, a process akin to entryism where 'radical actors hide behind surrogate causes that targeted similar audiences' (p. 6). In her view 'surrogacy was simply a rationally selected tactic that fit[ted] the existing structural conditions and that was discarded when no longer useful'. Like Holy, Dawson advances the post-independence loss of issue potency suffered by environmental concerns in support of her arguments. One clear example of this was the swift reverse in nationalists' stance towards nuclear power stations, which changed from symbols of 'imperial domination' to those of energy 'self-sufficiency' (Dawson, 1996: 8). Whilst it is clear that movement surrogacy (or environmentalism as means rather than ends, *sensu* Mitsuda and Pashev, 1995) has explanatory relevance in many of the countries of eastern Europe, our view is that the environment is more strongly bound into the structures and values of these societies than the surrogacy theory would suggest.

Despite the fact that Hungary, Poland and East Germany were also under Soviet tutelage, environmental protest in these countries has not been characterized by such nationalist sentiments. To some extent this may be understandable in East Germany, given the highly politicized question of German identity. In the other two countries, however, it may be thought more surprising, given the experience of Soviet intervention in Hungary in 1956 and the typical mythic construction of Polish self-identity as part of a continually oppressed and invaded nation. Indeed, in a typology by Offe (1996: 138ff.) both Hungary and Poland are characterized as having a 'high' level of national integration whilst in Czech society, in contradistinction to Holy, such integration is deemed 'precarious to non-existent'. However, by the time environmental issues had attained political salience, both Hungary and Poland had locally distinct forms of political and social compacts (either at an elite or mass level: Frentzel-Zagorska, 1990; Offe, 1996) which enjoyed enhanced legitimacy compared with countries such as East Germany and Czechoslovakia, which were guided more directly by policies from Moscow.

Poland, though having an early formalized commitment to nature conservation (the Liga Ochrony Przyrody or League for the Protection of Nature was founded in 1928), did not see any mass environmental consciousness emerge until the initial Solidarity revolution of 1980–81. Just as Gorbachev's policy of *glasnost* opened up modern Soviet environmentalism, so the relaxation of the ban on environmental data by the Polish government enabled Solidarity to mobilize popular environmental concerns. Mirroring the Polish opposition's precocious success in challenging one-party rule, this era saw the first major environmentalist victory in eastern Europe: the closure of the Skawina aluminium smelter near Kraków in January 1981 (see Wódz and Wódz, this volume). The end of the year saw Solidarity banned and martial law imposed, although the main ecological movement which sprang from Solidarity, the Polish Ecological Club (PKE), was allowed to continue its activities. In this sense, Poland presents an alternative, and possibly unique, model of regime opposition dynamics with direct political opposition prefiguring environmental mobilization. In many of the other countries considered here (Czechoslovakia, Hungary, East Germany, Bulgaria and the 'eco-nationalist' republics within the Soviet Union), mass environmental opposition has been generally observed to prefigure wider political mobilization.

In Hungary, the more consensual style of the Kádár regime gave another distinct element to eastern European environmentalism. In other countries we have noted the phenomenon of environmentalism as a means to an end – but usually as a tactic adopted by the opposition. However, the Hungarian state has been shown to have co-opted environmental issues as a way of defusing wider critiques emanating from the intelligentsia. Indeed, in the more open Kádárist society environmental groups were not always perceived as acting in opposition to the state; instead involvement in political deals can be interpreted as giving tacit support to the government. It has also been revealed that government officials in the environmental sphere actually encouraged the opposition in order to legitimize their own tasks and agendas (Szirmai, 1993; Enyedi and Szirmai, this volume), a possibly unique situation in eastern Europe[2] – though one that can be interpreted as fitting Ziegler's (1987) invocation of state corporatism. However, it is also clear that later environmental mobilizations (notably in the Danube Circle group opposing the Gabčíkovo–Nagymaros hydroelectric power and dams scheme) contained large numbers of political opportunists for whom the environment was a minor, or even irrelevant, issue (Szirmai, 1993; Hajba, 1994). This may explain the direct attack on social and political structures that this movement made, compared with the more subtle or oblique critiques made by earlier Hungarian groups (which also typified the form of environmental claims-making in the eastern bloc as a whole).

The tacit, even quasi-explicit, support of environmental activism by the state is a facet that also emerges from studies of environmental politics in Bulgaria, a country unfortunately not covered in any detail in this volume. In analyses presented elsewhere, Mitsuda and Pashev (1995) have suggested that the activities of the main Bulgarian opposition group Ekoglasnost (especially those surrounding the street protests in Sofia at the time of the October 1989 CSCE conference) may have been supported by key anti-Zhivkov elites within the regime as part of the efforts to isolate the leader and reform the system from within. Here a parallel may be drawn with the likely KGB manipulation of the 17 November student demonstration in Prague, although in the Czechoslovak case the situation unexpectedly evolved away from regime reform into total collapse and capitulation. As in Czechoslovakia, ecological activists played prominent roles in the newly elected parliament and administration (within the opposition Union of Democratic Forces coalition) but party political conflicts plus internal difficulties meant that the mainly centrist 'greens' were increasingly sidelined in terms of both political power and popular support. Typical of the evolution of environmental politics under post-communism, activism returned to its former extra-state and extra-parliamentary role as a mainly problem-led, minority or grass-roots activity.

The final country dealt with in this volume, East Germany, had little history of environmental activism until relatively late in the communist period. The country has also been characterized – perhaps uniquely in the region – as having an opposition movement that focused predominantly on the reform of communism, rather than its end (Joppke, 1995). Early opposition groups had mobilized around the peace issue since the 1950s, linked to Church support for conscientious objectors. In the 1970s, despite attempted dialogue with the government, Church criticism became more open, eventually leading to further state restrictions on independent initiatives.[3] By the late 1980s the peace issue was on the wane but the civic consciousness it had fostered now encouraged a wider activist agenda, including human rights, women's issues and ecology – the latter area of activity being catalysed in part by linkage with the West German greens and the Chernobyl issue (Tismaneanu, 1989; Holmes, 1992; Joppke, 1995: 108). For some time, discussion of green issues was tolerated and the government even tried to respond on specific issues as illustrated in this volume and elsewhere (Boehmer-Christiansen, this volume; Joppke, 1995: 115). Although most autonomous activities were stopped by another government clampdown in early 1988, by the summer of 1989 the pressure of civic initiatives had broken out again in massive street demonstrations as the state lost control and collapsed, finally being absorbed into a larger Germany in October 1990 (Maier, 1997).

East Germany has most frequently been analysed on the basis of its unique and rapid incorporation into western Europe, though some doubt the certainty of outcomes in this transitional metaproject (see Offe, 1996). With this modern *anschluss* came the claim that ecological modernization (in the original German sense: *ökologischer Umbau*) would be a guiding feature of the transformation (Boehmer-Christiansen, this volume). Instead it appears that the use of environmental issues in unification politics was largely rhetorical or self-serving, as evidenced by the use of pollution as a factor further reducing the asset value of East German enterprises to predatory West German capital – especially in the energy sector.

THEORIZING SOCIAL AND ENVIRONMENTAL CHANGE

The country-specific accounts have revealed the contingent nature of environmental issues as a site for conflicts between the party-state and the generally fragmented societies that existed in central and eastern Europe. The similarities and differences noted between countries remain to be linked to a theoretical model capable of general explanatory power for the environmental protest phenomenon in central and eastern Europe. This task has most frequently been attempted through various interpretations of civil society and we turn to these before advancing our own reformulation of these debates. Before entering into this exercise it is worth drawing attention to the main theoretical and material developments which complicate this task. There are three main constellations of theoretical concerns which make the task of identifying an integrated explanatory model complex and inevitably incomplete – even several years after the initial events. First, it is now apparent that the revolutions dealt with here were both a symptom and cause of a process of *globalization* (see also Lewis, 1997: 23–24). The initial conditions of the revolutions as symptom were established in the economic, political, military and ideological conflicts which defined the Cold War. The subsequent development of the revolutions and their *temporary* consolidation within post-communist governments have accelerated the processes of globalization. They have done so in at least five ways:

1. by exposing new nodes of capital accumulation within the global economy ripe for foreign direct investment, such as Volkswagen's buy-out of parts of the Czech engineering conglomerate, Škoda;
2. by contributing significantly to overall levels of global migration and the creation and consolidation of diasporas;
3. by enabling the integration of selected eastern and central European countries within the EU economic bloc;
4. by enabling the close alignment of Russia with key instruments of Western global governance, such as the G7, which Russian entry would re-dub G8;
5. by enabling the integration of selected eastern and central European countries within regional geopolitical alliances, especially NATO.[4]

These obvious contributions to processes of globalization are complemented by other less obvious ones. Amongst the most important of these is the exploitation of Russia's vast reserves of natural resources by modern means. The other significant global dimension relates to the unique experimental nature of the application of a western free-market model to countries which, from an historical perspective, seldom have the enabling social and cultural capital. This experiment is backed by powerful instruments of global governance such as IMF loans and World Bank structural adjustment funds.

Attention to the global domain makes addressing the processes of change dealt with here *purely* in terms of national criteria clearly inadequate. Unfortunately many of the social scientific concepts available to analyse these changes have been developed within specifically national frameworks. There is thus a particularly important need to identify empirically important processes and to either modify existing terms or generate new ones suited to prevailing conditions. We believe that the environment–society–economy nexus is one of the empirically important processes through which this impasse can be overcome. The neglect of the environment in accounts of eastern and central Europe from within long-established analytical traditions underlines this point. What is required is a fine understanding of the interaction between national characteristics and the global processes and agencies operating in each country.

The second and obviously connected set of concerns relates to the *decline of the nation-state*. As supranational agencies have grown in influence, the capacity of discrete nation-states to regulate economic activity, ensure security (including environmental security) and guarantee civil society have all declined. This decline in the coherence of the nation-state has been particularly intense throughout the region covered here, as the rise of both autonomy and nationalist movements testifies. Environmental issues have played a dramatic role in underlining the peculiar inability of the most powerful human institutions – nation-states – to deliver environmental security for their citizens. In Europe, where transboundary pollution of air and water are endemic, the demand for clean air and water assume particular importance in this respect.

Whilst environmental networks remained largely submerged within an immanent civil society,[5] their main objectives centred on halting the desecration of the environment by socialist industrialization and securing political and civil rights to protest. In the contemporary conjuncture, economic restructuring has closed many of the smokestack industries, producing a temporary amelioration of pollution levels. As the region is opened up to 'development' by global capital, environmentalism can be expected to regain some of its apparently lost potency. The environmental impacts of natural gas and oil extraction are set to become significant nodes for movement networks. Within the pockets of affluence centred on urban areas, increasing car ownership will introduce new concerns, familiar in the West, as air quality fails to improve in the long term. The fledgling democracies thus confront the tasks of simultaneously delivering economic growth, democratic freedoms, citizenship rights and environmental gains. These aspirations have all been framed in the context of national democracies in the West but are now pursued at precisely the point when global processes are rapidly undermining these very models and the social scientific concepts used to analyse them.

The third constellation which concerns us here is the *simultaneous fragmentation of political classes* within nation-states and the *rise of a variety of new identities* formed in relation to an extraordinarily diverse range of phenomena. There are two main elements to this process which appear in a number of variants in nations around the world. First, there is the emergence within advanced capitalist and ex-socialist countries of a large, economically marginal underclass. The common features of this underclass include unemployment and underemployment, low prospects of labour market entry and high dependency on welfare or private and charitable donations. Secondly, there has been a remarkable globalization of new social movement activity of all kinds. Environmental NGOs (ENGOs) have been accorded official recognition in global forums such as the UN Rio Earth Summit. Activist networks across the world are now closely linked by electronic communications. Such linkages serve to define both the identity of particular movements and their capacity to act. A particularly significant part of this global networking has been the early articulation of environmental concerns within the occupational and class transformation of modernizing economies (e.g. Brazil).

The increasing connectivity between the local, regional, national and global levels complicates the process of governance and analysis of agency within social and political systems. National governments are increasingly caught between pressures from above arising in regional and global geopolitical forums (e.g. the UN and the EU) and those from below as proliferating citizens groups press widely competing claims within national and local polities. The apparent effervescence of civil society within nation-states is complicated by the diverse nature of the claims, which far exceed the class-bounded origins of the concept. The input of issues and perspectives from outside a particular nation-state transform the sphere of civil society from a national to a global site. Agency and power become diffuse and it becomes difficult if not impossible to judge the social and political potential of apparently minor events.

Paradoxically civil society is the concept most widely utilized by scholars and commentators from both East (e.g. Michnik, 1985; Havel, 1986) and West (Arato and Cohen, 1988; Keane, 1988; Melucci, 1988; Miller, 1992; Joppke, 1995; Hicks, 1996) to address communist and post-communist societies. It is thus very important to outline the variety of ways the term is used within the literature on central and eastern Europe, drawing out some of the tensions and contradictions before advancing a schema which we believe may overcome some of these shortcomings.

CIVIL SOCIETY

Civil society is widely acknowledged as one of the most fashionable 'buzzwords' of eastern European politics in the 1990s (Miller, 1992). Given the variety of uses, from the analytic, political and instrumental dimensions to its normative capacity (Keane, 1988: 13ff), the term has become somewhat chimerical. However, it is generally used to characterize a realm of predominantly autonomous social activity interpenetrating the private and public spheres and providing a sphere between state and society. The communist systems of eastern Europe attempted, with varying degrees of success, to incorporate systematically such areas of autonomous economic, social, cultural and political activities within the interstices of the party-state. Indeed many authors attest to the destruction or repression of civil society in many communist states (including those of Asia: Miller, 1992), although it is conceded that vestigial structures remained in some eastern bloc countries, especially those with longer experiences of functioning, pluralist democracies.

As the voluminous literature on the topic of civil society attests, the application of the concept to capitalist societies has been deeply contested. However, in eastern Europe, where civil society has been defined as the articulation of society's interests independent of the totalizing state (after Schöpflin, 1993: 262), conceptual clarity is much enhanced, at least until the collapse of communism. As Schöpflin (p. 262) makes clear, 'in a system that required social atomisation as a necessary condition for its survival and reproduction', civil society (vestigial or otherwise) became 'public enemy number one'. In his interpretation, Schöpflin also suggests that civil society was 'highly effective in bringing about the demise of communism' (p. 262). There is thus a tension between the apparent extirpation of civil society under communism and a phoenix-like rise to dispatch the self-same regime which requires explanation.[6]

Various concepts of civil society were also used as an organizing principle within eastern European dissident movements. Notable amongst these was the 'new evolutionism' model of opposition proposed by Michnik (1985) on the basis of Gramsci's reworking of Hegelian civil society, and the Havelian view of 'living in truth' (Havel, 1986; 1988; see also Matraszek, 1989), an approach influenced by Konrád's (1984) concept of 'anti-politics'. The neo-Gramscian approach as characterized for eastern Europe (in particular in Poland: Pelczynski, 1988) envisaged elements of the opposition gradually opening up and taking over civic and political space in a manner similar to Gramsci's 'war of position' against capitalism. Although such formulations have difficulty in explaining the initial 1970s phenomenon of the Polish independent opposition, or what Pelczynski describes as the 'rebirth of *political society*' (Pelczynski, 1988: 369, original emphasis), from 1980 onwards Solidarity has been described as part of a new 'historic bloc', including the Church and other oppositional groups, which mounted a counter-hegemonic project against state repression and economic domination.[7] Rather than adopt the term 'political society' we prefer the term '*independent opposition*', which is also widely used to characterize this prefigurative sphere. The emergence of independent opposition movements codified and formalized an intellectual, and sometimes populist, critique of the Soviet system, fulfilling a role analogous to Gramsci's organic intellectuals.[8]

The role of environmental mobilization within such opposition 'blocs' is of central importance to us in defining the position of the environment in relation to civil society. As the natural environment forms the basis for all societies we define the environment 'as a site within which a number of social, cultural, economic and political forces intersect, compete and co-operate' (Welsh, 1996: 409). The environment thus becomes the necessary terrain upon which all expressions of civil society are forged. To the extent that the environment becomes a global site then it also becomes the site for a global civil society. This conceptual move thus suggests that the environment assumes a position of particular importance both as a global site and within reconfigured national civil societies.

For Poland the evidence seems relatively clear: the environment came to prominence as a sub-set of Solidarity's core values, reflecting the symbolic and material centrality of the environment within Polish civil society.[9] The environment remained a central element of the independent opposition in the guise of the PKE up to 1989. As an environmental organization the PKE continued to function in periods when Solidarity itself was banned. For example, when Solidarity, flushed with the success of continued political gains, proposed a 'self-governing republic' through a 'negotiated takeover of several parts of the old hegemonic state structure by civil society' (Pelczynski, 1988: 376), the response was the Soviet-backed imposition of martial law. This returned Solidarity to its underground status until social order broke down with the strikes of 1988, heralding the beginning of the end of communism in eastern Europe. In the interim the networks of the PKE acted as both an environmental movement and a surrogate for Solidarity's wider political programme.

Whilst Solidarity was able to engage in a war of position which sought to capture elements of the opposing state directly, few other countries achieved such an institutionalization of civic action. This then leads into the question of how significant were the far more fragmentary islands of independent opposition (dissidence) which typified countries such as Czechoslovakia and East Germany in the early 1980s (and Poland during the 1970s) and how did they relate to environmental mobilization? Here Havel's conceptualization of the post-totalitarian state is instructive.[10] In his writing Havel posed a stark moral choice between being compromised by the system ('living a lie') or rejecting it by 'living in truth', an action interpreted as an 'individual revolt [which] becomes the first step towards the re-establishment of civil society' (Matraszek, 1989: 43). This suggests that independent opposition is born on the margins of the private sphere with the potential to produce a 'nascent' civil society, although this evolutionary path is highly contingent on other external social and political conditions, some even beyond the borders of the state (e.g. Gorbachev's *glasnost*).

Clearly only a small proportion of the population of eastern European societies had the moral strength or the social circumstances to allow them to 'live in truth'. For example, in Czechoslovakia, during the twelve or so years of Charter 77's existence, its signatories numbered around 1900 from a total population of some 15 million (Prečan, 1990). In a Gramscian sense this easily distinguishes such dissident movements from a social force large enough to make a positional war feasible. Of course many citizens in communist systems withdrew into the private sphere, a way of 'living the lie' that was implicitly encouraged by the state. For many others, nature conservation and environmentalism provided an avenue of activity relatively untouched by social and moral stagnation, or a 'positive island of deviation' in society (Kundrata, 1992). The example of such movements in the Czechoslovak context illustrates a number of issues around the role of the environment in immanent civil society.

Early Czech conservation groups such as Tis (Yew) represented attempts to absorb institutionalized, pre-communist movements such as the decorative clubs into state conservation cadres. These groups therefore represented vestigial structures of a former civil society and as such did not enjoy a trouble-free existence in political terms (Kundrata, 1992). Increasing environmental awareness in the 1970s and 1980s brought conservationists into the realm of independent opposition, linking with dissidents and opposing state policy. Using the example of the Hungarian Danube Circle movement, Judt characterized environmental protest as intolerable to the state, taking place as it did '*outside* the official sphere, creating a *public* difference of opinion . . . [and] is thus implicitly an act of political pluralism' (Judt, 1988: 208, original emphasis). However, Judt regards the adoption of environmentalism by established dissidents as chiefly tactical, allowing them links to 'both a wider public and a younger one' (p. 208).

Although this tactical co-option may have been partly true of the Hungarian opposition, environmental issues had deeper resonances among Czech dissidents, and in particular Václav Havel. Havel (1986, 1988) approaches the environmental crisis in a much more profound manner. The state of the environment is symptomatic 'of a civilization that has renounced the Absolute, which ignores the natural world and disdains its imperatives' (1988: 389). In Havel's conception, post-totalitarian systems are not just an extremely ugly political and environmental cul-de-sac in the project of modernity but 'a convex mirror of all modern civilization and a harsh, perhaps final call for a global recasting of that civilization's self-understanding' (1988: 389). Such views have been mirrored sharply in more recent analyses of crises in global governance (see Welsh, 1996: 410). Havel's view of the environment also bears clear linkages with the humanist values which have been suggested as characterizing the post-normalization (1970s onwards) Czech and Slovak environmental movements (Kundrata, 1992).

As the political project of communism decayed further in the 1980s, state control relaxed in key areas, allowing more scope for social autonomy and the limited emergence of something approaching civil society (Schöpflin, 1993: 264–265). In the Czech and Slovak environmental sphere, this did not generally involve the creation of new, autonomous institutions as might be demanded by a Gramscian approach. Instead, mature organizations existing in the margins of the state *apparat* became re-energized, confirming the presence of an immanent civil society, not wholly engulfed by the totalizing Czechoslovak state. The same phenomenon has been noted in other spheres, most notably in relation to religious practice in Poland (Schöpflin, 1993: 265). These examples serve to suggest two things. First, that an immanent civil society persisted throughout central and eastern Europe. Secondly, that the environmental expressions of this civil society have autonomous and legitimate spheres of engagement which cannot be dismissed either by arguments of movement surrogacy or by arguments about the marginal importance of the environment as a political issue in the region.

A final point in the Gramscian analogy followed above concerns the relative strength of the state against which a war of position was enjoined. Gramsci based his analyses on an entrenched capitalist system which was unlikely to surrender power easily. This characterization has its best parallels with the Polish state and its opponents in 1980–81. Elsewhere, however, civil society looked decidedly thin on the ground, even immediately prior to the collapse of many country systems. This *apparent* absence of expressions of civil society helps explain the contradictory position adopted by commentators, such as Schöpflin and Havel, who declare civil society as *both* crushed by communism and responsible for its downfall.

Thus, ideas that Soviet communism banished civil society have proved to be profoundly misleading. Despite the totalizing nature of recent political systems in eastern Europe, historical models of social and political power (both pre-modern and modern: Szücs, 1988; Schöpflin, 1993: 263) seem likely to have had a major influence in structuring regional and national particularities of state and society under communism, the mode of transformation and the current trajectory of post-communism (Offe, 1996: 143). Significant elements of this immanent civil society have included environmental networks, the Church, and a variety of autonomous movements, including reformed communists, human rights and peace movements as well as various nationalisms. During the 1970s the advent of independent opposition added a further element, which we have described earlier as analogous to Gramsci's organic intellectuals. We would argue that the isolation of the independent opposition prevented both the capacity to gauge their political potential and enter into a war of position. During the 1980s 'emergent' civil societies became increasingly defined in different countries, being heralded first and most systemically in Poland with the rise of Solidarity.[11] The emergence of this phase of civil society can also be seen in the rise of environmental activism throughout the region, which as we and others (e.g. Hicks, 1996) have shown enjoyed a certain amount of tacit, even quasi-explicit, state involvement. The dynamic fusion of independent opposition and emergent civil societies throughout the region thus combined to precipitate the revolutions of 1989. The increasing confidence of large sections of the population – recognizing their collective voice within emergent civil society – added confidence to the independent opposition. The ensuing fusion of independent and environmental networks transformed both groupings. The leadership roles of organic intellectuals were significantly supplemented by the addition of trusted environmental activists, and crucially the capacity of the independent opposition to stage large mobilizations was significantly enhanced by the pre-existing environmentalist networks.[12] Without this capacity to mobilize through well-established environmental, youth and cultural networks, the popular revolutions would neither have cohered nor gathered sufficient momentum to achieve rapid ascendancy.

We would suggest that many of the analysts who have neglected the environmental and youth movements have fallen into a common problem with Gramscian models of civil society. This relates centrally to the balance between formal political contestation and wider socio-cultural factors. Emphasis on formal political contestation tends to produce an emphasis on the social forces controlling particular spheres of activity. It is this which enables many commentators to recognize Poland as a particularly strong example of these processes. An immediate problem for more culturally based contestation, including new social movement activities, is that once a movement becomes successful in terms of colonizing state space it arguably ceases to be part of civil society.

The role of youth and popular culture within the process of cultural contestation should not be underestimated. The social movement theorist Alberto Melucci has recently argued that states silence vast areas of social space and that increasingly it is those defining themselves as culturally young who breach these silences. Youth thus declares the stakes for the rest of society by revealing what is (Melucci, 1996: 127ff.). The generations who had experienced Soviet repression in the 1950s and 1960s were less willing to take to the streets in the 1980s until they were mobilized by their children. Another area of silence breached in the revolutions related to the gendered expectations around women's role in society. To the extent that a war of position was entered into it was fought on a number of fronts simultaneously and resulted in an uneasy armistice built around the promise of marketization and individual freedoms. It is in this sense that we argue that these were green revolutions linking demands for democracy and a more enlightened approach towards the environment. The introduction of market reforms, the opening of the frontiers of these countries to western environmental pressure groups and social movements, and the rapid decline in central planning combined to produce the appearance of modern, western civil societies. The gap between this appearance and the actuality assumes considerable analytical importance.

In central and eastern Europe, once transitional states had been established, civil societies were constructed in a profoundly different climate to their longer-lived counterparts in the West. Rapid marketization and individual freedoms were accompanied by the widespread collapse of both welfare provision and the ability to pay the salaries and wages of state employees regularly. It rapidly became apparent that formal political rights and freedoms associated with democracy left a considerable deficit in terms of nurturing meaningful civil societies. Though the prevailing political opportunity structures vary from country to country, the entire region has been left struggling to evolve towards a mature civic culture.

In contrast to civil society in the West, which has engaged with the limitations of developed western democracy in relation to issues of gender, sexuality, 'race' and environmental degradation, civil society in central and eastern Europe in the 1990s has largely failed to address such issues – producing longer-term democratic deficits. As our introduction suggested, the rapid marginalization of women after the initial revolutions has resulted in civil societies which are structured around gender difference in both the public and private spheres. Women are significantly absent or under-represented in the new political and economic institutions associated with the establishment of market societies. The public sphere is typified by masculinism. The construction of a public 'man's world' (Watson, 1993: 472) is paralleled by private patriarchalism. An important aspect of this patriarchalism is the subordination of women and environmental concerns to an agenda constructed around employment, economic growth and consumption. The absence of, and hostility to, feminist perspectives developed in the West reflects differing material, social and cultural circumstances during the post-war period.[13] Western feminism emerged within market-based liberal democracies and enjoyed significant periods of mobilization at times of particularly intense social and economic restructuring.[14] Eco-feminism, emphasizing the linkages between the exploitation of women and the organic environment, is a very recent development (Merchant, 1983, 1992) deeply indebted to contributors from the so-called 'third world' (Mies and Shiva, 1993). Now that the environmental movement is taken for granted in the West, the role of women in the formation of the movement has been somewhat obscured. In his early work Offe (1985), amongst others, pointed to the importance of women in the creation of the citizens' action groups, which initially campaigned for very local environmental gains in Germany during the 1960s. These small, largely urban groups concerned with traffic, road safety and clean air subsequently became a major source of recruits for first the anti-nuclear power movement and subsequently nuclear disarmament and environmental mobilizations.

In the former communist regimes, women had far greater access to a variety of occupations traditionally considered to be 'man's work', while in the West there was still a state-backed responsibility for biological reproduction. Watson notes that the response of many women at the end of this regime was to demand the right to a 'feminine' role built around motherhood and homemaking. Withdrawal and segregation within the private sphere of the family and the subsequent loss of economic status as a wage-earner effectively silenced women. Watson thus considers that 'civil society is being created in opposition to the domesticity of women, a process which is founded on the strength of pre-existing traditionalism' (Watson, 1993: 480).

To the extent that women are located within the private sphere of the family and stereotypic areas of the occupational structure within the transition societies, their voices will not shape the unfolding agenda of transformation and post-communism. In terms of the environment in the transition societies a further source of change prominent during the revolutions is thus lost. Given the diversity of the societies within which this process is taking place, this silence will end in a variety of nuanced ways. The only prediction we would want to make on the basis of historical and comparative trends is that this silence will be broken sooner or later. The overwhelming evidence of continued environmental degradation and human health impacts, particularly amongst children (see Feshbach, 1995), suggests that women will play a central part in challenging the acceptability of such practices. Home and hearth within marketized societies are sites of low status and low prestige, and as such they have been sites from which women all over the world have broken out (Pateman, 1970, 1988, 1989; Enloe, 1989). The transitional societies appear to have attempted to institute rather dated versions of 'modern' western societies. Central features of this dated approach assumes full-time male employment and a male-dominated polity, whilst the global marketization process is increasingly generating part-time female jobs in most western countries. Given this mismatch, gender politics seems to have the potential to transform the emergent civil societies, though time scales will probably vary.

Finally within this section, we return briefly to the influence of economic aspects of globalization – in particular, the idea (rapidly assuming the status of shibboleth) that democracy and the free market would automatically result in a better environment. The quest for civil society within discrete states had failed to accommodate the extent to which modernization would take place within the context of neo-liberal global restructuring.

The neo-liberal project to roll back the state, which became ascendant throughout Europe and America in the 1980s by curtailing welfare expenditure and reducing direct state employment, became widely applied as a condition of development loans. Paradoxically, as western European activists were increasingly turning to direct action to pursue political, environmental and social goals,[15] the selfsame objectives were pursued through formal political channels in central and eastern Europe. Indeed it can be argued in relation to the environment–society nexus that the trajectory of the revolutions in effect decapitated the environmental movement, which had been so important to their initial success. The incorporation of prominent activists within new state structures and the movement's faith in the thoroughgoing nature of its victory produced severe disappointment and demobilization. The seeming solidity of national societies in effect vanished as transnational capital negotiated directly with local 'leaders' for the rights to raw materials and resources. Lash and Urry (1994) have dubbed such regions 'wild zones' to denote the chronic weakness or total absence of formalized bureaucratic legal structures.

In this manner the entire region became a socio-economic experiment unequalled in scale since the introduction of communism. What then can we say about the nature of this experiment and its consequences for environment and society in eastern and central Europe? Have we witnessed the first failed green revolution or is this merely a stalled green revolution? Whilst it is clearly impossible to give definite answers to this last question, there are grounds for a not wholly pessimistic prognosis.

POST-COMMUNISM AND ENVIRONMENTAL POLITICS

In many countries, the initial transition period brought a novel prominence to national environmental issues and their regulation. New institutions emerged or were redefined (commonly at a ministry level) and these were often driven by charismatic environmental leaders who had emerged from the environmentalist–independent opposition nexus. Despite their undoubted influence in the transition democracies, their ability to deliver systemic reform of environmental policy and legislation was hampered by a series of factors, some specific to particular country circumstances, and some of a more generic nature. On a broad political level, the principal obstacle to fundamental environmental reform was economic, thwarting any moves extending beyond 'weak sustainability' towards a deeper, systemic reform.[16]

Often driven by external pressures from global economic institutions, most central and eastern European countries adopted liberalization packages of varying stringency. All prioritized macro-economic reform as the precursor to wider economic and political stability. In this sense, the introduction of the market would reap benefits first in a narrow fiscal sense, enhancing quality of life and introducing efficiency and competitiveness in regional and global markets; and second by catalysing wider democracy through new institutions, providing the underpinning for a modern, western-style civil society. In countries such as Poland and the Czech Republic, these policies enjoyed widespread political and public support, at least initially.

In this period, those for whom the environment was a prime concern acknowledged the necessity of economic reform but not at the expense of tackling issues such as energy policy, transport planning and new environmental standards. Such economy versus environment debates often became highly personalized (see Slocock, 1996: 508ff.). This polarization reflects the immaturity of political debate and the absence of a diverse opposition extending beyond the limited horizons of tribal party cultures reminiscent of the previous political system and typified by the Kádárist slogan 'Whoever is not with us is against us'. In this sense, environmentalists became as marginalized in the 1990s as they were under state socialism in the 1980s – even to the point of being explicitly labelled as a threat to the state (e.g.

in the Czech Republic: see Tickle and Vavroušek, this volume). This marginalization was not reserved solely for NGOs: in many countries in central and eastern Europe 'greens' were (and still are) viewed as an undifferentiated group ranging from state actors (ministers and officials) to the most radical activists, with the latter often being castigated as neo-Marxists for favouring hyper-étatist approaches to regulation (or 'the benevolent dictatorship of the ecologist kings': Dahrendorf, 1990: 149).

A further problem of post-communism which impacts disproportionately on environmental reform is the continuity of former state structures, both in an institutional sense and in terms of key elite actors such as the former *nomenklatura*. Resistance to change *per se* occurred widely across the state bureaucracy, driven mainly by common values and practices which had become deeply embedded during the communist era. Such material practices can be seen to operate as obstacles to the ascendancy of all new paradigms and policies, from neo-liberalism to environmentalism. As a further part of the restructuring of post-communist social space, the former bureaucratic class (mainly *nomenklatura*) quickly became transformed into a new elite to rival the intelligentsia-dominated politocracy (see Eyal *et al.*, 1997: 78ff.), especially in technologically related areas.

The continuity of such elites (also shown in the media: Sparks and Reading, 1994) is a serious obstacle to structural environmental reform, particularly in the heavy industry, chemical and energy sectors, which were also politically dominant in the former regimes because of their key role in delivering socialist industrialization. In countries such as the Czech Republic, powerful elites in key state sectors (e.g. energy production) continue to hold sway and, through tacit alliances with political actors, further entrench dominant demand-led paradigms of energy supply, illustrated by the continued support for nuclear power and antagonism to energy efficiency. The continuity of such elites and the residual inertia in social, though not political, structures begs wider questions as to whether less 'velvety', more politically 'violent' revolutions could have resulted in a more innovative and socially egalitarian starting point for post-communism.[17] In more environmentally specific terms, the marginalization and removal of former elites and their practices could be seen as removing some obstacles to ecological modernization.[18]

The political marginalization of environmental groups in post-communist societies has been variable across central and eastern Europe and has generally tended to mirror the degree to which quasi-authoritarian regimes have sought to restrict political freedoms, although civil society may still be active under such circumstances (Kaldor and Vejvoda, 1997: 77). In Belarus and Slovakia nationalist–populist leaders have imposed worrying restrictions on rights of assembly and protest through new legislation and sought to thwart the formation of civic associations through fiscal disincentives (prohibitive registration fees or sureties). In the Czech and Slovak Republics, NGO opposition to nationally prestigious economic projects such as nuclear power has engendered governmental wrath and state surveillance. This has been particularly evident where environmental groups have formed international coalitions to campaign against the national government, as in Slovakia, where national, Austrian and international NGOs successfully opposed multilateral development aid (from the European Bank for Reconstruction and Development) for the completion of the Mochovce nuclear power plant. This success has caused serious damage to Slovakia's perceived reliability as a partner for foreign investment and aid (Williams, 1995).

Lack of tolerance of autonomous civic groups has roots in the pre-1989 period and is related to a number of factors. In simple terms, such groups may be seen as imperilling economic progress with 'unrealistic' demands for strong environmental standards or new paradigms of production (e.g. clean technology or energy efficiency). Whilst this is a strong basis for the antipathy of the new governing elites towards environmental groups (mirrored the world over), central and eastern European NGOs also have other hurdles to mount which are more specific to post-communist conditions. First, as Wheaton and Kavan (1992: 183–186) have suggested in the case of the former Czechoslovakia, 'legitimate' democracy is perceived almost exclusively at the level of plurality of political parties, rather than a more direct mediation of interests with wider society through civic initiatives and other interest groups. This is related to such countries' totalitarian heritage: not only have governing elites sought to replace one hegemonic ideology with another (communism with neo-liberalism), but many citizens (the term is used guardedly), have retained their 'infantilization' born of the previous hyper-étatist regime, and are happy to continue to abdicate their own responsibilities in favour of the state (see also Horváth and Szakolczai, quoted in Lomax, 1997: 53). This mind-set does not bode well in terms of encouraging wider environmental mobilization, although economic hardship is clearly an allied problem. This is evidenced in part by a dearth of public financial support for NGOs, leaving groups dangerously reliant on foreign donors' grant programmes. Such grants are usually aimed at short-term institutional capacity-building and many are due to run out by the turn of the century.[19]

A second point is that post-communist politics has reasserted 'an emphasis on the nation as the key collectivity, rather than the rights of the individual articulated through civil society' (Schöpflin, 1993: 257). Whilst the restitution of national autonomy and traditions after the long domination of alien Soviet power is obviously welcome, chauvinistic attitudes are not easily reconcilable with pan-national environmental problems and the movements engendered by them, as illustrated above by the nuclear power issue in Slovakia. However, seen from the environmental movement's perspective (with their weak national profile), involvement in pan-national coalitions (often linked to claims-making in supra-national forums) is an attractive form of political engagement.

However, although environmental groups have struggled to compete in the new political conditions of post-communism, some positive changes have taken place which indicate that the movement is adapting and maturing. First, many new groups have formed since 1989, initially reflecting demands and concerns previously suppressed by the former political system. More importantly, the new groups have often arisen or adapted quickly to occupy specialized 'niches' in the environmental spectrum, often allied to specific single issues (e.g. forest protection, energy efficiency, traffic pollution) that would previously have been largely unaddressed or subsumed within the wider agenda of a more generalist environmental group. In some countries this has been augmented by a proliferation of grass-roots activist groups, often consisting of only a few concerned citizens organizing locally and autonomously on development issues. The burgeoning of this type of civic action is seen by some observers to be the most encouraging development in environmental politics since 1989 and, if matched by appropriate systems of local and regional political autonomy, could be a vital step in implementing 'bottom-up' sustainability action programmes such as Agenda 21.[20]

In addition, national NGOs have also adopted a markedly more professional attitude – particularly in relation to the new parliamentary democracies, where larger groups have utilized lobbyists to influence the legislative process with some success.[21] More recently, joint action by Czech NGOs through a consultation group with government officials, scientific experts and industry representatives resulted in two new stringent clauses being adopted in the 1997 Waste Act. The formation of such nascent policy communities, involving a wide range of actors in alliance and capacity-building, is a useful first step in delivering policy learning in interest networks. Such epistemic communities, recognized from other environmental forums (e.g. UNEP work in the Mediterranean: Haas, 1989), are considered vital in driving new paradigms through the stages of policy evolution (innovation, diffusion and persistence) to the point of institutionalization as orthodoxy (Adler and Haas, 1992).

However, the place of the environment within the post-communist regimes in the countries considered in this volume varies considerably. Perhaps unsurprisingly, Russia appears to be the country where the environment has become one of the most significant casualties of post-communism, although many of the trends discussed below are also present in part in most other former socialist states (e.g. Eyal *et al.*, 1997; Miszlivetz, 1997). Given the long, albeit discontinuous, tradition of Russo-Soviet environmentalism dealt with in this volume, this decline in status is particularly stark and requires some commentary.

In an analysis which broadly supports the conclusions of Mirovitskaya (this volume), Yanitsky (1997) has advanced a number of reasons for this. First, there is a cultural continuity within the dominant political group within Russia, which from the period of the Tsars has been accustomed to pursuing authoritarian modernization from above. Secondly, this group now comprises federal elites and regional elites with a 'principal goal' of accumulating capital by 'selling natural resources and robbery of all strata of [the] population' (Yanitsky, 1997: 10). Despite some differences in priorities, these composite elites, a mixture of the old *nomenklatura* and emergent entrepreneurs, represent the emergence of 'clan-corporate islands of modernization' (Yanitsky, 1997: 10). One such island can be seen in Russia's gas corporation, a huge modern extraction and distribution industry, which has close supportive links to Yeltsin at the federal level and collaborates closely with regional officials. Another significant island of modernization lies within the reconstituted media institutions which played an important part in securing the re-election of Yeltsin.[22]

Yanitsky characterizes Russia from 1985 onwards as a symbiotic mixture of 'a degrading techno-bureaucratic megamachine operating in self-support mode inside which "high modernity islands" and archaic associations were quaintly neighboring' in a social environment of 'counter-modernization' (1997: 4). In post-communist

Russia the islands of modernization have become islands of marketization favouring the 'most powerful clan-corporate structures' creating an immensely rich class fraction and an immense underclass of 'throw-away people' (Yanitsky, 1997: 9). Yanitsky argues that this underclass is a potential source of support for the forces of 'counter-modernization', rendering Russia a fragile and risk-laden society. In the absence of the adequately funded transition hoped for by Gorbachev, Russia presents the modern face of its 'clan-corporate elites' to the West to build business confidence and inward investment.

Two major organic and socio-political environmental concerns arise from this configuration. First, there is the likelihood that foreign direct investment, particularly that targeted on resource extraction and utilization, will be pursued at the expense of severe environmental degradation. Feshbach (1995) and others argue that Russian deforestation and despoliation of the fragile tundra and taiga biomes are globally significant ecological threats capable of contributing to global warming on a scale equivalent to forest loss in the southern hemisphere. Secondly, the insight that poverty and enhanced environmental degradation go hand in hand, originally advanced in relation to the developing world in the Bruntland Report, is increasingly being recognized as applicable to all societies. In part this is why contemporary analyses are highlighting the linkages between social justice and the environment (Harvey, 1996; Welsh, 1998). In this context the creation of a massive underclass in Russia acts as a threat to both the process of modernization and environmental politics. David Harvey argues that

> . . . the environmental justice movement has to radicalize the ecological moderniza-
> tion discourse. And that requires confronting the fundamental underlying processes
> (and their associated power structures, social relations, institutional configurations,
> discourses, and belief systems) that generate environmental and social injustices. (1996:
> 401)

In the current conjuncture the state has a key role in this process, which can be illustrated through the Russian case. Following the 1992 Rio Earth Summit Russia established a new State Environmental Policy and introduced the concept of Ecological Security of the Russian Federation in 1994. These priorities were formulated by the Russian Ministry for Ecology and Natural Resources, which declared that 'the policy of ecological security is a purposeful activity of the state, public organisations, judicial bodies and separate individuals' (*Zelony Mir*, cited in Mathews and Saiko, 1994: 224). The New Russian Law on Environmental Protection aimed to create a 'coherent regime of environmental legislation' within the context of marketization (Vartanov, 1992). The same law also addressed the 'rights of citizens to a healthy and favourable environment' through legal redress (Vartanov, 1992: 229). The post-Soviet government has thus created state instruments which – even if only rhetorical – will in the longer term undoubtedly be utilized by environmental activists and pressure groups.

There is, however, a need for a more pro-active stance in relation to the environment when sanctioning development plans. In this respect, the Russian state has a responsibility to secure the best available environmental package from all would-be foreign direct investors, including binding commitments to restore habitats disrupted by their activities. Thus the notion of ecological security developed in Russia could, given the necessary political will, be combined with the European concept of ecological modernization to create a strong sustainability approach to modernization. Nor is this a one-way street relying solely on the will of the recipient country. Western business has been quick to clamber aboard the green bandwagon by adopting a range of largely self-regulating environmental standards. This attempt at weak sustainability by business needs to be given some substance by being reflected in corporate investment and development strategies. If business is serious about the environment, then all the proposals to develop the natural resources of Russia and other countries in central and eastern Europe should automatically embody strong sustainability principles (underlain by appropriate techniques and technologies) capable of addressing the specific environmental conditions encountered. The idea that unbridled free markets can deliver this kind of ecological modernization, which inevitably has cost implications, is nonsensical. This is where individual states and supranational bodies such as the EU and the relevant bodies of the UN have a role to play.

However it is clearly utopian to expect economically distressed countries to impose conditions on inward investment. Investor or vendor states and their supranational agencies are, however, in a slightly different position in relation to this issue. The development of globally binding environmental conditions attached to agreements between transacting countries thus becomes an urgent priority within any ecological modernization scenario. The need to develop level playing fields in relation to this issue is one of the most urgent and important issues in terms of global trade and environment issues. The ideological commitment of the World Trade Organisation to free markets makes it supremely unsuited to this task and highlights the need for an environmental audit and realignment of the organizational and institutional configuration of modernity at all levels. At present the emphasis on local initiatives in areas like recycling attracts far too much attention, to the detriment of important sites of global strategic regulation such as intellectual property rights regimes (Purdue, 1995). In this dimension, the activist slogan 'Think global: act local' is inappropriate as it abandons the all-important strategic level to corporate players, governments and a small number of elite ENGOs whose representativeness and influence are often limited.

The need for improved global regulation of foreign direct investment must also be seen in the context of regional economic groupings such as the EU, which a number of the central and eastern European countries dealt with in this study are likely to join within the next five to ten years – the Czech Republic, Estonia, Hungary, Poland and Slovenia. Entry can only occur if the country concerned can 'assume the obligations of membership' (i.e. meet the '*acquis communautaire*') and fulfil a number of other clear demands related to democratic stability, human rights, a functioning market economy, endorsement of EU political objectives and competitive capacity (Commission of the European Communities, 1993: 2). In the field of environmental regulation, one of the most active EU policy sectors, this means that applicant states are obliged to match extant legal and policy instruments of the EU.

For many central and eastern European countries this will be a difficult process, though the more-forward looking states were quick to base new post-1989 regulations on EU frameworks. Thus by the time of accession, substantial environmental improvements should be in train, though successful implementation has always been a problem area for EU environmental law.[23] However, the widening of the EU eastwards is far from a universal panacea for the environment. As Baker (1996: 165) has suggested, despite the policy rhetoric of the European Commission and economic and cultural programmes of assistance (such as PHARE), which include funding of environmental projects and groups, 'environmental policy management by the EU is not primarily motivated by environmental considerations nor is it primarily directed towards environmental ends'.[24] We should be clear, therefore, in recognizing the paramount nature of the *economic community* that lies at the heart of the EU. This economic agenda fuels the drive towards a European political area where trade is liberalized and direct investment – both foreign and domestic – is aggressively pursued by investment in improved infrastructure such as trans-European networks in energy and transport (Commission of the European Communities, 1993: 6–7). In a wider context, the EU also seeks to maintain economic competitiveness within the global arena and this can also detrimentally affect environmental standards (Golub, 1998).

The experience of previous enlargements of the Community – involving large infrastructure projects with high environmental impacts in Spain, Portugal and Greece – does not represent grounds for optimism in terms of sustainable development in the new European periphery. Furthermore, although eastern Europe is usually known best for its areas of severe environmental degradation, there are also significant areas which – through lack of economic development and the retention of traditional practices (particularly in agriculture) – harbour unique landscapes now rare in Europe. Many such areas are found in border zones which are likely to be at risk from new transnational road developments.

TRANSITION AND SUSTAINABLE REGIONAL FUTURES

A number of authors have contended that the collapse of the state socialist system in eastern Europe portends a simple, linear evolutionary transition to western models of capitalism (e.g. Fukuyama, 1989; Michalak and Gibb, 1992). However, empirical evidence from a number of countries currently shows this not to be the case: change is instead contested with new forms of accumulation and regulation appearing that are strongly derivative of the social space and spatial economies of the former system (Smith, 1994, 1996; Eyal *et al.*, 1997). Imposed upon this background is the strong influence of globalization, either through the adaptation of enterprises to western markets or through selective foreign direct investment (Smith, 1995). As has been outlined elsewhere (Tickle, 1998), this trend will be influential in terms of the progress of sustainable restructuring in the region.

Away from the economic sphere, social space in terms of civil society has also undergone a profound transformation. Once again, transformation has not followed the direction predicted by analysts assuming a simple and benign progression towards societies strongly reminiscent of western liberal democracies. A multiplicity of other views range from those strongly critical of the role of civil society, either before or after 1989 (Lomax, 1997), and its influence, if any, on the state socialist system (Hirst, 1997), to those concerned at its apparently failed renaissance (Mislivetz, 1997). Others, by contrast, have noted positive features of renewed democratic and political participation by civic groups across a wide range of eastern European states (Kaldor and Vejvoda, 1997). As Lomax (1997: 44) and others have pointed out, part of the divergence of views is related to the adoption of eastern or western analytical perspectives. Within these varied perspectives overlap and, on occasion, confusion is also occurring between the theoretical and normative (instrumental) aspects of the civil society concept.

We have tried to overcome these problems by an analysis utilizing pre- and post-1989 intra-regional (often dissident) perspectives overlain by a wider extra-regional framework contextualized by social movement theories (particularly those of Melucci and Touraine) and social theory of risk in late ('high') modernity (e.g. Beck *et al.*, 1994). Through this approach we recognize the vital significance of the environment as a site of societal contestation in central and eastern Europe which, because of its unique political and temporal conjuncture within the failing project of Soviet socialism, assumed a salience seldom recognized in western environmental politics. Part of this salience can be attributed to the way in which Marxism–Leninism incorporated the environment within its ideology and rhetoric, thus opening a route for its contestation. In this process some party-states misjudged the political neutrality of the issue and, by engaging in environmental dialogue with society, opened up a much wider and ultimately open-ended debate undermining authoritarian rule (see Hicks, 1996).

Seldom has the power of the environment as an issue been so concentrated in time or space. In states and supranational forums outside central and eastern Europe, the development of environmental issues – though sharing a close epistemological roots related to advancing modernity (particularly the role of industrialization) – has taken place on a more incremental basis. This has given rise to an historically more engaged environmental movement which lately has been evolving partially in step with the still-unfolding processes of globalization. Analyses of NGO activity on the regional and global scale have recently sought to emphasize their role in less explicit forms of policy influence or governance characterized by the term 'social learning'. This role is considered vital as governments, with some exceptions, seldom act as leaders in environmental policy (Princen and Finger, 1994).

Further work by Wapner (1995) uses the concept of world civic politics which 'clarifies how the forms of governance in global civil society are distinct from the instrumentalities of state rule' (1995: 337). As Wapner accepts, this distinction is relative as 'activist efforts intersect with the domain of the state even if this is not the initial intention' (p. 339) – a situation amply illustrated in relation to the environmental movements in central and eastern Europe. However, activism outside formalized policy arenas, or in state socialist systems, where such forums were generally absent or inaccessible, is also important in propagating implicit messages related both to the issue addressed (in this case the environment) and to the need for new forms of participatory democracy. Indeed this study, amongst others, has illustrated how the wider independent opposition including environmentalists in central and eastern Europe prefigured wider participation in anti-state dialogues culminating in mass popular protest. Social movements' relevance in post-communism is also emphasized as their 'formation and success . . . is a measure of democracy, defined in substantive terms' (Pickvance, 1997: 139).

In attempting to move society towards the goals of social and environmental justice, NGOs – as Princen and Finger (1994) point out – also carry out a crucial task in *linking* the local *and* global through close epistemic links, which now include eastern and central European ENGOs. Confronted by an agenda which includes simultaneously delivering ecological modernization, market liberalization and social justice, it appears that the need to translate this into regional sustainable restructuring is only being recognized by a relatively fragile and insecure grouping within the civil societies of eastern Europe. The efforts of such groups must be reinforced by the active networking of those bearing similar demands for social and environmental justice in other countries throughout the world. Part of this agenda needs to be the promotion of environmental justice within the existing forums of global civil society. Beyond this we would argue that the creation of new institutions necessary to promote and *regulate* ecological modernization represents one of the most urgent political priorities not only for eastern and central Europe but for all nations. A prime candidate of central importance here would be the creation of institutions responsible for the application of stringent environmental audits to all development projects and large trade agreements. To have legitimacy, any such institutional constellation would have to be widely representative not only of northern and western interests but also the grass-roots recipients and partners to such transactions. As Power (1997) has argued, such environmental audits are one of the key means developed to address risk and development issues within discrete societies. By developing the notion of audits at a global scale and widening the constituency consulted within such processes, the potential for sustainability with social justice would be enhanced. This will require a rupture in current environmental politics that is contingent on wider political pluralism, both in terms of reconstructed notions of citizenship and state action and the ability of diverse national and international groups at all levels of civil society to challenge the environmental and social impacts of unfettered global capital.

NOTES

1. These were derived from nineteenth-century aesthetic/romantic movements in the Austro-Hungarian empire (see Kundrata, 1992 and Tickle and Vavroušek, this volume).
2. In a broad sense, this assertion can be contested. For example, Hicks (1996) has shown that the Polish state also utilized environmental discourses with non-state groups as part of its post-1981 normalization strategy.
3. Joppke's analysis suggests that although the Church was instrumental, as a non-state actor, in fostering autonomous movements, this was not an open-ended practice. He

instead describes ecology issues (together with 'third-worldism') as a substitute ('*ersatz*') for the less palatable human rights agenda that the Protestant Church felt ill at ease with (Joppke, 1995).

4. A less commonly addressed, though important, form of transition would see a steady convergence of interests between Russia and China as a response to any isolation imposed on Russia through western dominance of international forums. China's bid to control output of oil from the Caspian Sea can be seen as part of this process (see *The Guardian* 29 September, 1997: 11).

5. We use the term 'immanent' to describe a repressed and submerged civil society that often survives as a vestigial structure from the pre-communist period, though it may be augmented by additional autonomous movements arising under communism. We also describe a further 'emergent' phase of civil society under communism where opposition becomes more widespread and public.

6. The late Ernest Gellner also draws attention to the same contradiction in Havel's writing (Gellner, 1994: 125).

7. It should be noted that Pelczynski's conception of a 'political society' prefiguring civil society conflicts with Gramsci's association of political society with the state.

8. Unlike Gramsci's organic intellectual expressing a unified class critique, the independent opposition in central and eastern Europe was far more heterogeneous, drawn from decaying class factions as well as more liberal credentialized sources.

9. The Polish forests have, for example, served as a symbol of Polish nationhood and a material place of retreat throughout the country's history (see Schama, 1995: esp. 24–25).

10. Havel himself is aware of the imprecision with which he uses the term 'post-totalitarian'; he does not imply 'that the system is no longer totalitarian; on the contrary . . . it is totalitarian in a way fundamentally different from classical dictatorships, different from totalitarianism as we usually understand it' (Havel, 1986: 40–41) .

11. By 1989, the communist government entered into wide-ranging round-table negotiations with Solidarity. These included access to previously state-dominated institutions such as the media. Solidarity's initial negotiating position, a phased transition from state censorship to an independent broadcasting authority, was abandoned in exchange for independent production rights and limited weekly access to broadcast networks subject to usual censorship restrictions (see Sparks and Reading, 1994: 254–255).

12. This tendency is more clearly illustrated in some countries than others. For an account of these events in Slovakia see Pithart (1995: 215) and Podoba (1998).

13. Even radical liberals like Havel are quoted as regarding feminism as a refuge for 'bored housewives and dissatisfied mistresses' (Kaldor, cited in Watson, 1993: 477).

14. First-wave feminism coincided with the slowing down of economic growth and the associated crisis in the dominant political bloc in the UK. Second-wave feminism emerged within a wider crisis of political legitimacy of western states and gained momentum during the deepening economic crisis of the early to mid-1970s, which eventually pemitted the reassertion of class-related economic issues within the national political arena.

15. In the UK the introduction of a law requiring registered voters to pay a 'poll tax' resulted in widespread campaigns of civil disobedience and disorder. Throughout Europe direct action coalitions opposed the modernization of road infrastructure.

16. Some policy analysts take a more positive view. In the case of the Czech Republic, Slocock (1996) suggests remarkable progress in environmental policy-making, with new laws and instruments often surpassing in stringency those in force in some EU

states. In explaining the seeming ready acceptance of strict new standards by industry in both Poland and the Czech Republic, Slocock cites industrial managers' acquiescence in terms of the overall imperative of convergence with EU objectives.

17. This issue is explored at length by Offe (1996).

18. The term 'ecological modernization' is used variably in academic literature (see Simonis, 1989; Spaargaren and Mol, 1991; Weale, 1992; Hajer, 1996) but is generally taken to suggest that 'policies for economic development and environmental protection can be combined with synergistic effect (Gouldson and Murphy, 1996). In itself, however, this does not address wider issues of social justice and thus by its nature can only be seen as part of weak sustainability. For a critique of ecological modernization see Bludhorn (1997).

19. Funds have been made available from a wide variety of sources including bodies such as the EU (PHARE programme), national country 'know-how' exchange programmes and private/charitable foundations, such as the Soros Foundation (Kaldor and Vejvoda, 1997: 77) and the Environmental Parnership foundation administered by the German Marshall Fund on behalf of sixteen donors (mostly US-related) operating in the Czech and Slovak Republics, Hungary and Poland (Nadace Environmental Partnership, 1995).

20. For Russia and Hungary, Pickvance (1997), however, draws attention to the limited empirical evidence for associating decentralization and enhanced democracy.

21. In the Czech Republic groups such as Children of the Earth (Děti Země) and the Rainbow Movement (Hnutí Duha) were influential in lobbying for the 1995 decrees regulating ozone-layer-depleting substances.

22. Media events included the staging of rock concerts in front of the Kremlin, symbolically transforming Red Square – the centre stage of communist military and political power – into the site of a people's party.

23. The more relaxed attitude of southern European EU member states is commonly cited in relation to lax implementation, though north-western European countries also have patchy records in relation to key directives, particularly on habitat protection. However, it seems probable that new member states will be expected to demonstrate higher standards than those enforced in some current member states. This argument concerning double standards does not of course apply solely to environmental policy.

24. See also the similar arguments presented by Gowan (1995) described in the first chapter.

REFERENCES

Adler, E. and Haas, P.M. (1992) Conclusion: epistemic communities, world order, and the creation of a reflective research program. *International Organisation* 46(1), 367–390.

Arato, A. and Cohen, J. (1988) Civil society and social theory. *Thesis Eleven* 21, 40–64.

Baker, S. (1996) The scope for East–West co-operation. In *Environmental Policy in an International Context. 3: Prospects.* (eds A. Blowers and P. Glasbergen). Arnold, London.

Baumgartl, B. (1993) Environmental protest as a vehicle for transition: the case of Ekoglasnost in Bulgaria. In *Environment and Democratic Transition* (eds A. Vari and P. Tamas). Kluwer, Dordrecht.

Beck, U., Giddens, A. and Lash, S. (1994) *Reflexive Modernization: Politics, Tradition and Aesthetics in the Modern Social Order.* Polity, Cambridge.

Bludhorn, I. (1997) A theory of post ecologist politics. *Environmental Politics* 6(3), 125–147.

Bramwell, A. (1989) *Ecology in the Twentieth Century: A History.* Yale University Press, London.

Bryant, C.G.A. and Mokrzycki, E. (1994) *The New Great Transformation? Change and Continuity in East–Central Europe.* Routledge, London.

Commission of the European Communities (1993) *Background Report: Towards a Closer Association with the Countries of Central and Eastern Europe.* ISEC/B6/93, CEC, London.

Dahrendorf, R. (1990) *Reflections on the Revolution in Europe.* Chatto & Windus, London.

Dawson, J. (1996) *Eco-nationalism: Anti-nuclear Activism and National Identity in Russia, Lithuania, and Ukraine.* Duke University Press, Durham, NC.

Dreifelds, J. (1995) Latvia. In *Environmental Resources and Constraints in the Former Soviet Republics* (ed. P.R. Pryde). Westview, Boulder, CO.

Enloe, C. (1989) *Bananas, Beaches and Bases.* Pandora, London.

Eyal, G., Szelényi, I. and Townsley, E. (1997) The theory of post-communist managerialism. *New Left Review* 222, 60–92.

Feshbach, M. (1995) *Ecological Disaster: Cleaning up the Hidden Legacy of the Soviet Regime.* Twentieth Century Funds Press, New York.

Frentzel-Zagorska, J. (1990) Civil society in Poland and Hungary. *Soviet Studies* 42(4), 759–777.

Fukuyama, F. (1989) The end of history? *The National Interest* (Summer).

Gare, A. (1993) Soviet environmentalism: the path not taken. *Capital, Nature, Socialism* 4(4), 69–88.

Gellner, E. (1994) *Encounters with Nationalism.* Blackwell, Oxford.

Goldman, M.I. (1992) Environmentalism and nationalism: an unlikely twist in an unlikely direction. In *The Soviet Environment: Problems, Policies and Politics* (ed. J. Massey Stewart). Cambridge University Press, Cambridge.

Golub, J., ed. (1998) *Global Competition and EU Environmental Policy.* Routledge, London.

Gouldson, A. and Murphy, J. (1996) Ecological modernization and the European Union. *Geoforum* 21(1), 11–21.

Gowan, P. (1995) Neo-liberal theory and practice in eastern Europe. *New Left Review* 213, 3–60.

Haas, P.M. (1989) Do regimes matter? Epistemic communities and Mediterranean pollution control. *International Organisation* 43(3), 377–403.

Hajba, É. (1994) The rise and fall of the Hungarian Greens. *Journal of Communist Studies and Transition Politics* 10(3), 180–191.

Hajer, M. (1996) Ecological modernisation as cultural politics. In *Risk, Environment and Modernity: Towards a New Ecology* (eds S. Lash, B. Szerszynski and B. Wynne). Sage, London.

Harvey, D. (1996) *Justice, Nature and the Geography of Difference.* Blackwell, Oxford.

Havel, V. (1986) The power of the powerless. In *Václav Havel: Living in Truth* (ed. J. Vladislav). Faber and Faber, London.

Havel, V. (1988) Anti-political politics. In *Civil Society and the State: New European Perspectives* (ed. J. Keane). Verso, London.

Hicks, B. (1996) *Environmental Politics in Poland: A Social Movement Between Regime and Opposition.* Columbia University Press, New York.

Hirst, P. (1997) *From Statism to Pluralism.* UCL Press, London.

Holmes, L.T. (1992) The GDR: the search for autonomous patterns of development. In *The Developments of Civil Society in Communist Systems* (ed. R.F. Miller). Allen & Unwin, North Sydney.

Holy, L. (1996) *The Little Czech and the Great Czech nation.* Cambridge University Press, Cambridge.

Jancar-Webster, B., ed. (1993) *Environmental Action in Eastern Europe: Responses to Crisis.* M.E. Sharpe, Armonk, NY.

Joppke, C. (1995) *East German Dissidents and the Revolution of 1989: Social Movement in a Leninist Regime*. Macmillan, London.

Judt, T. (1988) The dilemmas of dissidence: the politics of the opposition in East–Central Europe. *East European Politics and Societies* 2(2), 185–240.

Kabala, S.J. (1993) The history of environmental protection in Poland and the growth of awareness and activism. In *Environmental Action in Eastern Europe: Responses to Crisis* (ed. B. Jancar-Webster). M.E. Sharpe, Armonk, NY.

Kaldor, M. and Vejvoda, I. (1997) Democratization in central and east European countries. *International Affairs* 73(1), 59–82.

Keane, J., ed. (1988) *Civil Society and the State: New European Perspectives*. Verso, London.

Klemenc, A. (1993) Co-operation between environmental NGOs and the government in Slovenia. In *New Horizons* (eds P. Hardi, A. Juras and M. Tóth Nagy). RECCEE, Budapest.

Konrád, G. (1984) *Antipolitics*. Quartet, London.

Kundrata, M. (1992) Czechoslovakia. In *Civil Society and the Environment in Central and Eastern Europe* (eds D. Fisher, C. Davis, A. Juras and P. Pavlovic). Ecological Studies Institute, London/Institut für Europäische Umweltpolitik, Bonn/ECO-Centre, Belgrade.

Lash, S. and Urry, J. (1994) *Economies of Signs and Space*. Sage, London.

Lewis, P.G. (1997) Theories of democratization and patterns of regime change in eastern Europe. *Journal of Communist Studies and Transition Politics* 13(1), 4–26.

Lomax, B. (1997) The strange death of 'civil society' in post-communist Hungary. *Journal of Communist Studies and Transition Politics* 13(1), 41–63.

Lowe, P.D. (1983) Values and institutions in British nature conservation. In *Conservation in Perspective* (eds A. Warren and F.B. Goldsmith). Wiley, Chichester.

Maier, C.S. (1997) *Dissolution: The Crisis of Communism and the End of East Germany*. Princeton University Press, Princeton, NJ.

Mathews, J.A. and Saiko, T.A. (1994) Environmental policies and public participation during transition periods: a comparison between Britain and Russia. In *Environmental Policy and Practice in East and West Europe* (eds I. Fodor and G.P. Walker). Centre for Regional Studies, Pécs.

Matraszek, M. (1989) Civil society, state, and opposition in eastern Europe. *Slovo* 2(1), 33–47.

Melucci, A. (1988) Social movements and the democratization of everyday life. In *Civil Society and the State: New European Perspectives* (ed. J. Keane). Verso, London.

Melucci, A. (1996) *Challenging Codes*. Cambridge University Press, Cambridge.

Merchant, C. (1983) *The Death of Nature: Women, Ecology and the Scientific Revolution*. Harper & Row, San Francisco, CA.

Merchant, C. (1992) *Radical Ecology*. Routledge, London.

Michalak, W.Z. and Gibb, R.A. (1992) Political geography and eastern Europe. *Area* 24(4), 341–9.

Michnik, A. (1985) *Letters From Prison and Other Essays*. University of California Press, Berkeley, CA.

Mies, M. and Shiva, V. (1993) *Ecofeminism*. Routledge, London.

Miller, R.F., ed. (1992) *The Developments of Civil Society in Communist Systems*. Allen & Unwin, North Sydney.

Miszlivetz, F. (1997) Participation and transition: can the civil society project survive in Hungary? *Journal of Communist Studies and Transition Politics* 13(1), 27–40.

Mitsuda, H. and Pashev, K. (1995) Environmentalism as ends or means? The rise and political crisis of the environmental movement in Bulgaria. *Capitalism, Nature, Socialism* 6(1), 87–111.

Nadace Environmental Partnership (1995) *Partnerství pro životní prostředí – česká republika [Environmental Partnership – Czech Republic]*. Environmental Partnership, Brno.

Offe, C. (1985) Challenging the boundaries of traditional politics: the contemporary challenge of social movements. *Social Research* 52(4), 817–868.

Offe, C. (1996) *Varieties of Transition: The East European and the East German Experience*. Polity, Cambridge.

Pateman, C. (1970) *Participation and Democratic Theory*. Cambridge University Press, Cambridge.

Pateman, C. (1988) *The Sexual Contract*. Polity, Cambridge.

Pateman, C. (1989) *The Disorder of Women: Democracy, Feminism and Political Theory*. Polity, Cambridge.

Pelczynski, Z.A. (1988) Solidarity and 'The Rebirth of Political Society'. In *Civil Society and the State: New European Perspectives* (ed. J. Keane). Verso, London.

Peterson, D.J. (1993) *Troubled Lands: The Legacy of Soviet Environmental Destruction*. Westview, Boulder, CO.

Pickvance, C.G. (1997) Decentralization and democracy in eastern Europe: a sceptical approach. *Environment and Planning C: Government and Policy* 15, 129–142.

Pithart, P. (1995) Towards a Shared Freedom, 1968–89. In *The End of Czechoslovakia* (ed. J. Musil). Central European University Press, Budapest.

Podoba, J. (1998) Rejecting green velevet: transition, environment and nationalism in Slovakia. *Environmental Politics* 7(1), 129–44.

Power, M. (1997) *The Audit Society: Rituals of Verification*. Oxford University Press, Oxford.

Prečan, V. (1990) *Charta 77 1977–1989: Od morální k demokratické revoluci [From a Moral to a Democratic Revolution]*. Scheinfeld, Prague.

Princen, T. and Finger, M. (1994) *Environmental NGOs in World Politics: Linking the Local and the Global*. Routledge, London.

Purdue, D. (1995) Hegemonic TRIPS: world trade, intellectual property and biodiversity. *Environmental Politics* 4(1), 88–107.

Schama, S. (1995) *Landscape and Memory*. Harper Collins, London.

Schöpflin, G. (1993) *Politics in Eastern Europe*. Blackwell, Oxford.

Simonis, U. (1989) Ecological modernization of industrial society: three strategic elements. *International Social Science Journal* 121, 347–361.

Slocock, B. (1996) The paradoxes of environmental policy in eastern Europe: the dynamics of policy-making in the Czech Republic. *Environmental Politics* 5(3), 501–521.

Smith, A. (1994) Uneven development and the restructuring of the armaments industry in Slovakia. *Transactions of the Institute of British Geographers* NS 19, 404–424.

Smith, A. (1995) Regulation theory, strategies of enterprise integration and the political economy of regional economic restructuring in central and eastern Europe: the case of Slovakia. *Regional Studies* 29(8), 761–772.

Smith, A. (1996) From convergence to fragmentation: uneven regional development, industrial restructuring, and the 'transition to capitalism' in Slovakia. *Environment and Planning A* 28, 135–156.

Sööt, S. (1995) Estonia. In *Environmental Resources and Constraints in the Former Soviet Republics* (ed. P.R. Pryde). Westview, Boulder, CO.

Spaargaren, G. and Mol, A. (1991) *Sociology, Environment and Modernity: Ecological Modernisation as a Theory of Social Change*. LUW, Wageningen.

Sparks, C. and Reading, A. (1994) Understanding media change in East Central Europe. *Media, Culture and Society* 16(2), 243–270.

Szirmai, V. (1993) The structural mechanisms of the organisation of ecological–social movements in Hungary. In *Environment and Democratic Transition* (eds A. Vari and P. Tamas). Kluwer, Dordrecht.

Szücs, J. (1988) Three historical regions of Europe. In *Civil Society and the State: New European Perspectives* (ed. J. Keane). Verso, London.

Tickle, A. (1998) Environmental geopolitics and shock-shift transition. In *Shock-shift in an Enlarged Europe* (eds F.W. Carter and W. Maik). Avebury, Aldershot. (forthcoming)

Tismaneanu, V. (1989) Nascent civil society in the GDR. *Problems of Communism* XXXVIII (2–3), 90–111.

Vartanov, R.V. (1992) A response to the new Russian Law on environmental protection. *CIS Environmental Watch* 2.

Waller, M. and Millard, F. (1992) Environmental politics in Eastern Europe. *Environmental Politics* 1(2), 159–185.

Wapner, P. (1995) Politics beyond the state: environmental activism and world civic politics. *World Politics* 47, 311–340.

Watson, P. (1993) Eastern Europe's silent revolution: gender. *Sociology* 27(3), 471–487.

Weale, A. (1992) *The New Politics of Pollution*. Manchester University Press, Manchester.

Weiner, D.R. (1988) *Models of Nature: Ecology, Conservation, and Cultural Revolution in Soviet Russia*. Indiana University Press, Bloomington, IN.

Welsh, I. (1996) Risk, global governance and environmental politics. *Innovation* 9(4), 407–420.

Welsh, I. (1998) Risk, race and global environmental regulation, In *Migration and Globalization* (eds A. Brah, M. Hickman and M. Mac an Ghail). BSA/Macmillan, London.

Williams, K. (1995) The foreign relations of independent Slovakia. *Slovo* 8(2), 87–108.

Yanitsky, O. (1993) Environmental initiatives in Russia: east–west comparisons. In *Environment and Democratic Transition* (eds A. Vari and P. Tamas). Kluwer, Dordrecht.

Yanitsky, O. (1997) Modernization and globalization from the perspective of a transition society. Paper presented at the International Sociological Association (ISA) Conference 'Sociological Theory and the Environment', Woudschoten, SISWO/ISA.

Ziegler, C. (1987) *Environmental Policy in the USSR*. University of Massachusetts Press, Amherst, MA.

Ziegler, C.E. (1992) Political participation, nationalism and environmental politics in the USSR. In *The Soviet Environment: Problems, Policies and Politics* (ed. J. Massey Stewart). Cambridge University Press, Cambridge.

INDEX

Reference to information in notes is listed as, for example: 26(n10)